"Any serious attempt to remove the present causes of war must concentrate on the roots of the Christian Religion and of Western Idealism."

F. C. S. NORTHROP: *The Meeting of East and West*

The Philosophy of

COMPASSION

THE RETURN
OF THE GODDESS

BY

Esmé Wynne-Tyson

FOREWORD BY

G. P. GOOCH

O.M., C.H., F.B.A., D.Litt.

LONDON
CENTAUR PRESS LTD

FIRST PUBLISHED IN 1962
BY VINCENT STUART PUBLISHERS LTD
© ESMÉ WYNNE-TYSON 1962, 1970

THIS EDITION PUBLISHED IN 1970
BY CENTAUR PRESS LTD,
FONTWELL, SUSSEX

SBN 90000072 4

PRINTED IN GREAT BRITAIN

Contents

To Curtis P. Freshel,
and to the memory,
beloved by us both,
of Emarel

Acknowledgments

For permission to use copyright material, the author gratefully makes the following acknowledgments:

To the University Press Cambridge, for permission to quote from *Origen: contra Celsum*, translated by Henry Chadwick. To Messrs. James Nisbet & Co. Ltd., for permission to quote from *The Teaching of the Twelve Apostles*, a translation with notes by Canon Spence, M.A. To Penguin Books Ltd., for permission to quote from *The Metamorphoses of Ovid*, translated by Mary M. Innes. To the Loeb Classical Library, for permission to quote from *Plutarch's Lives*, translated by Bernadotte Perrin; *The Works of the Emperor Julian*, translated by Wilmer K. Wright, Ph.D.; *Plato*, translated by the Rev. R. G. Bury, Litt.D.; *Plato*, translated by W. R. M. Lamb. To Messrs. Macmillan & Co. Ltd., and Mr. Diarmuid Russell, for permission to quote from *Imaginations and Reveries* by A. E. To Messrs. J. M. Dent & Sons Ltd., for permission to quote from *The History of Herodotus*, translated by George Rawlinson; *The City of God*, by Augustine, translated by John Helsey; *The Republic of Plato*, translated by A. D. Lindsay, M.A.; *Five Dialogues of Plato*, translated by Floyer Sydenham; *Discourse on Method, etc.*, by René Descartes, translated by John Veitch, M.A.; *Ethics: Spinosa*, Introduction by T. S. Gregory, M.A.(Oxon); *Plutarch's Lives* (Dryden edition revised by Arthur Clough); *The Eclogues and Georgics of Virgil*, translated into English Verse by T. F. Royds, M.A. (Everyman's Library.) To Messrs. Hodder & Stoughton Ltd., for permission to quote from *Christian Ethics and Modern Problems*, by W. R. Inge. To Messrs. T. & T. Clark, for permission to quote from *Origen and Greek Patristic Theology*, by the Rev. W. Fairweather, M.A. To Messrs. A. & C. Black Ltd., for permission to quote from Alexander Hislop: *The Two Babylons*. (S. W. Partridge & Co.) To Messrs. George Allen & Unwin Ltd., for permission to quote from *The Basis of Mortality*, by Arthur Schopenhauer, translated by Arthur Brodrick Bullock, M.A. To Messrs. Burns & Oates Ltd., for permission to quote from *The Confessions of St. Augustine*, translated by Sir Tobie Matthew, Kt. To Messrs. Longmans, Green & Co. Ltd., for permission to quote from *Prayer: Exhortation to Martyrdom by Origen*, translated and annotated by John F. O'Meara; *The Rise of Christianity* by E. W. Barnes. To the S.P.C.K., for permission to quote from *First Principles by Origen* (Koetchau's Text of De Principiis), translated by G. W. Butterworth; *Justin Martyr: The Dialogue With Trypho*, Translation, Introduction and Notes by A. Lukyn Williams, D.D.; *The Sibylline Oracles*, by the Rev. H. N. Bate, M.A.; *Selections from the Commentaries and Homilies of Origen*, by R. B. Tollinton, D.D.; *The Book of Enoch*, translated by R. H. Charles, D.D. To the Student Christian Movement Press Ltd., for permission to quote from *Alexandrian Christianity*, by J. E. L. Oulton, D.D. and Henry Chadwick, B.D. To Messrs. Faber & Faber Ltd., for permission to quote from *Plotinus: The Enneads*, translated by Stephen MacKenna. To Messrs. Routledge & Kegan-Paul Ltd., for permission to quote from *Lectures on the Philosophy of Religion*, by G. W. F. Hegel, Speirs and Sanderson translation; and from *Answer to Job*, by C. G. Jung.

FOREWORD

Some books, declared Bacon, are to be tasted, others inwardly digested. *The Philosophy of Compassion*, by Esmé Wynne-Tyson, clearly belongs to the second category. It is the ripe fruit of many years of study of philosophies and religions, of the saints and sages of all times and places. How far she has cast her net into the waters may be guessed from the rewarding bibliography. She has found exactly what she wants in Buddha and Jesus, Plotinus, the Neo-Platonists and the Mystics. She dares to hope that her conclusions may be of use to other seekers.

Darwin's proof of evolution, she assumes, has dethroned traditional orthodoxy and created a vacuum which materialism is incapable of filling. How then can it be filled? Back to Christ! is the reply. Back to the simple message recorded in the synoptic gospels, a message of purity and austerity, of unselfish service, of compassion, of nearness to the God of love. Was there ever a better Christian than St. Francis of Assisi? The author, like other mystics, has little use for the churches, for cannot the soul establish direct contact with the Divine Wisdom? The process of adulteration, she considers, began with Paul, and was continued by the theologians till their manifold additions transformed the original teaching almost beyond recognition.

Certain people have always been regarded as possessing special powers of penetration to see beyond the veil, and women, being as a rule less earth-bound than men, have always played a leading part in the quest. This erudite and challenging book is also a gallery with full comments on the most important portraits, among them Jakob Boehme and St. John of the Cross, Spinoza and Hegel. Among our twentieth-century theologians, Bishop Barnes and Dean Inge receive special commendation for their courageous attempts to find their way back to the fountain head, the saddest figure who, beyond all others, could claim to be the authentic voice of God.

The supreme merit of this volume is that it will compel its readers to ask themselves how much of their creed is dross and how much is pure gold.

G. P. GOOCH

Chalfont St. Peter

INTRODUCTION

The Impact of Darwin

Very appropriately, I am commencing this book in 1959, the centenary of the publication of *The Origin of Species*, for although the idea of evolution was not unknown in the West—George Louis Bouffon, for instance, having written on the theme in the eighteenth century—it was not until the advent of Huxley and Darwin that the idea was forcibly brought to the attention of a shocked general public.

The religionists—and most people in that era paid lip-service to religion—quickly averted their gaze from this sacrilegious theory that shattered the very basis of their theology. The idea that man, instead of being the unique work of a creator who produced the world and its contents in the space of six days, was physically a development from the lowest form of sentient life, was one from which the Western world has never recovered, and which, together with the influences of Karl Marx and Sigmund Freud, accounts for the almost total materialism of current Western thought, a materialism that has affected the religionists as well as the laity, since they cannot escape, and, owing to their faulty spiritual education, are unable to answer, the continuous doctrinal bombardment of scientific materialism.

This tragic state of affairs—for, as C. G. Jung assured us, it is the lack of an inward, spiritual life that chiefly accounts for the unhappiness and widespread mental disease of today that lead to both adult and juvenile delinquency, despite the unprecedentedly high standards of material living—need never have followed from the publication of this thought-provoking book had the religious instruction of the West not been so primitive and unrealistic. On the contrary, it could, and may even now, have quite the reverse effect; for the idea of evolution explains and elucidates almost every problem of human life, not excluding that of religion. The more thoroughly we examine it, the more clearly we come to see that it provides the clue for which mankind has been seeking throughout his entire sojourn on this planet. It suggests a reasonable answer to the "Why?" as well as to the "How?" Everything about us bears the mark of evolution, a striving for perfection, whether in the manufacture of things like automobiles, aircraft and armaments, or in the intellectual endeavour to improve on languages, political theory and material science. And that this urge is equally evident in spiritual matters can be proved by any student of Comparative Religion who turns from the primitive writings of the Rig-Veda to the teachings of the modern Vedantists, such as those of Swami Prabhavananda, Aldous Huxley and Dr. S. Radhakrishnan, and sees how the first lispings of the awakening human consciousness in the ancient Hindu Scriptures have evolved into the sublime utterances of a Perennial Philosophy, the highest point to which metaphysical thought has so far attained.

Unfortunately, such evidence of spiritual progression is lacking in the orthodox religion of the West, owing to the fact that the monotheisms of the Middle East—Judaism, Christianity and Islam—have, unlike tolerant and eclectic Hinduism, always been rigidly exclusive, each claiming to be the unique revelation of God to man, a revelation to which nothing may be added nor anything taken away, and without unquestioning acceptance of which salvation is impossible.

Such terms obviously eliminate any chance of evolution, as does the bibliolatry induced in the congregations of all these religions by ecclesiastical insistence that the Bible (or the Koran) contains the only veritable Word of God, and that everything in these primitive Scriptures is true and God-derived. Fantastic though this fundamentalism may seem to a scientifically-minded generation, such teachings have been reiterated with so much power and authority behind them for so many centuries (the Christians inheriting the already ages-long indoctrination of the Jews), that there are untold thousands of earnest Christians, even today, whose spiritual life and values depend on their belief in the infallibility of what is often alluded to as "The Book".

It was this attitude that accounted for the appalling harm done in the last century by the publication of *The Origin of Species*, an event that would have left the Vedantists and other Eastern religionists who had access to the wisdom of the *Upanishads* and the *Bhagavad Gita*, completely unmoved; for these works are wholly concerned with the subject of spiritual evolution, and their students have been familiar with the idea that so shocked the Victorians, at least since the days of Patanjali, who was known as the Father of Evolution. But it was also implicit in all the religions of the world, of the West as well as the East, that taught what was in ancient times, the almost universally accepted doctrine of metempsychosis, which is also a feature of those magnificent expositions of the perennial philosophy made by Plato and Plotinus that have been so inexplicably rejected by Western theologians in favour of the primitive theories of ancient Judaism and pagan Mithraism.

The Philosophy of Compassion will show that it is these extraneous and outmoded theories that have been shattered by the impact of Darwin, and not the original Creed of Christ which cannot possibly be affected by any theory of materialistic science, since, like the perennial philosophy, of which it is an evolutionary development, it is wholly concerned with immaterial life, and man the invisible, neither of which depends on the illusory, ever-changing, biological factors with which the author of *The Origin of Species* was concerned.

It is surely a striking proof of the weakness of the teachings of religious orthodoxy in the West that the very theory which caused a failing, and often complete abandonment, of faith among its congregations, should have been the means of that great spiritual eclectic, Mohandas Gandhi, living the sort of life that every Christian should, but all too seldom does, lead. For it was precisely because Gandhi believed both in evolution and reincarnation that he was inspired and enabled to lead such a deeply spiritual and selfless life in a densely materialistic age. He taught that "in our present state we are . . . only partly human; the other part of us is still animal; only the conquest of our lower instincts by love can slay the animal in us".* While of reincarnation he says, "I am a believer in previous births and rebirths. All our relationships are the result of the sanskaras we carry from previous births".† "Those who believe in the soul . . . know that the soul never dies".‡

In this last sentence we have what is probably the most fundamental difference between the teachings of the Western religions and those of the perennial philosophy and of the original Creed of Christ. He who declared, "Before Abraham was, I am", and who never rebuked the declared belief of his followers in reincarnation, (Matthew 16:13, 14 and John 9:2, 3), but indeed actually confirmed it when, in reply to his disciples' question:"Why then say the scribes that Elias must come first?" he answered explicitly, "Elias has come already" (to which, to avoid any possible doubt, Matthew adds, "then the disciples understood that he spoke unto them of John the Baptist") could obviously have had no part in formulating the completely untenable theory of orthodox Christianity, that a new soul is born with every body, dying with it and being resurrected on a suppositional Judgment Day. To substitute such a theory for the far more logical one formerly held throughout the ancient civilised world, of the soul's co-existence with its immortal source, as the ray co-exists with the sun, was to invite the atheism of today, for it not only outrages reason, which tells us that what has a beginning must inevitably have an end, but also denies that inner knowing by which such theories are tested, and which intuitively rejects the completely untenable.

* Quoted by René Fulop-Miller in *Lenin and Gandhi* (G. Putnam's Sons).
† *Harijan*, 18 August, 1940.
‡ *Young India*, 20 November, 1924.

An interesting sidelight on this subject was provided some years ago by the result of the enquiries made by Geoffrey Gorer for a book he was writing on the state of the Englishman's religion. He gained his information by means of 5000 questionnaires taken from a large cross-section of the public, and found, to his amazement, that a wholly disproportionate percentage of the population believed in reincarnation, in spite of the fact that in no Western Church, orthodox or unorthodox, was this theory taught. He wrote, "The prevalence of this belief was the most surprising single piece of information that came out of my research". And, in his report quoted in *The Observer*, he added: "A minority carry this belief to the logical point of stating that human souls can pass into animals". He found it quite impossible to account for the wide acceptance of what he referred to as this "Eastern" belief among people of the West, to whom it was never taught by their spiritual pastors. But, in fact, it was once as widespread in the West as it is in the East, and not only was it held by those most logical of all thinkers, the ancient Greeks, centuries before the birth of Jesus Christ, but it actually survived in the Catholic Church until A.D. 553 when, at the Fifth Church Council at Constantinople, it was anathematised, with other teachings of the great Alexandrian theologian, Origen, at the instigation of the Emperor Justinian.

That an idea which not only "makes sense", but now, as we find, is to some extent compatible with the scientific theory of evolution, should have been arbitrarily dismissed by a handful of State-serving churchmen who had nothing better, but indeed something considerably worse, to put in its place, is one of the greatest tragedies in the history of a Church that was supposed to be perpetuating the teachings and outlook of Jesus Christ.

But Truth has a tenacity that ensures its survival despite all the efforts made by often far from truthful theologians to conceal it. The abandonment of truth as a moral absolute is traceable at least as far back as Clement of Alexandria, who, quoting Plato, spoke of permissible "medicinal lies"—such as a doctor tells his patients for their good. This notion inevitably led to the concoction of fantastic dogmas, myths and legends supposed to be "good" for the souls of the simpler brethren, but which, in course of time, distorted Christianity out of all recognition. These untruths appeared to be necessary because the theologians themselves did not know the Truth. They had not discovered the clue of evolution which would have accounted for the many Biblical contradictions and illogicalities that they were continually having to explain away to pagan and other critics once it had been decided to accord to the Old Testament the same divine authority as to the New. Had it occurred to the Christian theologians that, together, these records of what were often two diametrically opposed ways of life constituted an historical chart of the evolution of primitive religious thought to the heights of God-realisation, the difficulties and perplexities would no longer have existed. The validity of the Old Testament could always have been tested in the light of the New, and teachings that did not conform to the Creed of Christ could simply have been discarded. But the determination to give the same authority to the former as to the latter obstructed the natural evolution of the spiritual hypothesis, nullified much of the purification of the Old Testament that Jesus had tried to effect, and hopelessly confused the mentality of those endeavouring to understand and follow the way of Christ.

The hampering clutch of an earlier tradition has always been the great obstruction to the evolution of religion. Unlike the evolution of a concrete article, such as a motor car, when all faults are ruthlessly discarded, and improvements constantly sought and, when found, immediately made, the development of religion has always been impeded by the clinging errors of the human mind that have become so sanctified by age and custom that few dare expose them; and primitive beliefs have been so firmly implanted in the consciousness of mankind that it seems impossible to dislodge them.

In the case of Christianity this is particularly evident, and the message of the New Testament bears the appearance of an angel whose strong and beautiful wings have been rendered powerless by, on one side, the tar of paganism, on the other, the ship's oil of Judaism. Christianity has never saved mankind as it was intended to do because it has never been allowed to soar, never been free to fulfil its divine function, owing to the fetters that have bound it to earth. Burdened by Tradition and the claim that Judo-Christianity is a unique revelation of God to man, instead of being, as it really is, an example of the evolution of the God-idea, it is almost impossible for that idea to evolve further within the Churches. Such progress as it has made has been through the persistence of the inner leaven of divine Wisdom functioning mainly outside the Church in what the Orthodox would describe as heresies and heretics, and in the experiences of the Mystics. Recently, as we have seen, it has been aided by the scientific theory of evolution protruded on our notice in the last century, but which, as an idea imperfectly conceived, has been latent in human consciousness from the beginning of recorded time.

In her recently published book, *Lascaux: Paintings and Engravings*, Annette Laming suggests that the cave-paintings of animals and beings half-animal, half-human, are something more than emblems of hunting magic, and may well be the substance of an early religion. If this is so, it seems likely that such a religion would be influenced by what pre-historic man (Lascaux is now dated about 13,000 B.C.) had retained in his consciousness of a former sub-human existence. This also seems to have survived in the ancient Egyptian religion, which was from the first despised by other religionists for the prominent part that animals played in its worship and ceremonial. We know, from Porphyry, that the animal masks worn in the Mithraic mysteries symbolised man's biological connection with the lower animals; and certainly the doctrine of metempsychosis, found from earliest times in India, Egypt, and, via Pythagoras, in Greece, must have resulted from an intuitive recognition of a link between physical man and the lesser creatures.

The idea of evolution seems to have been formulated in scientific terms for the first time in the West by Thales Milesius, one of the Seven Wise Men of antiquity, who taught that water was the single primal element from which everything had been formed. His disciple, Anaximander, a natural philosopher, was even more explicit, and taught that all living creatures were originally born of earth and water mixed together and heated by the sun—a materialistic version of the Trinity—and that man, who had gradually developed from the lesser creatures, was originally a fish.

This last theory, however, long preceded the men of Ionia who lived at a time when the Israelites were captives in Babylon, for it had appeared in the most ancient religion of Babylon and Chaldea, in which the spirit of the Ocean was worshipped as the supreme God, Ea. As W. St. Chad Boscawen wrote in *Religious Systems of the World:*

> Ea was the God ... of the mystic deep, the Oceanus, which surrounded the earth like a serpent, and which was his symbol ... (Men) heard his voice in the murmur of the ebbing and flowing tide ... They saw his anger in the stormy waves ... in the depths of its coral caves he dwelt invisible to man yet knowing all things.

It was during the reign of Ea, when all men were barbarians, that, according to Berosus, the Babylonian historian, a being half-fish, half-man arose from the Persian Gulf, or Red Sea, and civilised the Babylonians by teaching them arts and sciences, and instructing them in politics and religion. This sea-god was afterwards known as Dagon, the God of the Philistines,* and survived long enough to be included in the Roman Pantheon where he was identified with Janus, that name being derived,

* Judges 16: 3.

according to Macrobius, from Ea-nus, i.e., Ea, the original sea-god. The mitre worn by the Pope today is the fish-head of Dagon. His wife, or female counterpart, was named Derketo, for even in the earliest times the deity was regarded as androgynous, the Mother as well as the Father of all. And these two, who were essentially one, were the archetypes of the merman and mermaid of folk-lore. But the idea behind these symbolic forms may well have been the intuitive recollection that the physical man's origins lay in the sea, and the belief that at some period during the evolutionary process, he had appeared as half-man and half-fish. This theory is borne out by another fragment from Berosus, preserved by George Syncellus, describing the ancient chaos as portrayed by the Chaldeans. It reads:

> There was a time, they say, when all was water and darkness. And these gave birth and habitation to monstrous animals of mixed forms and species. For there were men with two wings, others with four, and some again with double faces. Some had the horns of goats, some their legs, and some the legs of horses and the fore-parts of men, like the hippocentaurs. There were bulls with human heads, dogs with four bodies ending in fishes, horses with dogs' heads; and men and other creatures with the heads and bodies of horses, and with the tails of fishes. And a number of animals whose bodies were a monstrous compound of the dissimilar parts of beasts of various kinds. Together with these were fishes, reptiles, serpents, and other creatures, which, by a reciprocal translation of the parts to one another, became all portentously deformed, the pictures and representations of which were hung up in the temple of Belus. A woman ruleth over the whole whose name was Omoroca, in the Chaldee tongue Thalath, which signifies the sea; and in the course of connexion, the moon.

This curious account from the deepest antiquity suggests the beginning of the worship of the Woman as the mother of all things. For if the sea were considered to be the Source of all, it became the birthplace even of the gods, and a female figure identified with and symbolising the sea, would have been regarded as the supreme Goddess, the mother of the gods.

The description of the monstrosities may conceivably be a picture held in the collective subconsciousness of the human race of the evolutionary force experimenting with forms. In his *Divine Legation* Bishop Warburton offers proof that these were the originals of the puzzling animal–human figures, an amalgamation of different species found on the wall of the temples, pillars and other buildings of ancient Egypt, and which were also depicted in the initiatory caves of the various Mystery Religions.

They certainly appear to bear a distinct relationship to the strange Apocryphal writings of Ezekiel, Daniel and St. John the Divine. Ezekiel 1:10.11 is a case in point. There we read of the four great beasts who came up from the sea: "The first was like a lion and had eagles wings . . . and a man's heart was given to it: . . . and to another like a leopard, which had upon the back of it four wings of a fowl", and so on.

Without the explanation provided by Berosus these fantastic writings are inexplicable, but as a race-memory of primeval chaos, believed by the lawmakers of antiquity to be important religious mysteries that must be most carefully preserved, they are not to be lightly dismissed in a scientific age.

They may even account for the Mosaic commandment regarding the making of graven images. Moses, well acquainted with the religion of Egypt, would have been taught their significance, and would have realised that this ancient evolutionary idea of man struggling against natural forces to a state of full biological manhood, could not possibly be equated with the theory of the six-day creation story and the special creation of man that was to base his legislative system. Therefore, unlike the pagan priests, he would not wish such a belief to be preserved, and the best way of destroying it was to forbid the pictorial reminders treasured by the pagans. Nevertheless, despite all that Moses and his devotees could do, there remained, even among the Jews, an apparently irresistible interest in the graven images of the gentiles which the most vigorous punishments of the jealous Lord God failed to quench. However, after the Dispersion, it went underground, and Christianity, especially of the early and Protestant variety, did all it could to deepen the entombment by a rigorous enforcement of the second clause of the Decalogue. Only in certain secret societies and heretical cults did any hint of the subject survive, and therefore little remained of the ancient knowledge to cushion the blow when, in the last century, science began to proclaim that the most intricate forms of life had developed from the plankton, and that man proveably had the salt of the sea in his blood.

The danger of Darwin's book lay not in its theory but in the fact that the mentality of orthodox Western religionists had been deliberately and persistently indoctrinated with a false idea that contradicted, and could not possibly be combined with it. The religionists of antiquity, with their awareness of the unity of being, and of the essential oneness of all life, that was inculcated by the teaching of the metempsychosis, would have been as unmoved by it as was Gandhi; but mentally fettered as they were to the Fundamentalist outlook, neither Christian churchmen nor their congregations gave the theory the serious consideration it so richly deserved. They either shied nervously from it or angrily rejected it out of hand.

The materialists, on the contrary, seized upon it with joy as the scientific confirmation of their own point of view. But the strange thing about it is that, if studied in depth, this same theory even more surely confirms the spiritual hypothesis. And had the religionists possessed more faith in Truth than fear of the vulnerability of their theology they would have found that, far from undermining religion, the idea of evolution not only explains it but proves it to be the sole means whereby man can achieve his destiny.

The figure of the Centaur, which is the Sign of Sagittarius, depicts man's evolutionary status, the hindquarters of the beast reminding him that his task is to slough the animalism which impedes his emergence to the state of full manhood, as the chrysalis impedes the creature within it from using its wings until it struggles mightily to free itself from the constraining sheath. The evolution of the butterfly demands physical effort; that of man requires mental and spiritual effort by means of the wisdom and discipline that are found in idealistic philosophy and true religion; true religion being the original teachings of those men who alone were capable of giving such instruction, since they themselves had taken the next step in evolution. These God-like men, notably Gautama the Buddha and Jesus the Christ, had made the transition from Centaur to full manhood, so that it could truly be said of their characters that they were the image and likeness of the Highest Good. Thus, they were capable of teaching others how to make the transition. In this very real sense, they were exemplars and saviours. They did not theorise about biological evolution, being concerned not with the flesh but with the spirit of man; but they triumphantly demonstrated that spiritual evolution to a higher state of being was possible, and, by their very existence, provided the evolutionary goal, or Mark, as Paul put it, for the rest of mankind. Their conception of religion was not a collection of myths, legends and ceremonial rites, but a way of thought and life whereby man could become something finer and better than an earthbound, frustrated Centaur.

There are many who believe, with Arnold Toynbee, that only a great spiritual revival can save the West. But if religion is to be revived, it must be in the form of the teachings of the great Masters and not in that of the inventions of the theologians or a mere emotionalism without thought, like that of the popular "Billy" Graham and other modern revivalists. In a scientific age religion, like everything else, needs a rational and intellectual basis. The despisal of intellect and reason which set in early in the history of the Church, and was deliberately encouraged by those who found intelligent questions difficult to answer, was, although the perpetrators did not recognise it as such, fundamentally a despisal of God. For every inspired religion and philosophy has explicitly, or implicitly, defined God as Mind, and therefore to substitute belief for knowing was to prevent conscious unification of the individual mentality with the great Parent and Source of all.

The Gnana Yoga of Hinduism, and the Gnosis of Alexandrian Christianity, as surely as Platonism and Neo-Platonism, insist that to *know* is the highest evolutionary achievement, since really to know is to *be* what man was destined to be. Clement of Alexandria, in describing the Two Lives lived within the Early Church, made it evident that the lower life was that of the believer, the higher life that of the Knower, or Gnostic. Therefore, before we can hope for an effective spiritual revival, we must learn what religion, or the spiritual life, really was, and is. We must at least know something of the history of religion, and face the fact that, so far, what has been called by its name has hindered as much as it has helped the evolution of mankind. Or, to be more explicit, that the teachings and lives of the evolved men have helped, and that the organisations set up in their name to perpetuate their teachings have eventually, and almost invariably, done the reverse, becoming serious obstructions on the evolutionary path. It was to this phenomenon that Jesus was referring when he said to the churchmen of his times:

> Woe unto you, scribes and Pharisees, hypocrites! For ye shut up the kingdom of heaven against men: for ye neither go in yourselves, neither suffer ye them that are entering to go in.*

Idealistic philosophy, the perennial philosophy of the Wisdom Religion, has done much to perpetuate the essence of the teachings of the evolved men; but this has usually been available only to the few, the intelligentsia, who are often the least willing to benefit by it, preferring to confine it to the realm of theory. The Unitarians, against great odds, have continued to bear witness to the unity of the Godhead. Certain esoteric cults, secret societies and other forms of heresy have managed to preserve various aspects of the Greater Mysteries in which the Wisdom Religion was taught in times of antiquity; but probably only the mystics have fully understood the original teachings, and their witness, coming from so many different Faiths, convinces by its unanimity.

Correct teaching and faithful practice are both essential to spiritual evolution, which is not, as some appear to imagine, something that hap-

* Matthew 23 : 13.

pens inevitably; nor does it proceed in a straight and direct line. Coastal erosion, perhaps, provides the best illustration of its course. Sometimes there is a tidal wave, with the advent of a great Teacher; but most of the time there is an ebb and flow. Certain individuals, such as Pythagoras in Italy and Plato in Greece, occasionally reach a high peak; then there is a recession, as though the evolutionary urge has exhausted itself. But looking back over a great distance of time, it is possible to trace a steady gain of ground in the general consciousness of the West. Fragments of the wisdom of the evolved men have reached and influenced the multitude, acting—to change the metaphor—as a leaven. This is particularly true of Christianity. The divine seed sown by the Master that was so soon buried deep under a mountain of reactionary teachings and misrepresentation, has nevertheless done considerable leavening work. The world at large is, perhaps, very little better than it was 2000 years ago in terms of social, national and international policy. Man's potentiality for destruction has increased beyond computation, and he seems as unfit as ever he was to be entrusted with materialistic knowledge. But individually people are kinder than they were, more sensitive to the sufferings of others than they were in the days of the Persian and Roman empires; and that kindness has resulted in the West largely from the leavening of the spirit of Jesus Christ.

The Welfare State, despite its many imperfections, is one of the fruits of this inwardly felt kindness. The concern for the under-privileged, the hatred of war, the revulsion from the death penalty, the many humanitarian movements, are others. None of these instincts and impulses would have been thinkable among the masses of pre-Christian Rome, except perhaps during the reign of Numa Pompilius, according to the accounts left to us of its policies and people.

Nor would such sentiments have been experienced by many of the Fathers of the Early Church, whose compassion seems to have been mainly cerebral. Their policies, indeed, led directly to the tormenting of men on the rack and the burning of women at the stake, not during the throes of total war, when such acts might be excused as "defensive", but as a considered policy against helpless human beings, in the attempt to propagate and universalise Jesus Christ's Creed of Compassion.

The advent of a man of some sensitivity, like Francis of Assissi, was considered such a miracle that he was made a saint. Today, people of far greater compassion and wisdom than this much-lauded man, go unrecognised about their business. In the present age such behaviour, especially as regards compassion for animals, is taken for granted by a great number of ordinary people; but few realise that, without the leaven of the spirit of Christ, it would not exist, and that such individuals, whether they know it or not, are evolving people, nearer in character than others to the original Model.

Evolution is essentially not a process in time but an inward quickening of awareness, an awakening. This may be the result of a long period of preparation, a steady breaking down of animalistic resistance, or a slow clarification of vision; or it may take the form of the religious experience known as conversion, which, when genuine, is spiritual awakening. True conversion is, in fact, true evolution. The individual is raised above the common consciousness to something higher. She, or he, sees for the first time with the Third Eye, which Philo Judaeus so well described as "the invisible and more divine eye which is placed in our Mind". It is with this eye that we perceive the kingdom of Heaven "at hand", i.e., in the very place that dense earthliness has seemed to be, and become aware of a state of being quite different from the one to which we have been accustomed, of a higher and more perfect life that alone can satisfy us once we have awakened to it. This is the Kingdom that Jesus revealed by his every act and word, a Kingdom ruled by compassionate Love, the one law of which was the law of harmony, where all the values of a world governed by violence and compulsion are reversed. This is baptism by the spirit of Christ whereby the initiate is enabled to take the next step in spiritual evolution.

In the course of this book it will be observed how persistently the spirit of compassion that existed long before the birth of Jesus of Nazareth, has been resisted throughout the ages, not only by the materialists, militarists and the masses, but by orthodox religionists. Yet, unmoved, it has "stood at the door and knocked", and here and there, in every era, there have been those who have opened their hearts and admitted it, and so have, to some extent, become one with what Christians term "the spirit of Christ".

The forms it took in the past, and in other Faiths, have gone largely unrecognised by Christendom, trained by jealous, narrow-minded priests to believe that the nature of God was, for the first and only time in history revealed in the person of Jesus, the Nazarene. But the refusal to believe that the Christ-spirit existed before the advent of Jesus is to misunderstand both the eternality of the Christ and the mode of spiritual evolution. Centuries earlier, the spirit of compassion and non-violence had appeared in the East, in the teachings of the gentle Lao-Tze, the harmless Mahavira, the wise and pitiful Buddha, Gautama. The temptation to refer to these great Teachers will not be easy to resist in writing this book, but to attempt to deal adequately with their philosophies, in addition to those of the West would be impossible in what must in any case be an outsize volume. Moreover, it is the evolution of religious thought in the *West* that *The Philosophy of Compassion* is intended to delineate, and this can be traced most clearly through the teachings of the Mystery Religions wherein the spirit of compassionate Love and Wisdom appeared in female form. It is with the original ascendancy, and subsequent repression and subjugation, of Woman and the feminine qualities—always so prominent in the characters of the evolved men—that this book is chiefly concerned.

Throughout the history of Western religion women have played, since the abandonment of the goddesses, such an inconspicuous part that they are believed to have had very little influence on it. With male teachers, prophets, saviours so much to the fore, it is forgotten, or overlooked, that the female deities, sibyls and other oracles of antiquity, as well as such legendary figures as Numa's Egeria and Socrates' Diotima, had an extremely potent, though often concealed, influence on the great men, and, through them, on the policies of their times. But the true gospel of the Woman has always lain in that "still, small voice", of compassion, so tragically ignored throughout the history of mankind, drowned in the clamour and shouts of the masculine way of life. Moreover, whenever it has appeared, either in female form or in the androgynous characters of the evolved men of all creeds, it has been fiercely resisted, silenced, and, sometimes, crucified. The reason for this fatal policy is that the true nature, status and qualities of Woman have never been correctly assessed, owing, again, to ignorance on the subject of evolution. Judging her externally, and therefore superficially, primitive man, to whom bodily strength was a supreme value, dismissed her as his inferior; and, until very recent years, this judgment has never been seriously questioned. Philo Judaeus, for instance, voicing the opinions of Persians, Greeks, Romans and Jews alike, stated that "the female is nothing else but an imperfect male".* The theory of evolution, however, has cast doubts on this dogmatic assertion; and a fine modern thinker, the late Rev. William Hayes, founder of the Order of the Great Companions, once wrote:

> Biologists tell us that woman has been the pioneer of progress from the beginning. In the upward path from the lower species she has led the way —in the decrease of hairiness, in the upright gait, in the shape of the head, and the face and the jaw. Just as woman has led in these purely physical improvements, she may lead in moral improvements . . . Woman is the civilizer.

* Fragments of the *Lost Works*.

This is surely an arresting thought, and seems to be related to the second chapter of Genesis, where woman is recorded as having been the last "creation" in the ascending order of evolution.

When answering the question of why the woman in this allegory was not made out of the earth like men and the beasts but out of the rib of the man, Philo wrote that it was "in order that woman might not be of equal dignity with the man".* But in the light of the theory of evolution, a truer answer might be that woman, being less of earth earthly than man and the beast, was made of something between earth and heaven. She might, in fact, be considered the highest form of evolution, and her innate and original virtues of gentleness, peaceableness, protective love and compassion may be just those that should have been most assiduously cultivated by humanity in general for its own good. If this is so, the age-old mistake about the nature and value of woman may well have proved as fatal as that made about the nature of God. In fact, the two subjects are closely related since the idea of God as Father–Mother, the divine equipoise of male–female qualities, has persisted, in theory, from the earliest times; but in practice, worship in the West has almost invariably been of an all-male God, and the masculine qualities of power, will, intellect, strength, and so on.

When Philo defined the most divine thing in man as Mind, he was making a statement that would have been acceptable alike to pagan, Greek, Roman and Catholic theologians; and when he declared that the mind which is in each of us is, in reality and truth, the man, he was merely echoing a conclusion reached by the greatest idealistic philosophers of the human race. But this was only one aspect of the deity—the male. Of the essential "better half", the female aspect of compassionate Love, which should influence and control the activities of the "male", and which was so evident in the characters of Gautama the Buddha and Jesus the Christ, Philo said nothing.

May it not be that this failure properly to evaluate Woman and her qualities is responsible for the present violent and power intoxicated age, so completely unbalanced by its all-masculine outlook and policies? Is it not obvious that what is needed above all else to redress the balance is just the acceptance and application of that truly maternal compassionate love, that reverence for life, which has been despised and rejected from the beginning of time, but for the lack of which humanity is now in danger of destroying itself? Since man-made religion and an all-male God have so evidently failed to civilise and tame humanity, is not the time now ripe for the return of the long-banished Goddess?

* *Questions and Solutions.*

Like Janus, who could suitably be called its symbol, religion has always been two-faced. Looking outward, it has presented its exoteric, or masculine aspect, the world-affirming doctrines of the patriarchs, priests and theologians whose intention has always been to make man conform to a law-abiding and orderly existence on earth. Looking inward, it presents the esoteric, feminine and world-transcending side, taught first by the goddesses of antiquity, and afterwards by the evolved men of the human race, which was intended to prepare man, by means of self-purification and other radical disciplines, for a mode of living far above what at present we conceive of as life. To use, once again, the simile of chrysalis and butterfly, the masculine aspect might be said to regulate the life of the chrysalis, while the feminine aspect aids the butterfly to emerge from its limiting sheath. The masculine perpetuates the *status quo*, the feminine is the way of evolution to a higher state. The masculine is for the man who is content to remain a Centaur; the feminine is for the initiate who aims at the status of Perfect Manhood.

Clement of Alexandria, having been accustomed to these distinctions in the pagan religion of which he is believed to have been an initiate before his conversion to Christianity, was probably the first to introduce the idea into the Catholic Church. As he saw it, the Christian community of his day was two in one, the inner life within the outer life, the esoteric Church within the exoteric Church. The ordinary believer lived the lower life based on fear, faith and hope, and was required to give unquestioning obedience to authority. But for the Gnostic, the man of knowledge, who understood what Clement called "the science of divine things"* there was the higher life of freedom, through joyous and complete surrender to the will of God.

Unfortunately he suffered from the delusion that the one life must inevitably grow out of the other. Although this may have been the case with the Mystery religions, and even in the Hellenised form of Christianity of Clement's day, it has certainly not been so since the time of Constantine, when the gulf between the orthodox believer and the Gnostic became so wide as to be virtually unbridgeable, organised Christianity constituting a cage from which the occupant could never hope to escape and soar into the upper air. And yet this cage, woven of outmoded dogma, primitive superstition and pagan myth, is what most people today regard as Christianity, or true religion. Is it to be wondered at that millions are ready to consent to the next generation being given an entirely secular and irreligious education? Unfortunately this means throwing away the immensely precious baby (Gnosis)

---

* "On Spiritual Perfection." *Strom.*, Book VII, Ch. I.

with the extremely stagnant and undesirable bathwater of man-made theology.

Only by the recovery of the perennial Wisdom-philosophy which contains the essence of true religion, the divine science that has always been the foundation of the spiritual life; only by the return of the Goddess always equated with Wisdom, can we hope to avoid the spiritual death planned for us by the modern Pharaohs whose evolutionary aim for mankind is its attainment to the status not of angels but of worker ants.

CHAPTER I

The Birth and Nature of the Mysteries

The Mystery Religions, or the Mysteries, as they were more generally referred to, are well named, for, from their foundation to the present day, they have been beyond all things mysterious, enshrouded in an atmosphere of profound secrecy.

As I pointed out in *Mithras: The Fellow in the Cap*, there are two main reasons for this. In the first place, it was because, from their inception, the initiates into these Mysteries were bound to secrecy on penalty of death, and secondly because the religion that eventually superseded them had very good reason to respect this wish for concealment, having both deliberately and unconsciously appropriated much of the old pagan religion and its rites while claiming to be a unique revelation from God to mankind, owing nothing to the teachings of other religions. But a third reason lies in the very nature of the Mystery Religions which always functioned on two levels, the esoteric and exoteric, known as the Lesser and Greater Mysteries, the former being in some important particulars a direct contradiction of the latter, so that those who judged them from their ritual, and orgiastic displays, gained an entirely erroneous idea of the true nature of what has generally and vaguely been thought of as "the pagan religion".

Nevertheless, despite all attempts of friend and foe to hide the true nature of the Faith that was superseded by Christianity much more has been learned of it by scholars than the general public has been allowed to know, and since my researches for the book on Mithras, I have discovered two experts on the subject of the Mysteries, both considerable linguists and scholars, who made it their business to examine every shred of evidence that they could glean from works of antiquity on the subject, and although more than a century separated them, came to a convincingly unanimous verdict.

Bishop Warburton, writing in the eighteenth century, devoted much of the first volume of his *Divine Legation of Moses* to a consideration and description of the Mysteries. He was writing at a time when an irreligious intelligentsia, disillusioned by what the Church had made of Christianity, had returned to a thorough examination of the pagan faith, and magnificent translations, from Homer to Ovid, were being made by such authors as Addison and Pope, fellow-guests with Warburton at Prior Park, where Ralph Allen—whose daughter Warburton married—

THE PHILOSOPHY OF COMPASSION

kept open house for the men of letters of his day. In this Roman setting, their researches into antiquity were exceptionally deep and thorough.

The second expert was the Rev. Alexander Hislop who, while he wrote much later, in the second half of the nineteenth century, does not seem to have drawn on the information in the *Divine Legation*, which makes the likeness of his discoveries to Warburton's all the more convincing. Of the two, Hislop's knowledge and scholarship in relation to the subject was infinitely wider, and his book, *The Two Babylons* gives the impression that his search for truth was unbiassed, while Warburton was writing principally in defence of the Jewish and Christian religions which prevented his going too far into the teachings of the older religion. As a consequence he convinced himself that the first Mystery Religion was founded by the Egyptian rulers, in which he differed from Hislop who, citing Biblical authority, as well as that of Josephus and Philo, made out an excellent case for the greater antiquity of the Chaldean Mysteries. Warburton once or twice touched lightly on this theory which in his day, as in our own, was held by a number of eminent scholars, including Sir Isaac Newton; but, for some reason, he preferred to ignore this evidence and to settle for Isis and Osiris as being the originators of the Mysteries.

Another marked difference between the two scholars is that Warburton, though naturally obliged to refer to the two Goddesses who were the principal figures in the Eleusinian Mysteries, refrained from examining the teachings and influence of these deities, and, in true Protestant manner, carefully avoided the subject of the connection of women with the pagan, or any other form of, religion. Whereas Hislop, who had studied further—though equally Protestant—was only too well aware of, and indignant about the power and influence of women in the formulation of the Mystery Religions. Therefore his thesis must be given priority in a book that primarily seeks to trace the influence of woman and her qualities on Western religion.

Hislop shows that, in order to understand the Mysteries, it is necessary to go back to the very beginning of history, to the time when Nimrod, the mighty hunter, looking about him on an unarmed world, decided that he would violate the unwritten law that then existed, of respecting the bounds of other men's habitations; and, having trained a large army of followers, began to hunt the unarmed human race, and soon acquired an extensive empire with the greatest ease.

We find an account of this first tyrant in Genesis 10:8–11 (King James' Version); but Moffat's translation is much more illuminating, and tells us that Nimrod was an Ethiopian, and the first man on earth to be a despot, being a mighty hunter before the Eternal; and that his empire began at Babylon and other places in the Land of Shinar, but that afterwards it extended to Assyria where he built the great city of Nineveh.

Nimrod was the son of Cush, who was the son of Ham and therefore the grandson of Noah, and in a footnote found in *Herodotus* (Book II:181), we find:

> The Chaldeans... appear to have been a branch of the great Hamite race of Accad, which inhabited Babylonia from the earliest times. With this race originated the art of writing, the building of cities, the institution of a religious system, and the cultivation of all science and of astronomy in particular.

Nimrod was, then, the founder of the first recorded civilisation, and from his chief city, Babylon, came the worship of the hosts of heaven, the first of all the great systems of religion, and one which inevitably permeated its successors so that much that it contained, both of good and evil, survives, although usually quite unsuspected, in all Western religions today.

Josephus, in his *Antiquities* depicts Nimrod as having been the first man to oppose the rule of God; and as he was an Ethiopian, and therefore black, and, being a hunter, is portrayed on Nineveh sculptorings as wearing horns, we are tempted to believe, with Dr. Hislop, especially after reading the description given by Josephus, that he may have been the earthly prototype of the devil. In *Antiquities*, Book I, Ch. 4: 2, we are told:

> It was Nimrod who excited them (the people) to such an affront and contempt of God. He was the grandson of Ham, the son of Noah,—a bold man and of great strength of hand. He persuaded them not to ascribe it to God, as though it were through His means they were happy, but to believe that it was their own courage which produced that happiness. He also gradually changed the government into tyranny—seeing no other way of turning men from the fear of God, but to bring them into a constant dependence upon his power. He also said he would be revenged on God if he should have a mind to drown the world again: for that he would build a tower too high for the waters to be able to reach! and that he would revenge himself on God for destroying their forefathers.

Devil or not, it may be deduced from this passage that Nimrod was the first scientific materialist, and, like so many of the inventions of his modern successors, his great achievement, the Tower of Babel, did nothing to add to the happiness of mankind. He was obviously the sort of man who had brought the retribution of the Flood upon mankind, since we read in Genesis 6:13 that it was because the earth was filled with *violent* men that it had to be destroyed.

Josephus goes on to tell us that "the children of Ham possessed the land from Syria and Amanus and the mountains of Libanus, seizing upon all that was on its seacoasts and as far as the ocean, and keeping it as their own. . . Nimrod, the son of Chus, stayed and tyrannized at Babylon". (*Ibid.*, Ch. 4:2).

In his *Posterity of Cain* Philo Judaeus confirms Josephus' opinion of the first tyrant when he "allegorises" the history of Nimrod, and writes:

> The sons of earth removing their minds from contemplation, and becoming deserters so as to fly to the lifeless and immovable nature of the flesh . . . abandoned the better rank which had been allotted to them as their own, and deserted to the worst rank which was contrary to their original nature.

This implies that the original nature was peaceable, and that men kept to their boundaries and lived and let live, for he adds: "Nimrod being the first to set the example of this desertion; for the lawgiver says, that 'this man began to be a giant upon the earth'."

The use of the word "giant" here is interesting and illuminating, for it proves conclusively what is meant by this term used in several places in the Old Testament. In Genesis 6:1, 2, 4, for instance, we read:

> And it came to pass that the sons of God (Moffatt translates this as "angels") saw the daughters of men that they were fair; and they took them wives of all that they chose . . . There were giants in the earth in those days . . . When the sons of God came in unto the daughters of men, and they bear children to them the same became mighty men which were of old, men of renown.

From this it is quite clear that the term "giant" which has sometimes given rise to fanciful ideas in the simple and credulous, is used to describe men great, not in body but in reputation; leaders and rulers of other men. This idea is evidently the Jewish equivalent of the one so prevalent among the Greeks and Romans, that a great man, such as Alexander or Augustus Caesar, must be born of a woman who has been visited by the sun-god. The Jewish idea may, indeed, have preceded the Grecian and Roman versions, the West deciding to "go one better".

Before leaving the subject of giants, it is interesting to note that Clement of Alexandria (Stromata, V:10) refers to the belief that truth first came to earth when the fallen angels confided it to the daughters of men that they had taken for wives. This is probably one of the earliest records of the tendency, found everywhere in the annals of antiquity, to regard woman as the source of wisdom.

Philo goes on to say of the first tyrant:

> The name for Nimrod, being interpreted, means desertion; for it was not enough for the thoroughly miserable soul to stand on neither side, but having gone over to its enemies, it took up arms against its friends, and resisted them, and made open war upon them; in reference to which fact it is that Moses called the seat of Nimrod's kingdom Babylon, and the interpretation of the word Babylon is "change"; a thing nearby akin to desertion . . . for the first step of every deserter is a change and alteration of mind.

Philo is here evidently making Nimrod a symbol of the turning of the mind from the contemplation of spiritual things to an absorption in material things. In other words, the abandonment of the spiritual for the material hypothesis. Nimrod is depicted as, and may well have been, the first dialectical as well as practical materialist, the opposer of God, playing Ahriman to the Lord God's Ahura Mazda, so becoming the devil or the father of lies.

In *Confusion of Languages*, XXVI, Philo describes the Tower of Babel as a turning away from God, and observes:

> Any strong building which is erected by means of plausible arguments is not built for the sake of any other object except that of averting and alienating the mind from the honour due to God, than which object what can be more iniquitous?

Some authorities cite Ninus as having been the first ruler of Babylon, but that this was merely another name for Nimrod seems obvious from a passage that Augustine quotes in *The City of God* from the works of Trogus Pompey. It runs:

> Ninus of Assyria was the first that followed the lust of sovereignty in breaking the old hereditary law of nations. He first warred on the adjoining countries, subduing the people (as yet unacquainted with arts military) as far as Lybia.*

As this has already been recorded of Nimrod, in the Scriptures as well as by Josephus and Philo, we can only assume that Ninus and Nimrod were one and the same person. Augustine goes on to say:

> It is certain by the record of other writers, that Ninus enlarged the Assyrian monarchy exceedingly: and that it continued longer than the Romans' hath done as yet. For as the chronicles do deliver up account, it was 1,240 years after Ninus' reign to the translation of this monarchy to the Medians.

* Trogus Pompeius (Latin historian 41 B.C.)

This is further confirmed by Lemprière, who tells us that Nino, the capital of Assyria called Nineveh in Scripture, was built by Ninus, an achievement ascribed to Nimrod in Genesis 10.

Dr. Hislop contends that Nimrod married his mother, Semiramis; which is possible, as this custom was afterwards practised by the rulers of Persia. But the traditional belief is that Ninus married the wife of one of his generals, in which case Semiramis may have acquired the title of the Mother of the God as the result of having had her husband deified as Nin after his death; in the sense that she was responsible for his existence as a God. During their reign they were known as Bel and Beltis, the Lord and the Lady, and when, at his demise, the reins of government fell into the hands of his wife, Bel became identified with the sun-god of the Babylonian religion, subsequently and variously known as Bel, Baal, Jupiter, Merodach and Tammuz. This would account for the common belief that Bel was the founder of Babylon.

Although it is possible that the identification of the earthly ruler with the sun-god originated in India, this was almost certainly the first instance of it recorded in the Middle East, from whence it spread, via Egypt, to the West. Wherever we turn in ancient history we find accounts of this practice. One of the early records is found in the text of Hattusilis, the Hittite king, who reigned c. 1275–1250 B.C., and which begins:

> Thus speaks Tabarna Hattusilis, the great king, king of Hatti, son of Mursilis, the great king of Hatti, descendent of Hattusilis, king of Kussara. I tell the divine power of Ishtar; let all men hear it, and in the future may the reverence of me, the SUN, of my sons, of my son's son, and of my Majesty's seed be given to Ishtar among the gods.

Here we have the complete identification of the king with the sun such as we find with the Egyptian Pharaohs, and which has never been entirely eliminated from the idea of monarchy that is primarily "rule by the Highest"—the highest on earth, as the monarch of the skies is the highest in heaven; the earthly ruler, when not wholly identified with the God, being his mortal counterpart and under his protection, as in Mithraism.

The Ethiopian Semiramis who was said by Hesiod to have played a considerable part in founding the Chaldean Mysteries, probably imported the idea from the East. Although Warburton differs from Hislop as to the actual identity of the Founder of the Mysteries, he is equally convinced that these cults originated from rulers and not from the priests. His reason for this is that the moral perfection which was taught to, and required from, the Initiate was wanted more by the legislator or Civil

Magistrate who had to keep order than by the priest. On this subject he quotes Locke as saying:

> The priests made it not their business to teach the people virtue; if they were diligent in their observations and ceremonies, punctual in their feasts and solemnities, and the tricks of religion, the holy tribe assured them that the gods were pleased, and they looked no further; few went to the schools of philosophers, to be instructed in their duty, and to know what was good and evil in their actions: the priests sold the better pennyworths, and therefore had all the custom: for lustrations and sacrifices were much easier than a clean conscience and a steady course of virtue; and an expiatory sacrifice, that atoned for the want of it, much more convenient than a strict and holy life.

This, put bluntly, has always been the difference between exoteric and false religion and the esoteric and true; between the teachings of the legislators and prophets and the theology of the churches supposed to be perpetuating their teachings.

Semiramis, who proved to be a great, wise and beneficent ruler, evidently realised, with the modern Einstein, that the only way to have a better world was to have better people, and the design of her religious system was to ensure this. The antiquity of this foundation is so great that we can only discover its nature through its offspring, the Mysteries of Egypt, Greece and Rome, all of which varied only in superficialities. When she died, after ensuring that Babylon was the most magnificent city in the world, Semiramis was deified with her husband, in relationship to whom she was depicted as Mother-Wife. In images that were set up everywhere and adored, she was depicted carrying her son in her arms. Together they were worshipped as Rhea, the Mother of the Gods, and Nin; and from these two the worship of Mother and Child spread throughout the earth. Isis and Horus appeared in Egypt; Ceres with Deois in Greece; Ishtar and Tammuz in Assyria; Kuan Yin and her Child in China; Tara and the Buddha in India; Ciocoatl and Quexalcoatl in North America; Rhea-Cybele with Attis, and so on. Hislop writes:

> As time wore away and the facts of Semiramis' history became obscured, her son's birth was boldly declared to be miraculous; and thereafter she was called Alma Mater, the Virgin Mother.*

This idea persisted in human consciousness far beyond the days of Ovid who, in his *Metamorphoses*, described the miraculous birth of Aesculapius. Saved from the womb of his dead mother, the pure Coronis.

---

* *The Two Babylons*, by Alexander Hislop. (S. W. Partridge & Co.)

by his father, Apollo, the child was taken to the cave of Chiron the Centaur whose daughter was a prophetess. The Addison translation of her prophecy regarding the demi-god reads:

> Once as the sacred infant she surveyed
> The god was kindled in the raving maid,
> And thus she uttered her prophetic tale:
> "Hail, great physician of the world, all hail;
> Hail mighty infant, who in years to come,
> Shall heal the nations and defraud the tomb;
> Swift be thy growth, thy triumphs unconfined
> Make kingdoms thicker and increase mankind.
> Thy daring art shall animate the dead,
> And draw the thunder on thy guilty head:
> Then shalt thou die.—But from the dark abode
> Rise up victorious, and be twice a God."

In Babylon and Egypt the Queen of Heaven was named Athor, the dwelling place or habitation of God, in which all gentleness and mercy lived. The names of her sons changed with their locality. Tammuz, the lamented son, Shamash, Merodach, Bacchus, Adonis, all were the identical offspring of the Mother of the Gods; all, as dying and resurrecting sun-gods, were the male counterparts of the Wisdom-Goddess, symbolised by the Moon.

In the Old Testament we find her as Astarte or Ashtoreth, the former name being derived from Asht-tart, meaning "the woman that made towers", and Ash-Turit, or Ashtoreth, meaning, "the woman that made the encompassing wall". In Phrygia, as Cybele, she was known as the Goddess of Fortifications, the Idaean Mother of the Gods, being depicted, like Diana of the Ephesians, with a mural crown. In *Opera*, III, and *Fasti*, IV, 219–221, Ovid explains Cybele's crown of towers by saying that it was accorded her "because she first erected them in cities", having already stated (*Metamorphoses*, IV, 58, Pyramus and Thisbe) that Semiramis was the first queen of Babylon to have surrounded it with a wall of brick.

Like her husband, Semiramis was a huntress and warrior, but, unlike him, she was credited with outstanding benevolence. In addition to her battlements, she is said to have made extensive roads and aqueducts, bringing irrigation to deserts. At her death she was believed to have been changed into a dove. This bird was always the symbol of Semiramis, as it was of the Queen of Heaven in her role of Venus. Diodorus says that the name Semiramis is derived from the word for dove in the Syrian dialect (Assyrian: Summatu = Dove), and under the form of this bird, she was worshipped in Babylon. The third member of the Assyrian Trinity is represented by the wings and tail of a dove.

This gentle, harmless creature was ever the bird of the Queen of Heaven, as the powerful, soaring Eagle was the Bird of the Sun. With its qualities of gentleness, mercy and peaceableness, the Dove symbolised the female aspect of deity, as the Eagle symbolised the strength, power, majesty and dominion of the masculine aspect of God. For both Jew and Christian the Dove was identified as the Holy Spirit of God from the time of Noah, but of its Babylonian origin and its derivation from the Mysteries, there can be no doubt.

Hislop writes that, according to Hesiod (*Theogonia*, V:453, p. 36), "the grand distinguishing feature of the ancient Babylonian system was the Chaldean Mysteries (which) can be traced up to the days of Semiramis, who lived only a few centuries after the Flood. . . In the Mysteries, which she had a chief hand in forming, she was worshipped as Rhea, the great Mother of the Gods".

Thus, in addition to all her other achievements, this remarkable woman played a great part in founding the Mysteries that, for centuries, were to influence the minds and lives of mankind, openly from her own days to those of Theodosius the Great, who extinguished Vesta's fire and closed her Temple, and secretly, to a considerable degree, up until the present time.

Referring to the system of the Chaldean Magi, Layard wrote in *Nineveh and Its Remains*, (Vol. II, p. 440):

> Of the great antiquity of this primitive worship there is abundant evidence, and that it originated among the inhabitants of the Assyrian plains, we have the united testimony of sacred and profane history. It obtained the epithet of PERFECT, and was believed to be the most ancient of religious systems, having preceded that of the Egyptians . . . The identity of many of the Assyrian doctrines with those of Egypt is alluded to by Porphyry and Clemens.

The aim of the Mysteries since their inception seems to have been the most exalted that has ever occurred to the mind of man—that of obedience to the demand made thousands of years after their foundation: "Be ye therefore perfect. . . " which, in modern terms, might be described as the evolution of man to his highest potential.

In an Appendix to Ouvaroff's *Eleusinian Mysteries*, Christie writes:

> Mr. Ouvaroff has suggested that one of the great objects of the Mysteries was the presenting to fallen man the means of his return to God. These means were the cathartic values—(i.e. the values by which sin is removed),

by the exercise of which a corporal life was to be vanquished. Accordingly the Mysteries were termed *"Teletae"*, "Perfections", because they were supposed to produce a perfectness of life. Those who were purified by them were styled *Teloumenoi* and *Tetelesmenoi*, that is, "brought to perfection", which depended on the exertions of the individual.

Warburton quotes Tully as saying of the institution of the Mysteries:

In my opinion your Athens . . . has . . . given nothing better than those Mysteries, by which we are drawn from an irrational and savage life, and tamed, as it were, and broken to humanity. They are truly called INITIA, for they are indeed the beginnings of a life of reason and virtue. From whence we not only receive the benefits of a more comfortable and elegant subsistence here, but are taught to hope for and aspire to a better life hereafter.

This clear description of the process of evolution through religion could hardly be bettered. The Mysteries were, then, the means of spiritual evolution so far as this was understood in times of antiquity. We have abundant evidence that all the Mysteries—those of Babylon, Egypt and Greece—were basically similar. Ouvaroff writes (*Ibid.*, Sect. II, p. 20):

The Mysteries transplanted into Greece and there united with a certain number of local notions, never lost the character of their origin derived from the cradle of the moral and religious ideas of the universe.

Layard confirms this when he quotes Birch as saying:

The Zodiacal signs . . . show unequivocally that the Greeks derived their notions and arrangements of the Zodiac (and consequently their mythology that was intertwined with it) from the Chaldees. The identity of Nimrod with the constellation of Orion is not to be rejected.

The many names that are given to the single character of Nimrod brings us to the most confusing aspect of the Mysteries—the constant resolving of the One into the Many and the Many into the One, which was the central theme of the worship of the hosts of heaven. Hislop tells us that:

The Mysteries set out with the doctrine of the unity of the godhead . . . At bottom they recognised only Adad, the one God. Adad being triune, this left room . . . for three forms of divinity—(Father, Mother, Son); but all the multiform divinities with which the pagan world abounded . . . were resolved substantially into so many manifestations of one or other of these divine persons . . .

Upon this extremely important point Warburton and Hislop are in complete and absolute agreement. The Lesser Mysteries, intended for

26

the general public, taught, according to them both, the worship of the gods. In the Greater Mysteries, taught only to the most trustworthy, these gods are revealed as deified men, and the final truth of the divine unity is made known: God is One, the soul and spirit of all; the so-called lesser gods, inasmuch as they are good, being but attributes or aspects of the ONE. Warburton insists that this was the deepest secret of all the Mysteries, the violation of which was so dangerous to civil government that it was punished by the death penalty. He writes:

> In the Eleusinian rites there were two Mysteries, the Greater and the Less . . . We are told that the lesser mysteries were only a kind of preparatory purification for the greater and might be easily communicated to all— that four years was the usual time of probation for those greater mysteries, in which . . . the secrets were deposited.

And the most closely held secret was that which denied the polytheism that has always been ascribed to the pagan religion, by affirming the unity of the godhead. It was contained in an Orphic hymn quoted by Clement of Alexandria and Eusebius, and addressed to Musaeus, a disciple of Orpheus. It begins:

> I will declare a secret to the initiated, but let the doors be shut against the profane . . . Go in the right way, and see the sole governor of the world, he is one, and of himself alone, and to that one all things owe their being. He operates through all, was never seen by mortal eyes, but does himself see everyone.

Isocrates called the Mysteries the thing human nature principally stands in need of, since their teachings are aimed at taming and purifying that nature. Warburton quotes Epictetus as saying of them:

> Thus the Mysteries became useful; thus we seize the true spirit of them when we begin to comprehend that everything therein was instituted by the ancients for instruction and amendment of life.

He goes on to say that "Porphyry gives us some of these moral precepts, which were enforced in the Mysteries, as to honour their parents, to offer up fruit to the gods, and to forbear cruelty towards animals. . . It was required of the aspirant that he should be of a clear and unblemished character. . . To come at the truth he was severely interrogated by the priest or the hierophant impressing him with the same sense of his obligation to conceal nothing, as is now done at the Roman confessional".

Elsewhere he writes:

> Proclus tells us that the Mysteries and the initiations drew the souls of men from a material, sensual, and merely human life, and joined them in

communion with the gods. Nor was a less degree of purity required of the initiated for their future conduct. They were obliged by solemn engagements to commence a new life of strictest piety and virtue; into which they were entered by a severe course of penance, proper to purge the mind of its natural defilements.

So we see that primarily the Mysteries aimed to restore the soul to its original purity and perfection. In order to do this the mind of the initiate must be freed from the primitive beliefs and superstitions of the rest of mankind. In a world where licentious gods and goddesses were forever setting a bad example to their devotees, the people had a good excuse for immorality in claiming that they were emulating the gods. But for the initiate there was no such excuse. He knew the truth and was therefore free from illusion. Warburton tells us that the instruction was given by the priestess of the Eleusinian Mysteries, who, in the place of Proserpine, conducted the aspirant through the initiation. He writes:

> The Mystagogue taught them, that Jupiter, Mercury, Venus, Mars, and the whole rabble of licentious deities, were only dead mortals; subject in life to the same passions and infirmities with themselves; but having been on other accounts, benefactors to mankind, grateful posterity had deified them; and with their virtues, had indiscreetly canonised their vices. The fabulous gods being thus routed, the supreme cause of all things naturally took their place. Him they were taught to consider as the creator of the universe, who pervaded all things by his virtue, and governed all by his providence . . . What (was overthrown) was the vulgar polytheism, the worship of dead men.

The initiated, he tells us, were hereafter called by a Greek word indicating " one that sees things as they are " instead of as they had formerly seemed to be.

That Saint Augustine was well aware of this secret doctrine of the unity known to the pagans is shown in his *City of God* (Book VI, Ch. 2) where he comments on it in the words:

> Let Jupiter be one . . . Let him be Jupiter in the sky, Juno in the earth; Neptune in the sea . . . Pluto in the earth, Proserpina in the earth's lowest parts, Vesta in the household's fire, Vulcan in the smith's shop, Sol, Luna and the stars in the spheres. Apollo in divination, Mercury in traffic, in Janus the porter, in the bounds Terminus, in time Saturn, in war Mars and Bellona, in the vineyards Bacchus, in the corn Ceres, in the woods Diana, in men's wits Minerva . . . Let Jupiter be all these that I have reckoned . . . If it be so . . . what should they lose if they took a shorter course, and adore but one God? . . . They say that the stars are all and every one real parts of Jove . . . If they worshipped all the stars inclusively in Jupi-

ter's particular person, they might satisfy them all by this means in the adoration of him alone.

It is impossible to know when and how this ancient metaphysical game of resolving the many into the One first occurred to the human race. The thought of a supreme God seems to have existed in the primitive nature–religion that preceded the universal worship of the hosts of heaven. It was the golden Being that emerged from the watery wastes at dawn and returned to them in the evening—believed at first to be the son of God, but gradually superseding the Father and becoming God Himself—that raised the thought of man from the earth to a contemplation of the starry heavens. We cannot guess when mankind first had a suspicion that the many lights above emanated from the One, which seems to have been the basis for the concept of monotheism; but Plutarch plainly states that the Pythagoreans held that "the earth is neither motionless nor situated in the centre of surrounding space, but that it revolves in a circle about the central fire, not being one of the most important nor even one of the primary elements of the Universe".

That this scientific fact may also have been known to the early Chaldeans is strongly suggested by the fact that, in the Mystery religions, the Moon was understood to be the female counterpart of the Sun—two manifestations of a single light. It is quite conceivable that men living so much nearer to the psychic animal kingdom than modern man may have had an instinctive realisation that there was but one light of which all the celestial orbs were but reflections, even as their intuitive realisation of the one Life resulted in the doctrine of the metempsychosis; and from the inner sense of the basic oneness of things may well have evolved the notion that all gods were but attributes of the one Supreme Deity.

The single root of the legends of Rhea, Cybele, Ishtah, Isis, and Diana of the Ephesians with her castellated crown is obvious enough; but the myth of the greatest of all the mysteries of the West—those of Eleusis—seems to have been originally of a different order, concerned more with earth than with heaven until, amalgamated with the rites of the sun-god, it became yet another form of the worship of the hosts of heaven.

When primitive man was first initiated into the arts of agriculture he may well have marvelled at the miracle of sowing and reaping. Tiny seeds cast into the dark earth reappeared in the course of time as fields of golden corn, which became the bread of life for man. Earth was then perceived as the Great Mother who abundantly fed her children, and, as such, she must be placated and worshipped. The original myth upon which the Eleusinian Mysteries were founded seems to have sprung from this concept. Ceres, or Deo, has a beloved daughter, the Maid, or Proserpine, who disappears into the earth, or underworld, where she has been taken by Pluto, the ruler of those regions, and is mourned by her mother as lost. But owing to the intervention of the King of Heaven, i.e., the Sun, the daughter is released once a year, and appears every spring to spend six months with her mother. Thus the Sun was introduced into the agricultural myth. Men perceived that as his golden Majesty penetrated the earth, it began to bud and blossom; therefore the Sun was recognised as generator, or Creator-God, and the Great Mother, or Earth, was regarded as his wife, being impregnated by him. This raised her to the status of the Queen of Heaven, and identified her with that paler, lesser luminary who appears at night and cools the ardours of the day. From this concept evidently grew the idea of the Queen of Heaven being, in her divine aspect, Wisdom, the restraining Mother of the God, or Gods.

In the earliest Greek legend the interest was focussed primarily on the female figures, with Pluto and Zeus as subsidiary characters. But when the Cult of Cybele and Attis was, as it is said, brought to Greece from Phrygia by Eumolpus, and amalgamated with that of Deo and the Maid, the emphasis gradually changed. The two goddesses were recognised as being embodiments of one and the same Wisdom, while the dying or mutilated God entombed in the cave of matter and rising again, was seen as a variation of the theme of seed fallen into the ground, dying and resurrecting. It was the recognition by Erechtheus, King of Athens, of Ceres and Cybele as being but two aspects of the same Wisdom-Goddess, the teacher of agriculture to whom his country owed so much, that led him to ordain their mutual worship in the Eleusinian Mysteries.

With the passing of time this amalgamation seems to have resulted in the figure of Kore or Proserpine being superseded by that of the young God. Iacchus, Dionysus, or Bacchus, as Attis seems to have been variously renamed by the Greeks, was said to have been the son of Zeus and Semele, or Proserpine, corresponding to heaven and earth. Semele being killed by the lightning of the King of Heaven, Zeus bore the babe in his thigh until he was ready to be born. In the descent of Dionysus to the underworld to bring back his mother from the shades, we have another version of the story of Orpheus and Eurydice. Orpheus, of whom Aristophanes wrote: "Orpheus taught us the Mysteries, and to abstain from murder, i.e. from a life of rapine and violence, such as men lived in the state of nature," was also identified with Dionysus in the manner of his death. Both, like Adonis and Osiris, were torn to pieces; all were represented by a bull which, known as Serapis in Egypt and Rome, also played a prominent part in the Mysteries of Mithras, the animal symbolising the god's procreative nature. In all these cults omophagia, the eating of raw flesh, was practised in the endeavour to assimilate the virtue of the god represented by the animal victim, its blood being drunk for the same purpose.

By the time of Herodotus, Iacchus had evidently become the most prominent figure in the Eleusinian Mysteries, for in Book VIII:65, he speaks of the religious procession travelling from Athens to Eleusis, crying out "Iacchus". In *Antigone*, 1119, Sophocles identifies Iacchus with Dionysus. The names might change, but the male figure was always that of the son, or sun, of God who came to show mankind how to escape from the earthly spell by which they had been trapped. Ceres, or Proserpine, like other suffering mothers, from the mother of Tammuz to the Catholic Virgin, suffers through her child, and the cup drunk in the early Mysteries was to commemorate the suffering of the Mother.

But in the orgies attending the masculine cults that grew out of the originally woman-founded Mysteries, woman is represented as something infinitely remote from the spirit of Wisdom, Love, mercy, unity and compassion with which she was originally equated. Women now frenziedly tear the god apart and sacramentally drink his blood, the fruit of the vine. Or, hordes of harpies, discovering that Orpheus has become homosexual, will have nothing to do with him and tear him to pieces. This is a far cry from the gentle Isis who bitterly mourned the dismemberment of Osiris, and strictly forbade blood-sacrifices, as did Ashtoreth and other manifestations of the Queen of Heaven. But these perversions and distortions of the original Mystery teachings are the inventions of the poets of whom Plato so disapproved that he allowed them no place in his Republic.

Despite these popular fantasies, however, the truth was still to be discovered in the Mystery teachings at a deeper level. Orphism, for instance, taught that Zeus had by Proserpine a wonderful child, Zagreus, who was eaten by the Titans. He could only win salvation from this disintegrated state by ridding himself of the Titan element through self-purification, which included the avoidance of funerals or the taint of birth, since the imperfect creature known as man was not fit to be perpetuated, abstinence from all animal food, and the wearing of white linen garments that had not been acquired from the lesser creatures.

Whatever the myth might be that attached itself to these cults, the aim to escape from "the circle of birth or becoming" seems always to have been the decree of Wisdom, or the Goddess.

It was after the fall of Troy that Aeneas took the god and goddess of the Mystery Religion of Phrygia into Italy. Here Cybele became known as Vesta, or the Great Mother, being worshipped, as we know, in the days of Romulus and Numa Pompilius. Attis was identified with Phoebus. We are helped on this point by an illuminating passage in *The City of God* (Book I, Ch. 4), where Augustine observes: "Nor could Troy itself that was ... the mother of Rome's progeny, in all her hallowed temples, save anyone from the Grecian force and fury, *though they worshipped the same gods*"; which indicates that the Eleusinian Mysteries had been established in Greece long before the fall of Troy.

The equation of Woman with Wisdom, which made her the Mother of the Gods, since Wisdom must precede and control all else, has been obscured by the emphasis that has always been laid on the earthward aspect of the Great Mother. It was thus that she was represented to the unillumined mind in the rites of the exoteric pagan religions of the East as well as of the West. In these she was depicted as the earth-goddess, the fecund generator of all living things, the Mother whose very name, Ma, or Mater, is derived from matter. The prominence given to her lower aspect, the nature-goddess, now cruel, now kind, as depicted in such hideous forms as the Indian Goddess Kali, has almost totally concealed what may be called her divinity, or heavenly nature, as understood by the initiate, and has therefore given as unbalanced a portrait of the Queen of Heaven as one of the sun-god would be if it only stressed his burning and destructive features. The virtue and wisdom of the goddess, her nature as revealed by the esoteric teachings of the Mysteries, seem, from the time when she was ejected from Zoroastrianism and angrily opposed and banished by the Jews, to have been purposely and deliberately concealed from humanity, only being referred to by a few great men— idealistic philosophers and world-teachers—who, whether they were aware of it or not, preached her gospel, the one basic Wisdom-religion upon which all the different forms of the Mysteries were founded.

As we have already seen, woman appears to have been identified with Wisdom from the earliest times, in the earthly as well as the heavenly sense, for the goddesses of the Mysteries were all believed to have been originally extremely wise human beings, owing their deification to this fact. Ceres was said to have brought the art of agriculture to the West, instructing the Grecian king's son, Triptolemus, how to reap, sow, plough, make bread, and care for the fruit trees, for which she was deified by the recipients of her benefactions as the goddess of corn and harvests. She was also reputed to have been a great legislator. Semiramis, as we know, was a woman remarkable for many achievements that would have required super-human wisdom in those early times to perform; while Cybele was later described by the Neo-Platonist Emperor Julianus as "the intellectual principle", the very fount of wisdom. Of the deification of Isis Augustine wrote in *The City of God* (Book XIV, Ch. 3):

"Some write that she came out of Ethiopia to be Queen of Egypt, and because she was mighty and gracious in her reign, and taught the subjects many good arts, they gave her this honour after her death, and that with such diligent respect, that it was death to say she had ever been mortal".

As we have already been told this of Semiramis, or Rhea, this passage, particularly as regards its allusion to Ethiopia, seems amply to confirm Hislop's theory that these goddesses possessed one and the same human archetype.

The unanimity of the esoteric teachings of these many deities certainly proves their oneness of mind. Those early observers of nature and her works appear to have discovered, together with the useful and practical information that they were able to impart to mankind in general, other far less agreeable secrets that could only be taught to the priests and the highest initiates, those spiritually prepared to bear the burden of such knowledge. Having seen nature in all her moods, and noted the cruelty and violence that lay behind the beautiful veil of the visible world—each sentient creature preying on another in order to live—these women were evidently realists. As actual or potential mothers, they must have come to realise that to bring another human being into such a world was to subject it inevitably to suffering, misery and death, and so arrived at the conclusion proclaimed to the world by Sophocles in his *Oedipus Coloneus*, that,

> Not to be born is past all prizing—
> But when a man hath seen the light
> This is the next best by far, that with all speed
> He should go thither whence he came . . .

a sentiment evidently shared by his contemporary Euripedes, who wrote:

> When a man is born we ought to assemble only to bewail
> His lot in coming into so much evil.
> But when one dies and comes to the end of troubles
> Then we should rejoice and praise his happy departure.

These poets perceived what the great Greek philosophers taught, that this world was not a place in which to linger, or something to be perpetuated, but a fallen condition to be outgrown as soon as possible by means of the Mind which was the highest good, while matter was the source of all evil. This teaching, which so surprises, and usually

c

33

antagonises, modern man when he finds it in the works of such great men of wisdom as Plato and Plotinus, undoubtedly had its birth in the Mystery Religions. For however much they differed in other respects, the persistent core common to them all was the great emphasis placed on continence and purity.

Here we have again a complete reversal of what we have been taught to believe about the pagan religions which are usually depicted as orgiastic revels of completely amoral gods and goddesses. But this erroneous impression was given by the exoteric religious celebrations and the stage plays that were based on the myths found in the works of the Greek poets; but it was certainly not true of the Mystery Religions themselves that were noted for their celibate priesthoods. The castration practised by the priests of the Goddess, which so shocked and horrified the world-affirming Jews, dated, according to Ammianus (L. XIV. c. 6) from the days of Semiramis. In Gibbon's *Decline and Fall of the Roman Empire*, (Vol. II, Ch. 19) a footnote states that Ammianus "imputes the first practice of castration to the cruel ingenuity of Semiramis", suggesting that purity, of which such a practice was the outward and visible sign, was from the first a basic demand of the Mystery Religions, and that Semiramis, as part-founder of the Chaldean Mysteries, instituted a practice that was later found among the priesthoods of all the Mystery religions in Egypt, Phrygia and Greece.

The gibe of both Jewish and Christian critics directed at the Galli, the castrated priests of Cybele's cult, and the celebrated Eumolpidae, the hierophants of the Eleusinian Mysteries, was that they made themselves like women, wearing feminine robes, which appears to have disgusted the masculine-minded monotheists with their determinedly patriarchal view of God. But it seems that these priesthoods who so deeply reverenced their goddess, wished to become like her, even as the worshippers of Mithras later moulded themselves on the masculinity and violence of the sun-god. The priests of the Mysteries may intuitively have realised what William Hayes declared, that the woman, with her qualities of peaceableness, tenderness, non-violence and gentleness, is a more evolved being than the belligerent, animalistic male, and that, as Wisdom, she must not only be worshipped but emulated. But to the Jew, militaristic Greek and Persian, for whom man was always the superior sex, compared with whom woman was a poor, feeble, creature, such submission to a feminine deity was unthinkable. And for a man to deprive himself of his power to procreate was, in their view, to rob himself of his manhood and likeness to divinity. Whereas, for the Galli and Eumolpidae, this practice was merely the outward and visible sign of their acceptance of the goddess's demand for inward purity. As the initiated Emperor Julianus was later to explain in his *Hymn to the Mother of the Gods* (487):

> She (the Mother-Goddess) bade me cut off no vital part indeed of my body, but . . . all that was superfluous and vain in the impulses and motions of my own soul.

Like other Gnostics, Julian was well aware that desire is not killed by physically preventing its indulgence, but only by a purification of thought —which he himself triumphantly practised—that eliminates the desire.

The demand of the goddess was, therefore, for the cleansing of consciousness, the casting off of the animalistic habits that impede man's spiritual evolution. But primitive mentalities are capable only of literal interpretation, and spiritual teachings, materialised, often have unfortunate results. It may well be that, like Origen, the great Alexandrian Father of the Church whose self-mutilation caused such a scandal among his peers, the pagan priests felt that in mixed company it was as well to take no chances of breaking one's vows!

In Greece and Egypt, however, where the shedding of blood was forbidden by the goddess, a preparation of hemlock was applied, instead of the knife, with the same effect. It was this materialisation of an exalted concept, this debasement of highly metaphysical teachings, that led to some of the revolting rites of exoteric paganism of which its critics complain. But it must be pointed out that the idea lying behind the practice of self-mutilation was not only found in the original Gospel of Jesus Christ (Matthew 19:12), which Origen took a thought too literally, and in the writings of Paul who made it quite obvious that chastity was a superior state to matrimony, but it persisted for many centuries in the Catholic Church after the incorporation of the myth of the Virgin Mary. The Mother of the Gods having become the Mother of God, was understood to have made the same demands on her devotees as her pagan prototype, to judge by such descriptions as that of Meschler in his *Life of Saint Louis of Gonzaga* (French translation by Lebriquier, 1891), where he writes of the saint:

> The inspiration came to him to consecrate to the Mother of God his own virginity—that being to her the most agreeable of possible presents . . . Joyous of heart and burning with love, he made his vow of perpetual chastity.

But the idea of perpetual chastity existing in a Church that makes a sacrament of marriage, and accepts the order to increase and mutiply as referring to matter and being the will of God, leads to a confusion and double-mindness on the subject of sex that did not exist in the Mystery religions. The Mother-Goddess provided a clear, if unpopular, sense of direction. But the Catholic theologians have always avoided facing the embarrassing fact that if everyone adhered to the ideal, and followed their celibate Exemplar, the end of the world that he promised to his followers must inevitably have come about with the universal acceptance of Christianity.

The esoteric pagan teachings on this subject are found in the Emperor Julian's description of the cult of Attis, in his *Hymn to the Mother of the Gods;* but as in his *Hymn to King Helios*, which precedes it, there is a most illuminating explanation of the relation of Wisdom to deity as understood by an initiate into the Mysteries, it would be as well to examine this before passing on to the subject of the Cult of Gallus.

An age-old idea persistently referred to in the works of antiquity is that Minerva, or Athene, sprang whole from the brain, or head, of Zeus, the Supreme God. This statement, so lightly dismissed by the literal-minded Augustine as being "merely poetic", has never received the attention from Christians that it deserves, for it is obviously a pagan version of the birth of the Logos that is described in the Gospel of John in the words:

> In the beginning was the Word, and the Word was with God, and the Word was God.

Both pagan and Christian statements mean that God, or Divine Mind—(Iamblichus speaks for the pagans when he defines the sun as the "mind" of the universe)—and the Wisdom that emanates from it, are one and inseparable; a reasonable explanation that would have saved the theologians at the Council of Nicaea a great deal of time if they had accepted it in its simplicity. But what never seems to have been noticed either by Christians or Jews is that the Logos for the pagans was one of the feminine gender, and that throughout the ancient world, this divine Wisdom, this daughter or Word of God, was always equated with, and symbolised by, the goddess, whether Minerva, Athene or Cybele.

In his *Hymn to King Helios* (407), Julian speaks of the relation of this Wisdom to the most High God who, whether he be called Horus, Apollo, Jupiter, Jove or Helios, "everywhere makes all things perfect . . . and marshalling together this great army of the gods into a single commanding unity, he handed it over to Athene Pronoia who, as the legend says, sprang from the head of Zeus, but I say she was sent forth from Helios whole from the whole of him, being contained within him".

Here we have the idea of the inseparability of the child from the Father that we find in John 10:30. Julian then goes on to describe Athene as the god's intelligence in perfect form who therefore

> binds together the gods who are assembled about Helios, the King of All: and she distributes and is the channel for stainless and pure life throughout the seven spheres.

It is Wisdom that resolves the many into the One, and that purifies and clarifies all things. Seven being the number of completion, the "seven spheres" denote total purification. "She is", Julian finally says of the goddess, "in very truth, a synthesis of the heavenly gods, and in their harmony she is the spirit of love and unity."

Here we have a portrait of the goddess who is the subject of this book, and who was, for Julian and the rest of the cultured world, the Holy Spirit of God and the Mother of the Gods; the giver not of earthly and fleshly life with its sufferings, agonies, and inevitable death, but of deliverance from this imperfect state through the Wisdom that is Life Eternal. It is of the relation of this Mother-Goddess, as Cybele, to the sun-god in his *role* of Attis that Julian writes when he describes the cult of Gallus, or Attis, in his famous *Works*.

In a footnote to the *Hymn to King Helios*, we find the following description of Julian's conception of the sun-god:

> Julian conceives of the sun in three ways; first, as transcendental in which form he is indistinguishable from the Good in the intelligible world, secondly as Helios-Mithras, ruler, of the intellectual gods, thirdly as the visible sun.*

This was the esoteric teaching of the true nature of the deity of the almost universal sun-worship known to us under the vague appellation of "the pagan religion".

It may be objected that the above quotation is a description that could only have been made after the purification and elucidation of the pagan faith effected by Neo-Platonism. Even if this were true, I would say that to obtain a correct view of anything, including a religious system, one should examine it in its most perfect form, and not as it may seem to be during the process of evolution. Or, to quote William James:

> Interesting as the origin and early stages of a subject always are, yet when one seeks earnestly for its full significance, one must always look for its more completely evolved and perfect forms.†

---

* *The Works of the Emperor Julian*, Vol. I (Loeb Classical Library), edited by T. E. Page and W. R. D. Rouse, Litt.D., with an English translation by Wilmer Cave Wright, Ph.D. (Heinemann, MCMXIII.)

† *The Varieties of Religious Experience*, by William James. (Longmans, Green & Co.)

But we have no evidence that any radical change was made by Neo-Platonic philosophy in the essential teachings of the Wisdom-religion. Religion and the philosophy of religion are two modes of expressing the same basic idea, the latter being the rationalisation of the former in which the idea of a trinity in unity was, from the earliest times, discernable. From Plato it found its way into the writings of those great theologians of the Early Church, Clement of Alexandria and Origen.

In the old Persian religion from which the cult of Mithras sprang, it was in his second form, as Helios-Mithras, that the sun-god was known; for there he was one of the seven spirits of God, the Amshaspands. As Julian put it:

> Kronos, Zeus, Aries, Helios, Aphrodite, Hermes, Selene are the seven planets. Though Helios guides the others he is counted with them.

The number seven was a significant one in all forms of sun-worship, and always seems to be related to the planets, or "the seven spirits of God"; seven aspects of the divine nature. Vesta was evidently accorded six vestal virgins in order to identify her as the female counterpart of Helios.

It is, however, in the third form, that of the visible sun, that Julian conceives of Attis. In his *Hymn to the Mother of the Gods*, he writes:

> But him who I call Gallus, or Attis, I discern of my own knowledge to be the substance of generative and creative minds . . . Now there are many substances and very many creative gods, but the nature of the third creator (Helios) who contains in himself the separate concepts of the forms that are embodied in matter . . . I mean that nature which . . . through its superabundance of generative power descends even unto our earth through the upper region from the stars, that is he whom we seek, even Attis.

He goes on to explain that Cybele is Forethought, or Wisdom, among the intelligible gods, and so is superior to Athene who is forethought among the intellectual gods; and that the true meaning of the myth of Cybele and Attis is that the Mother of the Gods conceived a passionless love for the creative and generative cause (Attis, the Sun), and wished to save him from descending to generation in matter, desiring that his attention should be given only to herself, the divine Wisdom:

> Therefore she commanded that cause to beget offspring rather in the intelligible region, and she desired that it should turn towards herself and dwell with her, but condemned it to dwell with no other thing. For only thus would that creative cause strive towards the uniformity that preserves it, and at the same time would avoid that which inclines towards matter. And she bade the cause look towards her . . . and not to be dragged down

or allured into generation. For in this way was mighty Attis destined to be an ever mightier creation seeing that in all things the conversion to what is higher produces more power to effect than the inclination to the lower.

This is what is meant, Julian tells us, when it is said that, "the Mother of the Gods exhorted Attis not to leave her or to love another". Helios must, in other words, ascend to his higher nature in order to be himself at his greatest—a thoroughly evolutionary concept! But it was the nature of the sun's rays to leap and dance unrestrainedly in its great generative power; and Attis descends into the cave, which plays so great a part in all the Mysteries, where he is wedded to the nymph, or matter. Whereupon the Mother, seeing no other way to save the situation, demands his castration; and this is the act symbolised by the cutting down of the pine-tree. Atonement for infidelity to the Highest frees the soul from generation, and Julian describes the mutilation and resurrection of Attis which takes place at the Spring Festival, in the words:

> The sacred tree is felled on the day when the sun reaches the height of the equinox (March 22nd). Thereupon the trumpets are sounded (March 23rd), and on the third day the sacred and unspeakable member of the God is severed (March 24th). Immediately after the castration the trumpet sounds a recall for Attis and for all of us who once flew down from heaven and fell to earth. And after this signal, when King Attis stays his course by his castration, the God bids us root out the unlimited in ourselves and imitate the gods our leaders, and hasten back to the defined and uniform, and, if it be possible, to the One itself. After this the Hilaria must by all means follow. For what could be more blessed, what more joyful than a soul which has escaped from limitlessness and generation and inward storm, and has been translated up to the very gods?

The symbolic descent into the cave, and re-ascent, occurs in all the Mystery Religions. Julian gives its esoteric meaning in one line: "The association of Attis with matter is the descent into the cave". This fall of consciousness to the physical realms from the spiritual, which is the soul's natural habitat, this downward attraction to matter instead of remaining in perpetual contemplation of the Good, or God, is the main theme in Greek philosophy from the time of Pythagoras who doubtless took it both from the Brahmins and from the Egyptian priests, who, as we have seen, were so early in touch with the Chaldean Mysteries. The fall of man, or mind, from a higher state to a lower, as an explanation of human suffering, seems, therefore, to have been an idea in the consciousness of humanity from the earliest times, so that relatively at least it might be considered an "eternal" truth. It is, perhaps, the most reasonable answer to the perpetual question of: "Why, if God is good, do we experience so much evil?" Whether it takes the form found in the Egyptian *Book of the Dead*, or of the descent of Orpheus, Aeneas or Proserpine into the nether regions, the symbolism is always the same, and the re-ascent is intended to illustrate the emergence of the soul from a life lived in matter to the life of the Spirit; the means being always the same: total purification from animalism.

Of the cult of Ceres and Proserpine which he calls "the most holy sacred Mysteries of Deo and the Maid", Julian writes:

> As in the festival of the Mother the instrument of generation is severed so, too, with the Athenians, those who take part in the sacred rites are wholly chaste, and their leader the Hierophant foreswears generation; because he must not have ought to do with the progress of the unlimited but only with the substance whose bounds are fixed so that it abides forever and is contained in the One, stainless and pure.

Since the whole aim of the Mystery Religions, as, indeed, of all the great World-Faiths, is the at-one-ment of the initiate with the Supreme Being, purification from all unlike that One, which is Spirit, is obviously an essential condition for its achievement.

Referring to the cutting down of the pine-tree, Julian makes what is at once a most interesting and tantalising statement when he says, "The cutting down of the tree belongs to the story of Gallus (Attis) and not to the Mysteries at all. But it has been taken over by them".

The tantalising thing about it is that he does not say *when* the myth was taken over by Mithraism, to which, as a Mithraist, he was obviously referring. He could hardly have been alluding to the early amalgamation of the cults of Ceres and Cybele, as he has already spoken of those as being separate Mysteries from his own.

In his book, *The Mysteries of Mithra*, Franz Cumont writes:

> It was undoubtedly during the period of moral and religious fermentation provoked by the Macedonian conquest that Mithraism received approximately its definitive form.

But it seems doubtful whether at that time, and coming from Persia, there could have been the same emphasis on absolute continence that was so prominent in Roman times. Cumont himself remarks that chastity and militarism are seldom synonymous, yet continence was one of the chief requisites in a soldier of Mithras.

Zoroastrianism, the parent Faith, though it demanded morality in its followers, was far too world-affirming to impose celibacy on them. It seems very probable that Mithraism came to this position through its contact with the Mother Goddess, and Cumont suggests a possible date for this amalgamation when he writes of Mithraism that 'from the moment of the discovery of traces of the Persian cult in Italy, we find it intimately associated with that of the Magna Mater (or Great Mother) of Pessinus, which had been solemnly adopted by the Roman people three centuries before".

The Mithraists may well have found that the converts they wished to make were too much attached to the idea of the familiar Queen of Heaven to be weaned from her by an all-masculine cult from which she was totally excluded. In fact the masculinity of Mithraism was so extreme that by making its initiatory tests too physically arduous for women to perform, they denied the hope of salvation to half the human race. Therefore, having already a high ethical code as regards sexuality (Cumont writes of this that "resistance to sensuality was one of the aspects of the combat with the principle of evil"), they probably saw fit to go a step further and accept the absolutist position demanded by Cybele.

The establishment of the Taurobolium in which the ceremonies of Mithras and Cybele were performed, is sometimes ascribed to the latter. This is curious for, as we have seen, there was nothing in the Cult of Attis to demand such an institution, whereas the central feature of Mithraism was the slaying of the bull by the sun-god. Moreover, it is difficult to associate such a practice with the non-violent policy of the Queen of Heaven who would not even allow her followers to wear garments that had necessitated taking life, and whose demand from the first had been "unbloody sacrifices", in the form of drink-libations and honey-cakes, or *boun*, which were small round cakes, symbolising the sun and marked with the Southern Cross. We find them illustrated in Cumont's *Mysteries of Mithra*, on a fresco depicting the sun-god's Supper, where they appear on a tripod in the foreground, and are evidently the pagan ancestors of our familiar hot cross bun.

Referring to this sacrifice being made by Empedocles, Diogenes Laertius (p. 227 b.) writes: "He offered me one of the sacred cakes called *boun* which was made of fine flour and honey." We read of these sacrifices being offered to Ashtoreth in Jeremiah 7:18, and 44:19. This was the great distinction between the goddess and her male counterpart whose priests were continually offering bulls in his honour. As Dr. Hislop puts it:

> The Goddess-Queen of Chaldea differed from her son ... He ... delighting in blood ... She, as the mother of grace and mercy, as the celestial "Dove", as the hope of the whole world, was averse from blood.

Nevertheless, we know that, from the earliest times, the priests of the goddess continually consecrated oxen to her. Lucian speaks of the animal sacrifices offered to the Syrian goddess, and the Sicilian priests of Ceres offered up sacrifices of oxen in honour of Proserpine's return from underworld. But the practice seems to have emanated from the priests, and not from the teachings or disposition of the goddess. Perhaps, like other hierarchies, having their eye more on the quantity of their congregations than the quality and purity of their deity's teachings, they may have decided that they must accommodate themselves to the popular rites and practices of the more virile and bellicose male god whose rising in the public esteem seems to have been in direct ratio to the moon's waning.

In the early agricultural times when the Eleusinian Mysteries were founded, the pacific, gentle wisdom of the seed-sowing goddess suited the climate of thought in the West; but when men turned their ploughshares into swords, and especially after the devastating invasion of the Persians, the non-violent wisdom of the goddess may well have seemed like suicidal unwisdom. Enquiries would have been made into the nature of the gods that had ensured victory for the enemy. As we know, the chief of these was Ormuzd, who, as we find in *Herodotus*, Book VII:53, was worshipped so assiduously by Xerxes and his armies, the principal aide of Ormuzd being Mithras, the warrior sun-god, easily identifiable with Apollo, the Grecian god of the Delphic Oracle. Whereupon the male god, the god of victory and power, became for many the symbol of the highest wisdom, and the priests of the goddess may have decided to hitch their wagons to this ascendant star, and to have established practices entirely at variance with the Wisdom-teachings of their deity.

There is a hint of this amalgamation of gentle goddess and warrior god in the disclosures made by Apuleius in his strange book, *The Golden Asse*, which probably contains as much as has ever been revealed to the general public of the nature of the Eleusinian Mysteries as they were celebrated in the early part of the second century. Here, the chief deity, Ceres, was said to have a high priest called Mythra, the name of the high priest always being that of the male deity who must otherwise be nameless. The refusal to name the principal god worshipped in any cult is one of the peculiarities found in the initiates of all the Mysteries. Throughout his *History*, Herodotus consistently refused to write the word "Osiris", although it was perfectly obvious to which God he was referring. Macrobius wrote that the Romans never revealed the real name of the chief deity of their worship lest their enemies should call upon him and he should go over to their side. This may explain the fact that although, as the excavated, architectural remains have proved, Mithras was the most popular god with the Romans and their legions during the first four centuries of our era, we find so little mention of his name in either pagan or Christian literature of the period; Apollo, Jupiter or Zeus being the names usually given to the supreme deity.*

In *The Golden Asse* Lucius Apuleius tells us how, having indulged his animal habits and lusts, he was turned by his mistress, who had promised to transform him into a bird with wings, into an ass instead, in which shape he had to live like the beast he had inwardly become, until through repentance and purification—symbolised by plunging himself seven times into the sea—he resumed his natural form by the power of the goddess to whom he had appealed. Apuleius's description of Ceres provides complete proof, if that were still needed, that deities believed by the unlearned to be many, were recognised by the initiates as One.

The eleventh book starts with the identification of the Moon with Ceres:

> I ... saw the Moone shining bright, as when shee is at the full ... then thought I that that was the most secret time when the goddess Ceres had most puissance and force ... Then with a weeping countenance, I made this Orison to the Puissant Goddesse, saying, "Oh blessed Queene of Heaven, whether thou be Dame Ceres ... or whether thou be the Celestial Venus, I pray thee, to end my great Travaile and misery."

And when the goddess appears, she says:

> I am she that is the natural mother of all things, chiefe of powers divine ... Queene of Heaven, the principal of the Gods celestial. ... My name, my divinity is adored throughout all the world in diverse manners, in variable customs and in many names, for the Phrygians call me Mother of the Gods: the Athenians, Minerva: the Cyprians, Venus: the Candians, Diana: the Sicilians, Proserpina: the Eleusians, Ceres: some Juno, other Bellona, other Hecate: and principally the Aethiopians. .. and the Aegyptians ... call me Queene Isis.

We have already seen something of the process of resolving the many into the One in the writings of Augustine and Julian. The former showed

---

* On this subject Plutarch writes (*Roman Questions*, 61); "How cometh it to pass, that it is expressly forbidden in Rome, either to name or to demand ought as touching the Tutelar god, who hath in particular recommendation and patronage the safetie and preservation of the citie: nor so much as to enquire whether the said deity be male or female? .... It is in regard of a certain reason that some Latin historians do alledge: namely, that there be certain evocations and enchantings of the gods by spels and charmes, through the power whereof they are of opinion that they might be able to call forth and draw away from the Tutelar gods of their enemies, and to cause them to come and dwell with them: and therefore the Romans be afraid lest they may do as much for them? ... so the Romans thought, that to be altogether unknown and not once named, was the best means, and surest way to keepe with their Tutelar god.

how the god was presented in female *roles* as well as male, while the latter concentrated on his male aspects. Apuleius, however, describes only the unity of the goddess, and it should be noticed that Ceres–Isis speaks of herself as being the "chiefe" of all beings divine.

Owing to the androgynous nature of the Supreme Being, it was just as permissible to represent it in female as in male form. In Egypt, the Queen and not the King of Heaven was most generally depicted as the One. An inscription found in one of the temples of Isis reads:

> I am all that has been or that is, or that shall be. No mortal has removed my veil. The fruit which I have brought forth is the Sun.

Here Horus is clearly the secondary deity, an emanation of the One, and that One, the goddess.

Yet, however presented, the One always contained the power, will and creativeness of the male as well as the wisdom, love and protectiveness of the female. Even Mithras, the essentially male god, also appeared as Mylitta. These two-in-one were Mediator and Mediatrix between Ahriman and Ahura Mazda, or between man and the Supreme Being. This accounts for what is usually considered to have been a mistake made by Herodotus when he wrote (Book I, Ch. 131):

> Mylitta is the name by which the Assyrians know the goddess, whom the Arabians call Alitta, and the Persians Mithra.

Mylitta was Mithras when worshipped under his female form. Mithras is sometimes depicted as a lion—the Sun at its full strength in Leo, July—with a bee issuing from his mouth; and Mylitta is sometimes spelt Mylissa, derived from a word meaning "Bee". It was evidently the honey of this "Word" that was placed on the lips of the Soldiers of Mithras during their initiation. In his book, *Le Culte de Mithra*, M. Layard writes of the priestess who assists at the initiation of the Mysteries: "Her cap is tipped by the sun-star, but she also wears the crescent to show the hermaphrodite nature of Mylitta".

Osiris–Isis; Cybele–Attis; Mars–Bellona; Jove–Juno; Jupiter–Minerva, are the male–female names for the One, and so are—and frequently were—interchangeable, Ceres or Isis being paired, as we have seen, with Mithras, as Cybele was afterwards to appear as the Keeper of the Keys with Janus, having held that position hundreds of years previously under the name of Cardea. We can only control the sense of bewilderment and confusion caused by this constant deific reshuffling and re-aligning by keeping in mind the basic monotheism of the pagan idea.

But to return to the subject of Apuleius who, after receiving a promise of help from the goddess, goes to watch a procession made in her honour. Describing it, he refers to the blowers of trumpets which were dedicated to Serapis, the bull-headed symbol of Osiris, the Egyptian sun-god, and speaks of a priest who carries "the secrets of their religion, closed in a coffer", which were almost certainly the sacred relics of Osiris–Dionysus–Attis. There is also a reference to the pine-tree in the description of a boat launched by the Priest, of which he says: "The mast was of a great length, made of a pine-tree, round and very excellent with a shining top".

After his deliverance from the form of an ass, Apuleius felt that he should enter the service of the goddess who had freed him; but "the feare of the same withheld me", he writes, "considering her obeysance was hard and difficile, *the chastitie of the priests intolerable*". Later, however, he tried to get the priest to initiate him into the Mysteries. But the Hierophant recognised the need for further purification, and only when this was achieved, did the goddess appear to say that she had appointed her principal priest, Mythra, to be minister to him in his sacrifices. Then followed purification by water, abstinence from flesh and wine, and the usual lustrations. A linen robe was put upon him, and he was taken to "the most secret and sacred place of the Temple". Of what happened there, Apuleius writes that it is unlawful to tell, but he permits himself to admit:

> I approached neere unto Hell, even to the gates of Proserpina, and after that I was ravished throughout all the Element, I returned to my proper place. About midnight I saw the Sun, I saw likewise the gods celestial and the gods infernal ... behold now I have told thee, which although thou hast heard, yet it is necessary thou conceale it.

He emerged from what reads like the equivalent of the Twelve Tortures of Mithraism, "sanctified with Twelve Stoles". Twelve, like seven, was a particularly important number in all forms of sun-worship, relating primarily to the signs of the Zodiac, and, later, to the months of the year. Apuleius wore a cope upon his shoulders embroidered with beasts. He specifically mentions a Gryphon which was one of the degrees of the Mithraic Mysteries. He carried a light torch, as does the sun-god, and, indeed, writes: "I was adorned like unto the sun". The initiate was identified with the deity.

Nevertheless, when worshipping his goddess he declares, "Thou givest light to the Sunne". This, while reversing the order of nature, was true for those who perceived that Wisdom was the supreme Enlightener.

After embracing the great priest, Mythra, whom he refers to as his "spiritual father" owing to "the good which he hath done to me", Apuleius sails for Rome where his greatest desire was to make his prayers "to the soverign goddess Isis, who by reason of the place where her temple was builded was called Campensis"—yet another title of the Queen of Heaven!—"and continually adored by the people of Rome. Her minister and worshipper was I, howbeit I was a stranger to her Church, and unknown to her religion there".

In a further vision he was informed by his goddess that he must go through a second initiation since he was "only religious to the goddess Isis, but not sacred to the religion of the great Osiris, the sovereigne father of all the goddesses, between whom, though there was a religious unitie and concord, yet there was a great difference of order and ceremony".

Again, we are given little information except that Apuleius speaks of the "sumptuous banket (banquet) of mine entrie". Frescoes showing such a banquet being partaken by the sun-god and his followers, have been unearthed with other Mithraic remains, as we see from the illustrations in Franz Cumont's work. Once more Apuleius had to purify himself and "abstaine from all animal meats, as beasts and fish", which ruling was certainly an inheritance from the Chaldean Mysteries, for, as Porphyry tells us (*De Abstinentia*, ii, 56, lv, 16) of the Magi: "The highest and most learned neither kill nor eat any living thing, but practice the long established abstinence from animal food". The reason for this being, as he goes on to explain:

> For in all the highest grades the doctrine of metempsychosis is held, which also is apparently signified in the mysteries of Mithra; for these through the living creatures reveal to us symbolically our community of nature with them.

Here we find one of the most profound, important and remarkable features of the Mysteries, the idea of the metempsychosis, or the recognition of physical man's relationship to the lesser forms of life, owing to the essential oneness of that life. From the premise that the many different forms were but manifestations of the same Essence in varying degrees, the ancients deduced not only the necessity for man to evolve to something higher than his "Centaur" state, but also the possibility of his devolution to the lower forms of life if he did not progress spiritward but indulged his animalism instead of exercising his God-like mind. This possibility is the central theme of Ovid's *Metamorphoses*, sometimes dismissed as mere fantasy by the uninitiated and ignorant modern critic. But the cruelty, treachery, violence and lust that turned men into wild beasts, the bird-minded, gossiping women who became magpies, and the self-loving, useless, but beautiful Narcissus who became a flower, were all expressions of a deeply metaphysical truth known to the initiates of all Faiths: we become what we inwardly are.

For the pagans, what we now think of as evolution to a higher state was salvation through man becoming god-like, while devolution was the price paid for unwillingness to become what each man potentially is—a manifestation of the Highest. The primitive and illogical concept of a punishing god was therefore unnecessary. Under the law of justice man became what he had built up by his thinking and mode of living, sometimes the Centaur man or human being, sometimes, if he degenerated, the animal that his own form of bestiality chiefly represented; or, if he became one of the Tetelesmenoi, or Perfected, he achieved at-one-ment with his idea of God, whether simply the sun-god in the form in which he worshipped him, as, for instance, Osiris, Apollo or Mithras; or, if still further advanced, with Ultimate Reality, which, as Julian conceived of it, was The Good of Plato.

Apuleius assiduously pursued the upward path, having had enough of "ass-hood", and was finally admonished by the God Osiris to receive a third order of initiation, which, the god told him, was "right necessary if thou mean to persevere in the worshipping to the Goddesse". After which, having become a full initiate, he ends his book by saying that Osiris "appointed me a place within the ancient palace . . . where I executed my office in great joy with a shaven crown".

The tonsure worn by the priests of both god and goddess was at once the symbol of the sun, and, as Apuleius put it, "the terrene star", which even today adorns the head of Catholic monks.

This account by Apuleius is particularly valuable since it shows that, even in the Mysteries of the second century, the goddess was still, as she proclaimed herself, "*chiefe* of the powers divine", and had not been wholly deposed by the sun-god. It was evidently a transitional period before the male and militaristic cult of Mithras had supplanted the gentler Mysteries of the Mother Goddess. For it is obvious from the excavations that the Roman legionaries were interested not in the ancient goddess of agriculture and peace, but in Mithras who was "also a soldier", and the killer of the Bull from whose divine tail emerged the three ears of corn that had always been the symbol of Ceres and Isis, their constant appearance in the Mysteries being apparently to show their connection with the Eleusinia. It was as though Mithras were definitely dispensing with the service of Woman, whom he is said to have hated, for, according to

Mithraism, it was the Bull's blood that had originally produced all herbs and grain, and every good form of sentient life.

In the climate of thought obtaining in Imperial Rome, the masculine god was all-powerful and all-sufficient, although Vesta was still allowed to go on tending his fire. But the usurpation of the chief place in religion by the male god in the Grecian cults had started many centuries previously with the appearance of Iacchus, Dionysus, Orpheus, and other male figures who became the chief deities of the orgiastic cults.

In the Oracles, as we shall see in the next chapter, the same change of emphasis, with the passing of time, is apparent. Founded originally by priestesses, the god became gradually the most important figure until the priests of Apollo, God of the Delphic Mysteries, virtually dictated the policies of the civilised world.

CHAPTER II

The Oracles

Further evidence of the equation of women with Wisdom is provided by the many legends surrounding the Sibyls of antiquity, the oldest and most celebrated of whom was the Sibyl of Cumae in Italy, who, as Tertullian pointed out, was older than all literature, her evidence being the "testimonia divinarum literarum". So that not only are women believed to have been the first bearers of Wisdom to the world through the confidences made to them by their angelic husbands, but also to have been the first to produce poetry and religious teachings, or, as they were called in the remote past, "Oracles".

The Sibyl of Cumae was said to have been about 700 years old when Aeneas met her, and she instructed him as to how he might find his father in the infernal regions and return in safety. She had then still 300 more years to live, for she had not always been so wise, and when in her youth she asked Apollo, who loved her, to allow her to live as many years as she had grains of sand in her hand, she forgot to ask at the same time for eternal youth and beauty, and therefore had to live most of her lifetime in an old and decrepit state.

Of her many oracles only comparatively few survived her. These were greatly prized by the Roman State, and kept in the Temple of Jupiter in the Capitol at Rome. But they were burnt in a fire that destroyed the Temple in 82 B.C., whereupon commissioners were despatched all over Greece to collect whatever verses could be found of the inspired writings. The eventual fate of these is not known, but for centuries they were preserved and held in the greatest reverence by the rulers of Rome who constantly went to them for advice. That they survived at least as long as the reign of the Emperor Aurelian is proved by a passage from a letter of his quoted in *The Life of the Emperor Aurelian*, by Flavius Vopiscus of Syracuse. It is written to the Senators, and runs:

> I wonder that you, holy fathers, have so long hesitated about opening the Sibylline books, just as if your consultations were held in some church of the Christians and not in the temple of all the gods.

They were also known to, and quoted by, the theologians of the Early Church, but the pagans insisted that they had been tampered with by the Christians or that they were forgeries composed in the second century by a Christian writer. These may still be read in a short book entitled *The Sibylline Oracles*,* and whether they emanated from the Sibyl of Cumae or not, they certainly contain some prophecies that are startingly relevant to the present age.

The Sibyl delivered her own oracles under inspiration, but the manner of giving out these oracular sayings, a practice that spread throughout the West and was also a religious rite of the Jews, varied not only from country to country but from shrine to shrine. As we learn from Exodus 25 : 18–22, they were believed to have been delivered to the Jews direct from God, presumably through the medium of the priest at the mercy seat in the tabernacle.

At the first oracles to be established in Greece, that of Dodona, which was served by priestesses, the questions of the votaries were often answered by the birds and trees, and even by the waters of the fountain in the Forest of Dodona. This shrine was said to have been founded by a black dove, who came to Dodona and demanded that it should be built for her. She was thought to have been one of two Egyptian priestesses who had been carried off by Phoenicians and afterwards transformed into these birds. But since we know that the symbol of Semiramis, or Rhea, was a dove, and that she, like the Egyptian goddess Isis, was said to have been an Ethiopian, this legend may be taken to mean that the shrine of Dodona was founded by a priestess of the Mother of the Gods who had come to Greece for the purpose of extending the Mysteries to other countries; a sort of missionary venture. The custom of oracles was certainly known in Egypt. Herodotus speaks of the oracle of Latona in Buto, which he describes as being the most veracious of all the oracles in that land (Book II : 152).

According to one tradition, the seven daughters of Atlas were first installed as priestesses of Dodona; but later, after Jupiter, to whom the shrine was dedicated, had become the lover of Dione, he allowed her to receive divine honours there, and from that time three old women delivered the oracles. This shrine was extremely ancient, and was destroyed by Dorimachus, 219 B.C.†

The second dove was said to have established the famous oracle of Ammon in Libya, in the temple of which there were more than one hundred priests, the elders among them delivering the oracles. Herodotus refers to both of these shrines when in Book I : 46, he writes that:

> Croesus resolved to make instant trial of the several oracles in Greece, and of the one in Libya . . . so he sent his messengers in different directions, some to Delphi, some to Abae in Phocis, and some to Dodona;

---

* *The Sibylline Oracles*, translated by the Rev. H. N. Bate. (S.P.C.K.)
† *Herodotus*, Book II. 52–55.

others to the oracle of Amphiarous, others to that of Trophonius; others again to Branchidea in Milesia.

But the most famous and enduring of all the oracles was that of Apollo in Delphi. As Eusèbe Salverté writes in *Des Sciences Occultes:*

All the Greeks from Delphi to Thermopylae, were initiated in the Mysteries of the Temple of Delphi. Their silence in regard to everything they were commanded to keep secret was secured both by the fear of the penalties threatened to a perjured revelation, and by the general confession exacted of the aspirants after initiation—a confession which caused them greater dread of the indiscretion of the priest than gave him to dread their indiscretion.

This not only explains one of the reasons why the secrets of the Mysteries were so well kept, but suggests the origin of the Catholic practice of Confession, which cannot be traced to any teaching of Jesus Christ, and shows how, in the case of both pagans and Christians, it led to priestly power.

Curiously enough, at Delphi as at Dodona, we find two doves concerned with the founding of the shrine. According to mythology, Jupiter loosed two birds from the two extremities of the earth, and they met at the place where the temple was built, so Delphi was thought to be the centre of the earth. But, according to another legend, a goat-herd discovered the underground stream over which the temple was afterwards erected, and inhaling the steam that came from a fissure in the earth, he became inspired and began to utter prophecies. The shrine, however, was built and destroyed so many times that both stories might have roots in fact, for it is said that many deities were in possession of it before Apollo. The names of these include Terra, one of the most ancient forms of the goddess, and her daughter, Themis; so that the doves, or priestesses, may have originally founded a shrine for the goddess whose priests, in the course of time, may have been replaced with those of the sun-god.

It was, however, during the time of the patronage of Apollo that Delphi counted among its clients some of the greatest rulers and wisest men of the ancient world. Gyges, Croesus, Alyattis, Xerxes, Lycurgus were among those who craved advice and aid from the famous oracle that was a real power, politically as well as spiritually, in times of antiquity. But its methods differed very considerably from those of the all-feminine shrine of Dodona. The medium who delivered the oracle at Delphi was always a woman, but she was served by male priests and inspired by a male god, the radiant Apollo, in the form of a serpent, or python.

Owen (apud *Davies's Druids*, in note p. 437) writes:

> In the mythology of the primitive world, the serpent is universally the symbol of the Sun.

But it is always the sun as Wisdom; the healing wisdom of Aesculapius, the sun incarnate, for instance, being represented by a serpent coiled about a rod. Aesculapius himself was known as the man-instructing serpent, giving mankind the knowledge of good and evil. In *De Proescript adv. Hoereticos*, cap. 47, Vol. II (of Ophites) Tertullian writes:

> These heretics magnify the serpent to such a degree as to prefer him even to Christ himself; for he, they say, gave us the first knowledge of good and evil.

One of the Mithraeums unearthed in Ostia is known as the Serpent Temple, and has a large serpent engraved on the mosaic floor. It was in this form that the sun-god appeared to the women whose sons he "fathered", as in the cases of Alexander the Great and Augustus Caesar. Bacchus, too, was supposed to have been born as the result of his mother's relationship with a speckled snake. But at Delphi the sun-god's spiritual bride was known in the days of Herodotus as the Pythoness, and later as Pythia. When the shrine was first founded, this prophetess had always to be a virgin, an arrangement that was changed only after a Thessalian called Echecrates did violence to one of these young girls, from which time only women above the age of fifty years were allowed to hold office. Nevertheless, the idea of the spirit of God visiting a virgin and so producing the Logos, or Word, was maintained by dressing these elderly women as virgins.

The Word, or spirit of the serpentine god was conveyed to the Pythoness through a tripod placed over a small aperture in the floor of the shrine directly above the stream of the Cassotis from which vapours arose. Upon this the naked medium sat, the vapours apparently inducing in her a state of frenzy, in which condition she conceived and delivered the Logos or Word of the god. As Origen disapprovingly and rather crudely describes it in *contra Celsum*, Book VII:111:

> Of the Pythian Priestess—the oracle that seems to be more distinguished than others—it is related that while the prophetess of Apollo is sitting at the mouth of the Castalian cave she receives a spirit through her womb; after being filled with this she utters oracular sayings supposed to be sacred and divine.

These sayings that were in answer to questions raised by her clients, were taken down by the priests in charge, and given to a poet to arrange in hexameter verse. Some of these were so enigmatical that they had to be interpreted, and then if the prophecies proved to be inaccurate, the blame could always be laid on the interpreter.

But the important thing to be noted here is that it is now the god who has become synonymous with Wisdom. The Woman, or virgin, is no longer equated with Wisdom itself but has become a deliverer of the Word. She is still the instructress, and apparently has great power. Her sanction was required before wars were undertaken or any colonisation entered into by the monarchs of the earth. The Persians as well as the Greeks sent to Delphi for advice, and had the peace-loving goddess, with her disinclination for blood-shedding, been allowed to speak and advise, the course of history might well have been different. But the Pythoness had only the *appearance* of power; the reality belonged to the god and his priests, the former providing, and the latter editing, the Wisdom. The prophetess, therefore, was but a medium for the will of the god. It was masculine wisdom that hereafter was to sway the fortunes of the civilised world, as can be seen from the oracles that have survived. Though some were happy and suggested great prescience, we can search in vain for any recognisable teaching of the goddess. The moon waned, and Apollo of the radiant crown rose to the seat of power. The god's approval of Lycurgus, referred to by Herodotus (Book I: 65), shows how far his taste in men was from that of the Queen of Heaven. Herodotus tells us that no sooner had the Spartan lawgiver entered into the sanctuary than the Pythoness hailed him with the words:

> O! thou great Lycurgus, that com'st to my beautiful dwelling,
> Dear to Jove, and to all who sit in the halls of Olympus,
> Whether to hail thee a god, I know not, or only a mortal
> But my hope is strong that a god thou wilt prove Lycurgus.

In point of fact, few men could so have retarded the evolution of mankind to a purer and more harmless species than this famous legislator who trained the Spartans so assiduously into homicide and homosexuality, ensuring that they did so well in war that they were looked upon as models for the rest of the Western world.

Plutarch leaves us in no doubt as to the achievements of Lycurgus. Like some modern tyrants, he demanded the total subordination of the individual to the State. "He trained his fellow citizens to have neither the wish nor the ability to live for themselves", Plutarch writes, "but like bees they were to make themselves always integral parts of the community, clustering together about their leader, almost beside themselves with enthusiasm and noble ambition, and to belong wholly to their country"*—a statement that might have been made about Hitler in the 1930s.

In his economy Lycurgus was communistic:

> Determined to banish insolence, envy, crime, and luxury, also poverty and wealth, Lycurgus persuaded his fellow citizens to make a parcel of all their territory and divide it up anew, and to live with one another on a basis of entire uniformity and equality in the means of subsistence.

This policy produced a standard of living so austere and low that no modern Communist would tolerate it for a moment. Any but the most essential personal possessions were firmly discouraged, and, indeed, made impossible. His foreign policy, too, provided the blueprint for Stalinism. Plutarch writes that he did not permit the Spartans "to live abroad at their pleasure . . . imitating the lives of people who were without training and . . . under different forms of government. He actually drove away the multitudes which streamed in there for no useful purpose . . . that they might not become . . . teachers of evil. For along with strange people, strange doctrines must come in . . . from which there must arise many feelings and resolutions which destroy the harmony of the existing political order".

His avowed intention of banishing crime sounds curious to those who have Plutarch's evidence that the Spartans were deliberately trained into it—if violence and unnatural vice are to be considered as crimes.

Parents were considered to be merely guardians of their children whom they held in charge for the State to which all belonged. The father was obliged to take his newborn infant to a place called Lesche where it was examined by a committee, and if found to be strong and healthy, the father was allowed to keep it; if weakly or deformed it was destroyed at Apothetae, "a chasm-like place at the foot of Mount Taygetus". At the age of seven, boys were taken from their parents, enrolled in companies and forced to live a most austere existence suited only to the training of a nation of super-commandos, sleeping on bare boards and eating the plainest of food.

> The boy who excelled in judgment *and was most courageous in fighting*, was made captain of his company; on him the rest all kept their eyes, obeying his orders, and submitting to his punishments, so that their boyish training was a practice of obedience,—

a description that reads very like the training of our modern juvenile gangsters. "Of reading and writing", Plutarch tells us, "they learned

* *Plutarch's Lives*, Vol. I, translated by Bernadotte Perrin. (Heinemann.)

only enough to serve their turn; all the rest of their training was calculated to make them obey commands well, endure hardships and conquer in battle".

In other words, they were trained to despise and neglect the things of the mind, and the wisdom of the Mother-goddess, and to concentrate on fitness of body and brute strength, for the sole purpose of slaughtering other men.

At the age of twelve, they were just as thoroughly trained into homosexuality, or, as Plutarch puts it, "they were favoured with the society of lovers from among the reputable young men", to whom they became not only concubines but unpaid servants. They were obliged to steal food for their "Masters", and if discovered, they were flogged, not for thieving but for being so unskilful as to be found out. "One boy", Plutarch tells us, "who was carrying under his cloak a young fox which he had stolen, suffered the animal to tear his bowels out with its teeth and claws, and died rather than have his theft discovered".

The boys were supposed to emulate and model themselves upon their male lovers in order to become the hardened criminals that Lycurgus considered noble. Endurance and toughness were the qualities reverenced above all others. During their training, the young men were scourged at the altar of Artemis Orthia, their inhuman parents looking on and urging them not to murmur or weaken. Plutarch observes that he himself has seen many "expiring under the leash".

All of which is very nearly related to the practices and outlook of the Mithraists, in which the Spartan ideals were preserved up to a very late date, but none of it could conceivably have been sanctioned by the Mother-goddess who demanded reverence for life, and whose influence in Egypt produced men as different from the Spartans as they could possibly be. Yet, without any of the Spartan austerities, they were, according to Herodotus, Book II: 76, the healthiest people in the world. They were also the most unwarlike. He tells us that "Sesotris . . . inscribed on pillars an emblem to mark that they (Egyptians) were a nation of women, that is unwarlike and effeminate." Book II: 102.

Like the Jews and Persians, the militaristic Greeks considered the woman the lesser creature because of her lack of prowess in, and disinclination for, war; and it was considered the greatest insult to call a Persian man "worse than a woman". It never seems to have occurred to these primitives what a much happier world it would have been if all men were, in that sense, "womanish". Herodotus describes Telines of Telos, who was a high priest, as "a soft-hearted and womanish person", as though only women were capable of compassion. That such softness is not necessarily the pre-disposing cause of homosexuality is proved by the universal indulgence of this vice by the extremely hard-hearted, brutal and all-male Spartans. Plutarch writes that homosexual love "was so approved among them that even the maidens found lovers in good and noble women", the adjectives revealing a curious sense of values!

Nor were the women allowed to adopt the wisdom of the goddess. They, too, were deliberately hardened and coarsened, and trained into an irreverence for life. In order that they should have hardy children, they were made to run, wrestle, cast the discus and hurl the javelin. They had great power as they were left in sole control at home while their menfolk were away at their frequent wars. They inevitably became unsexed, dominating and arrogant. Plutarch relates that in reply to a foreign woman who observed that the Spartan women were the only ones who ruled their men, the wife of Leonidas said, "Yes, we are the only ones who give birth to men." Her curious conception of manhood shows how far from the wisdom of the goddess, with its demand for purity and peaceableness, the women of Sparta had strayed.

Despite all this, Lycurgus was looked upon by the rest of the Western world as a model legislator, and his views and policies were still greatly affecting the social habits of the Greeks in the time of Plato. Like Hitler, he committed suicide, but unfortunately the evil that this particular man was responsible for lived all too long after him. The Pythoness may have pronounced a blessing on him, but it certainly came from Apollo and not from Isis.

It was the Delphic Oracle, too, that encouraged Croesus—one of its best customers, who had filled Apollo's temple with treasures—to engage in the fatal war with Cyrus that lost Croesus his kingdom and nearly his life. When Cyrus enquired who it was that had persuaded him to lead an army into his country, Croesus was said to have replied, "If there be any blame it rests with the god of the Greeks who encouraged me to begin the war."

One of the consequences of that ill-advised war was the devastation of the West by the armies of Xerxes in the following century.

But despite its many mistakes, and the frequent destruction and re-building of the shrine, the Delphic Oracle survived to be eventually plundered of its treasure by Constantine the Great. This suggests that its successes must have been more numerous than its failures. And, in-deed, in spite of its obvious potentialities for swaying the policies of the world in favour of Greece, it seems to have remained extraordinarily impartial, which is probably why it won, and kept, the patronage of the barbarians from all parts of the world. Only twice was it reported that the Pythoness of the day had been convicted of venality, and both offences were most severely punished.

But that the wisdom of the Oracle was that of the serpent, or male order, and not of the goddess, is evident from the nature of the verses that have survived. As in the case of the Mysteries, a gradual change of emphasis took place in the Oracles with the passing of time, the goddess and her peaceful policies giving way to the militant, triumphant sun-god.

It would probably have seemed to the people of those long-past ages, as well as to many modern critics, that this was an inevitable "historical necessity". Continually beset by the onslaughts of predatory empire builders, the Persians, the Macedonians, and the Romans, the peaceful goddess of the ploughshare must have seemed something of an anachronism in a world dominated by the sword.

There appears, moreover, to have been a positive move in Greece to subordinate woman as a sex, as well as a deity; for, as Augustine relates, when a name had to be chosen for Athens, the choice lay between Neptune, symbolised by a fountain, and Minerva, or Athene, symbolised by an olive tree. The women loyally cast their vote for Minerva, and being more numerous than the men, won the day. This so outraged Neptune that he flooded all the Athenian lands, and, to appease him, the women incurred three penalties. "First, they must never hereafter have a vote in council. Second, never hereafter be called Athenians; third, nor even leave their name unto their children. Thus the ancient and goodly city, the only mother of arts and learned inventions . . . by a female victory obtained by women, was enstyled Athens after the female's name that was victor, Minerva"—or Athene.

So for women their victory was bought with a heavy price. Their loyalty to their goddess, or their concept of the highest god—Wisdom—was ill-rewarded by the loss of prestige and power which this incident strongly suggests was much greater in the most ancient times than is generally believed. Indeed, the fact that before the naming of Athens women had a vote, and left their names to their children, gives further support to the idea that a Matriarchy in which the agricultural goddesses with their policy of peace, love, and unity, ruled the then known world, preceded the patriarchal era.

Nevertheless, women achieved their ambition of making the chief city of Greece a stronghold of Wisdom. The subsequent history of Athens fully justified their judgment—although no commendation seems to have been accorded them for their foresight—for this great city became the spiritual centre of the world, its chief deities being Ceres and

Demeter whose Mysteries superseded those of all other gods. Warburton writes:

> But of all the Mysteries, those which bore that name by way of eminence, the Eleusinian, celebrated in Athens in honour of Ceres, were by far the most renowned, and in process of time, eclipsed and, as it were, swallowed up the rest. . . . We are told in Zosimus that "these most holy rites were then so extensive, as to take in the whole race of mankind". Aristides called Eleusis the common temple of the earth. And Pausanias (declares that) the rites performed there as much excelled all other rites instituted for the promotion of piety as the Gods excelled the heroes. How this happened is to be accounted for from the nature of the State, which gave birth to these Mysteries. Athens was a city the most devoted to religion of any upon the face of the earth. On this account their poet Sophocles calls it the sacred building of the Gods, in allusion to its foundation. . . . Hence in these matters Athens became the pattern and standard to the rest of the world.*

Thus Minerva justified her penalised daughters and devotees. An interesting pendant to her election by the women of Athens is found in Plutarch where, in his essay on Cicero, he remarks that "his own house was taken up by the women, who were celebrating with secret rites the feast of the goddess whom the Romans call The Good, and the Greeks, "The Women's Goddess". For the Good was the Supreme God of the Platonists and Neo-Platonists who, above all men, worshipped Mind and Wisdom.

* *The Divine Legation of Moses*, by W. Warburton, D.D. (J. & P. Knapton, London, MDCCLV.)

CHAPTER III

The Apostles of the Goddess

The idealistic philosophers of antiquity appear to have built up their systems of thought on the basis of the current religious notions. By eliminating the superfluous—the legends, myths and superstitions—they exposed the underlying truth in all its purity. In fact, religion and the philosophy of religion have always been two sides of the same coin. They were the Two Lives of Clement of Alexandria, the exoteric and esoteric aspects of religious experience. And had all men been genuine mystics ceremonial and superstitious religion would long ago have given place to its philosophy, which supplies the rules for self-government and makes men independent of organisations that inevitably impede spiritual evolution.

The first of the philosophers of the West to preach the Gospel of the Goddess was Pythagoras of Samos. He is believed to have been born in the sixth century B.C., but Plutarch is one among many who suggest that he lived at a much earlier date, before the founding of Rome, since the influence of his philosophy is so apparent in the life, teachings and customs of Numa Pompilius. Plutarch makes out such a good case for this in his *Life of Numa* that, as it is now impossible to verify dates of such antiquity, I am going on this supposition. In any case, the influence of the goddess is so evident in the teachings of both men that it hardly matters which influenced the other. They are flowers sprung from the same divine root.

Born into a distinguished family, Pythagoras received an excellent education, and early revealed signs of great intellectual powers, showing particular aptitude for astronomy. He was said to have been the disciple of Pherecydes of Syros, who, as Lemprière informs us, "was acquainted with the periods of the moon and foretold eclipses with the greatest accuracy. The doctrine of the immortality of the soul was first supported by him, as also that of the metempsychosis".

Presumably the writer meant that Pherecydes was the first openly to support these doctrines in the West, for, as we have seen, they based the Mystery Religions, and long before the days of Pherecydes, had been known and accepted in India, Persia and Egypt. Herodotus (123) says that the idea that the soul is immortal, and of transmigration, came from Egypt, and writes, "There are Greek writers, some of an earlier, some of a later date, who have borrowed this doctrine from the Egyptians, and put it forward as their own." This may well refer to Pherecydes and Pythagoras, although the latter openly acknowledged his debt to Egypt, to which he retired at an early age, despite the admiration and popularity accorded him in Greece, in order to learn the secrets of its priests, and the means by which they so successfully ruled both their rulers and the people.

When he returned as a teacher to the West, he wore garments like those of the priests of the Egyptian gods, thus revealing himself as a devotee of Isis. In his *Life of Apollonius* Philostratus writes:

> They who admire Pythagoras of Samos say of him that he wore no clothing taken from animals, and that he forbade the use of animals in food and sacrifice, offering up only cakes with honey and frankincense and hymns.

It is related that when Pythagoras was hailed in the public assembly as *Sophist*, or Wise Man, he rejected the title, and said he would prefer to be known as the *friend of Wisdom*, i.e., of the Mother of the Gods.

It seems possible that at some time Pythagoras was in contact with the Brahmins of India. E. J. Urwick in his book, *The Message of Plato*, points out that the perennial philosophy found in the Pythagorean system was essentially that of the highest teaching of Hinduism. He writes:

> Every one of the doctrines which we know formed the "gospel" of Pythagoras and the Pythagorean brotherhood of Crotona, was an almost exact reproduction of the cardinal doctrines of the Indian Vidya and the Indian Yoga. ...So much so that the Indian Vedantins today do not hesitate to claim Pythagoras as one of themselves, one of their great expounders whose very name was only the Greek form of the Indian title Pitta Guru, or Father-Teacher.

While this may only be yet another proof of the universality of Truth, it might well have been from India that Pythagoras gained his strong convictions as to the importance of, and necessity for a harmless diet. He believed, indeed, that men could be educated through their diet, and proved his theory among his students, arguing that if they could be persuaded to be harmless and compassionate in their feeding habits, this attitude would eventually affect and permeate their whole lives and outlook.

For Pythagoras, life was a unity, a theory that he had deduced from a study of the hosts of heaven, which had also revealed to him the idea which later got Galileo into so much trouble—that instead of the universe revolving about the stationary earth, the earth was an inconspicuous planet revolving about the sun.

In that tolerant age, or perhaps because he kept it a close secret among his students, Pythagoras was not persecuted for such teaching, like the unfortunate Galileo; and it is not surprising that he recognised the relationship of this scientific fact to the universal worship of the sun-god.

But that worship had led to undue reverence for masculinity, and to the perpetual slaughtering of sacrificial beasts. Moreover, his scientific explorations of nature had not only assured him that the sun was the central power to which all physical life was subservient, and upon which it depended, but they had also revealed the underlying horrors of the material plan of creation, with life forever being sacrificed on the altar of life. Therefore he looked higher than the sun-god for the supreme Good, and found it in the invisible, uncreated Being, the unfettered, unchanging Spirit, which the sun and his fire symbolised.

He taught that "the first principle of being was . . . invisible and uncreated, and discernable only by the mind"; and that the supreme God was of the nature of mind, or intellect, beyond sense and feeling. In other words, Cybele, Vesta, Isis, Rhea, or whatever name was given to the feminine Wisdom-aspect of deity, was the highest Good. The sun-god was responsible for the world of appearances, the visible world of metamorphoses, of constant flux and change, the illusory life—Pythagoras was probably influenced by the Brahmanical teaching of *Maya* on this point—while Mind, or Wisdom, was responsible for the immortal, the permanent, the unchanging, the real and eternal life.

Mind, or Spirit, was the real Unit, the one fact that lay behind all appearances, that which ensured the unity and oneness of Being, for all things were expressions of this invisible One. Since the sun illustrated this unifying power, its light could be used to keep men in mind of what it symbolised. Plutarch tells us that the Pythagoreans place at the centre of the universe "the element of fire, and call it Vesta and Unit". Vesta, as we have seen, was but another name for the Mother of the Gods, the Idaean Goddess, and, during her long reign in Rome, she was identified with the Magna Mater.

It is significant that Pythagoras elected to settle and found his sect—which became known as the *Italian*—in Italy, where the sacred fire of the Goddess Vesta had first been brought by Aeneas at the fall of Troy, in which city she had been more particularly known as the Goddess of the Hearth, the warming, golden flame, a ray of the celestial Being on high. But to Pythagoras, the household god of Aeneas was something greater and higher than the Trojans, blinded by their ferocious, animalistic masculinity, ever guessed. They instinctively worshipped the power giving sun; Pythagoras exalted and enthroned the Wisdom that restrained this power, as Cybele restrained Attis.

It is symptomatic of our materialistic times that whenever Pythagoras is referred to, it is almost inevitably in connection with his scientific and mathematical achievements, while his far greater importance as philosopher, social reformer and humanitarian, is forgotten or ignored. Yet although it is recounted that once, after making an important geometrical discovery, he was so jubilant that he made an offering of a hecatomb to the gods—the oxen being tiny figures of wax, in deference to his merciful goddess—Pythagoras, like Plato after him, considered that materialistic science was greatly inferior to the divine wisdom that enabled men to live rightly.

Certainly his greatest achievement for the people of his time was not his scientific teaching, but his influence on the characters of his students and the inhabitants of luxury-loving Crotona, where he settled at the age of forty. His eloquence, reputation, teaching and example so impressed a lascivious populace that they completely amended their ways, the women becoming modest, the young men temperate, paying deference to their parents, which was one of the strict Pythagorean rulings. The simplicity and harmlessness of their diet was reflected in their manner of living, and his sect soon became so renowned and admired that rulers throughout the Western world boasted of being his disciples, and would fully have agreed with one of his biographers who declared that "a greater good never came, nor ever will come, to man than that which was imparted by the gods through Pythagoras".

In *Satire*, XV, complaining of Roman gluttony many centuries later, Juvenal wrote:

> What would not Pythagoras denounce, or whither would he not flee, could he see these monstrous sights—he who abstained from the flesh of all other animals as though they were human.

It was just because he refused to differentiate between animal and human flesh and blood, discerning the common origin of both and the similarity of the suffering of all sentient creatures, that the Sage of Samos so vigorously advocated non-violence and reverence for life. Detesting the practice of warfare among men, he clearly perceived the connection between the slaughtering of animals and the killing of human beings, "for those accustomed to abominate the slaughter of other animals as unjust and unnatural, will think it yet more unjust and unlawful to kill a man, or to engage in war".

His belief in the doctrine of metempsychosis led him to regard flesh-eating as literally a sort of cannibalism. In *The Metamorphoses* of Ovid, Book XV, he is represented as expounding his philosophy in the words:

> Our souls are immortal, and are ever received into new homes, where they live and dwell, when they have left their previous abode. . . . All things change, but nothing dies: the spirit wanders hither and thither taking possession of what limbs it pleases, passing from beasts into human beings, or again our human spirit passes into beasts, but never at any time does it perish.

Here we have the first clear Western enunciation of the doctrine that Geoffrey Gorer found still flourishing in Britain in the present decade. But Pythagoras did not only teach it as a theory; he declared that he could actually recollect previous existences, such as when, as a participant in the Trojan war, he had been speared in the chest, which may well have accounted for the intensity of his distaste for violence of all kinds. In his incarnation as Pythagoras he actually recognised his own shield that he had used when he was known as Euphorbus, the son of Panthous.

The narrator in Book XV of *The Metamorphoses* says of him that, "in his thoughts he drew near to the gods . . . and with the eyes of the mind he gazed upon those things which nature has denied to human sight". Which, in modern terms, may be interpreted that he possessed an extremely advanced metaphysical and scientific mentality, intuitively recognising man's biological relationship to the lesser creatures.

His strong feeling of what Porphyry describes as our "community of nature" with the lower animals, caused Pythagoras to plead eloquently with mankind to adopt a non-carnivorous diet, which he believed was natural to them. In *The Metamorphoses* he is depicted as begging his fellow men not to defile themselves with sinful food, going on to describe how bountifully nature has provided mankind with banquets that involve no bloodshed; "innocent foods", such as grain, apples, grapes, herbs and vegetables, milk and honey; and he reminds us that only the most ferocious beasts, "Armenian tigers and raging lions, bears and wolves", demand slaughtered food, continuing regretfully:

> Alas, what wickedness to swallow flesh into our own flesh, to fatten our greedy bodies by cramming in other bodies, to have one living creature fed by the death of another! In the midst of such wealth as earth, the best of mothers, provides, nothing forsooth satisfies you, but to behave like the Cyclopes, inflicting sorry wounds with cruel teeth! You cannot appease the hungry cravings of your wicked, gluttonous stomachs except by destroying some other life.

Pythagoras did not, like the common run of men, supinely accept the pattern of nature—life sacrificed upon the altar of life—as the correct regimen for humanity. It was true that all about him he could see in the realm of nature the diabolical cruelty of one creature preying on another; but the fact that he could criticise and disapprove of such a plan evidently convinced him that there was that in him which was above and superior to it. And, like the god of the first chapter of Genesis, he was convinced that the natural diet for man was a harmless one. He continually speaks of a Golden Age where people "did not defile their lips with blood", where there was no violence, no fear of treachery, and all lived in peace, until someone envied the lions their diet and "swallowed down a meal of flesh into his greedy stomach".

This Golden Age has often been thought of as a Utopia of the past, a sort of Garden of Eden which existed before men fell, but it seems equally likely that, in the Pythagorean system, it was equivalent to the Republic of Plato, or the Kingdom of God of Christianity, a state which existed in the mind—the realm of reality—and could "come to earth" only when its laws were accepted, entertained and obeyed by the individual.

Pythagoras emphasises the ingratitude and treachery involved in slaughtering the friendly, trustful, herbivorous animals, like the sheep, who have given man their milk and wool, and the oxen who have contributed their labour, helping to plough the fields for food. And then he expatiates on the enormity of attributing to the gods, as men did, a liking for the sacrifice of harmless animals, and on the appalling habit, said to have been introduced into Italy by the Etruscans, of prognostication by means of examining the lungs, liver or entrails torn from the living beast. This habit was still being indulged by the militarists and Mithraic priests in the reign of the Roman Emperor Julianus, and today has its scientific equivalent in such medical practices as cellular therapy, and the sacrifice of millions of harmless animals per annum on the altars of Aesculapius.

All such behaviour filled the Sage with foreboding as well as horror. "I beg you heed my warnings and abstain." He could foresee the retribution that must inevitably follow such practices since every living thing was so inextricably inter-related.

> The heavens and everything that lies below them change their shape, as does the earth and all that it contains. We, too, who are part of creation, since we are not merely bodies but winged souls as well, can find a home in the form of wild beasts, and be lodged in the breasts of cattle. Therefore let us leave unmolested those bodies, which may contain the souls of our parents or of our brothers, or those of other relatives, or at least the souls of man.

64

If the Sage's realisation of the kinship of all life, the eternal oneness of things, was a more sentimental one than that of Darwin and his followers, it nevertheless led to that all-important reverence for life the lack of which is now threatening the existence of humanity, a contingency that the superhumanly wise Pythagoras appears to have foreseen.

But the jungle world lay all about the little coterie of evolved people at Crotona, and in it stalked many beasts of prey in human form who revelled in their animalism and had no wish to dispense with it. One of these—if Plutarch is right in believing that Pythagoras ante-dated Numa—was Romulus, said to have been the foster-child either of a wolf or of a bestial woman, who founded the chief city of Pythagoras's adopted country by methods of the jungle, so that the tide of evolution inevitably receded in Italy.

CHAPTER IV

The Reign of Wisdom

We are told that the young Duchess of Burgundy, when she was sent to the Court of Louis XIV as a child, delighted the King and Madame de Maintenon by declaring, as she hopped about: "When a queen is on the throne, the men rule; when a king is on the throne, the women rule".

If we are to believe the word of Numa Pompilius—and there is no reason to doubt his veracity since he was reputedly the most virtuous of kings—this was certainly true of his reign, the most ideal and peaceful of any Western monarch, comparable only with that of the Emperor Asoka in the East. For he insisted that he gained all his wisdom from Egeria, the nymph, or goddess, with whom he consorted. What her advice was may, at least in part, be deduced from its effects on Numa's character, ideas and policies, during the forty-three years of his exemplary reign.

Numa, the son of Pompon, an illustrious native of Cures, a city of the Sabines, was born on April 21st—the day that Rome was founded by Romulus. According to Plutarch, he seems from the first to have been possessed of every virtue, being pacific by nature, the very reverse of the barbarian ideal of his time, which was that of the predatory, conquering warrior. He early devoted himself to the study of wisdom, and, as a philosopher, he believed that the greatest victory was the conquest over a man's own passions.

Tatius, who had been the royal colleague of Romulus, gave Numa his daughter, Tatia, in marriage; but when they had been married for thirteen years, she died, after which event Numa became more of a recluse than ever. As Plutarch, who spoke of him as "the gentlest and justest of kings", put it:

> Then Numa, forsaking the ways of city folk, determined for the most part to live in country places . . . in groves of the gods. . . .

It was evidently in this sylvan solitude that he met his Egeria who taught him the wisdom that enabled him to become the wisest king the West has ever known. She may, of course, simply have been the spirit of Wisdom to whom Numa, as a philosopher, was "wedded"; and Plutarch seems largely to have taken this view, being convinced that Numa derived his wisdom from Pythagoras, despite the common belief that he lived many centuries before the Sage of Samos was born.

Plutarch certainly assembles convincing evidence to prove that the justest of kings was a Pythagorean; but, as we have already seen, the gospel of the goddess was to be found in the Mysteries many centuries before it was preached by Pythagoras. And if Egeria was a living woman, she may either have been an initiate in the Mysteries who, conceiving for Numa the platonic love that, long afterwards, was to be advocated by Diotima, the teacher of Socrates, imparted to him the wisdom of the goddess.

Ovid, however, in *The Metamorphoses*, Book XV, definitely states that Egeria was Numa's wife, and that after she and the Muses had guided him throughout his life, at his death she left the city and hid herself away in the woods of Aricia, and, at last, prostrate with grief, died at the foot of a mountain, melting away in tears, her body being dissolved through the power of a compassionate goddess into a cool spring whose waters were everlasting. This is obviously a flight of poetic imagination. It is extremely unlikely that so wise a woman who, as a Pythagorean, would have been well aware of the oneness and immortality of the soul, would have indulged in such immoderate grief, or would have imagined that the essential life of her noble and beloved husband was at an end. But the chief interest of the story lies in its evidence that Numa was supposed to have been married to his nymph.

According to Ovid, Numa was instructed in the views of Pythagoras by a native of Crotona; but, however he may have acquired his humanitarian wisdom, it is quite certain that, like Solomon, he regarded it as being of the feminine gender, and gave his Egeria and the Muses full credit for his knowledge as well as for his virtues, which were certainly of the gentle, passive, protective, non-violent and pacific variety that were considered in those days as "feminine".

When he was offered the throne of Rome by the Senators who had formed the "interregnum" government after the death of Romulus, he at first refused, reminding them that his disposition was the very reverse of king-like. His love of seclusion, his constant studies, and his inveterate love of peace and religion, were, he pointed out, surely most unsuitable for a governor of the Romans to whom the acquisitive and violent Romulus had bequeathed the habit of warfare, filling them with a desire for conquest. Such a people needed a strong, warrior king who could lead its armies; whereas his policy must always be to serve the gods and to teach men to honour justice and to hate violence and war. Eventually, however, he was persuaded by his friends that his influence was needed to train these fiery, ambitious people into a milder way of life. This task he magnificently accomplished, chiefly by first reforming the religion, and then directing the people's energies to agriculture and arts and crafts, and so away from military pre-occupation and dreams of conquest.

In reforming the religion he, in true Pythagorean style, forbade the use of images in worship, since the eternal, uncreated invisible God could only be seen by the mind, therefore He must never be represented in human or animal form, since it was impious to liken higher things to lower. Nor must there be any painting or graven image of deity, who could be comprehended only by the intellect. Also, in the manner of Pythagoras and the goddess, he taught that sacrifices to the gods should be of flour and drink-offerings, not of blood.

He instituted the order of the priests known as Pontifices, the word being derived from *potens*, signifying powerful; and in his reign these servitors of the gods were indeed all-powerful. He, himself, as Pontifex Maximus, not only taught the people and directed the sacred rites, but acted the part of prophet in interpreting the divine will. This all-important office has, since his reign, always been a feature of the Roman religion, represented since the defeat of paganism by Christianity by the papal power. And it was Numa who ordained that the head of the State should automatically become the head of the Church, as the custom was for so long in Rome, and as it exists in Britain today.

There can be no doubt at all that Numa worshipped Vesta who was already a venerated deity in Italy since we know that the mother of Romulus and Remus was supposed to have been a vestal virgin.

But Numa built a temple to the goddess, installing therein six vestal virgins to tend and guard the holy fire. The number is significant as, with Vesta herself, it makes seven, and so identifies the goddess as the female aspect of the sun-god who, in his Persian manifestation, as Mithras, was as we have seen chief of the seven Amshaspands, or spirits of God.

Plutarch tells us in *Camillus*, XX, 2–5, that Numa, the king, appointed the ever-living fire to be worshipped as the first cause of all things:

> The Principle of fire . . . Numa, who was an extraordinary man, and whose wisdom gave him the repute of holding converse with the Muses, is said to have hallowed and have ordered to be kept sleepless, that it might image forth the ever-living force which orders the universe aright.

If ever the sacred fire was allowed to go out, it could never be relighted from other fires, but must be taken direct from the rays of the sun by the Pontifex Maximus himself, by means of metallic mirrors.

The temple was circular in shape and faced East, "and a very prevalent story had it that the famous Palladium of Troy was hidden away there, having been brought to Italy by Aeneas. There are some who say it is the Samothracian images that are hidden there, and they tell the story of Dardanus bringing these to Troy, after he had founded that city, and consecrating them there with celebration of their rites; and of Aeneas, at the capture of Troy, stealing them away and preserving them until he settled in Italy."

The need for chastity in those who served the goddess was emphasised in this case by the Vestal Virgins who were vowed to chastity for thirty years, after which they could, if they pleased, marry. But it is said that few took advantage of this permission. Both they and their chastity were highly revered and honoured. Special privileges were granted to them by Numa, who was their overseer, such as permission to make their wills in the lifetime of their fathers, and to manage their own business affairs. They travelled in chariots, and a guard accompanied them wherever they went. If by accident a criminal passed by them on his way to execution, his life was spared. They were given the best seats in the festivals and the games, and great deference was paid to them by the magistrates, consuls, and other prominent men.

In the reign of the Emperor Tiberius, his mother, Olivia, esteemed it a great honour when the Senate accorded her the title of Vestalium Mater, which enabled her to sit among the Vestal Virgins at plays. The maintenance of their chastity was, however, of such vital importance to their office that if the vow was broken, the offender was entombed in an underground chamber. Before it was sealed, she was provided with a bed, lighted lamp and a little food, evidently in order that it should not be said that she had been actually "killed", since homicide was against Numa's policy.

The institution of Vesta and her Virgins survived longer than any other cult of the pagan religion, and ended only when the Emperor Theodosius the Great extinguished the fire and closed the Temple. Numa's royal house, or Regis, was built in its vicinity, and here he spent most of his time in contemplation and instructing the priests. By inducing a genuine respect for and devotion to religion in the people, Numa, as head of the Faith, achieved authority to rule by means of the teaching of the gods; and he was similarly wise in his social reforms.

When he took over the reins of government, there was bitter enmity between the Sabines and Romans, and the city was therefore dangerously divided against itself. To unite the two factions, Numa decided to obliterate these two most dangerous distinctions by dividing the whole body of the people into many other distinguishing groups. Classing them under various arts and trades, such as carpenters, musicians, goldsmiths, dyers, leather-workers, potters, and so on, he encouraged them to think of themselves according to their trades and occupations rather than as Sabines or Romans, a plan that resulted in the harmonious co-existence of what had once been implacable enemies.

Realising that respect for the boundaries of other men's fields and lands—the unwritten law that Nimrod had so fatally violated, and which Romulus had more recently flouted—was essential to the preservation of peace, Numa built temples to a couple of new gods, Faith and Terminus. The worship of these led to respect for the bounds, or terminus of other people's property. The sacrifice to this God was a bloodless one "since Numa reasoned that the god of boundaries was a guardian of peace and a witness of just dealing, and should therefore be clear from slaughter".

The land that Romulus had acquired by the spear, Numa divided up among the unemployed classes of Rome, wishing to remove the poverty that led to crime, and to turn the attention of the populace to agriculture instead of to military ambition, for he believed that a farmer's life induced a desire for peace.

He also established the *Fetiales* as guardians of peace, who were to seek peace by conference and negotiation, and were given power to forbid either king or warrior from taking up arms until the *Fetiales* had decided without shadow of doubt that such an act would be justified. In that way, no irresponsible individual or ambitious ruler could plunge the city into war.

Even the calendar was altered in honour of peace. In the reign of the war-like Romulus the first month had been Mars, or March, and Plutarch brings evidence to show that the year then consisted of ten months, as is indicated by the name of the last, December. According to this theory, Numa added January and February, the name of the former being derived from Janus once believed to be the supreme God (Ea), who was "said to have lifted human life out of its bestial and savage state"; while February, according to Plutarch, was connected with *purification*, this being the nearest derivation of the word.

In Rome, the temple of Janus had double doors known as the gates of war. These always stood open in times of war. Perhaps on account of the honour accorded to him in giving him precedence, Janus saw to it that these doors remained closed during the entire period of Numa's reign.

It is said that not only were the Romans tamed by the virtue and wonderful example of their king but that the people of the surrounding cities felt as though "some salubrious wind were wafted from Rome", and all wished to have a similar government so that they could bring up their children in peace and attend to their religion. Thus by following the advice of, and giving due reverence to, "feminine" Wisdom, Numa induced in a war-like people a love of peace, and by his personal obedience to the dictates of his Egeria, became the sort of man that other men could respect and wish to emulate. His implicit belief in the power and protection of the gods is illustrated by his reply to those who told him that Rome was in danger of being attacked: "But I am sacrificing", he said.

Plutarch suggests that Numa believed there was no need for threats or compulsion in dealing with the populace, for if their ruler's life was blameless and an example to all mankind, they would of their own free will seek his wisdom and way of life. He died as gently as he had lived, from old age. He was over forty when he came to the throne, and reigned for forty-three years. The people mourned for him as though they had lost their dearest relative.

By his order, the sacred books he had written, said to be twenty-four in number, were buried with him in a separate coffin; for he believed, with Pythagoras, that the Mysteries should not be revealed indiscriminately in lifeless books that might fall into anyone's hands, but should be perpetuated by the memory, teachings and practice of his students and followers. The books, however, came to light about four hundred years later when, during torrential rains, the coffins that were buried under the Janiculum were flooded. One coffin was found to be empty, and the other full of books, which when the Praetor, Petilius, had read he took to the Senate, expressing the opinion that the writings should be suppressed, and they were accordingly burned.

The wisdom of the goddess, therefore, disappeared from Rome with her devotee, although such institutions as the Temple of Vesta and her Virgins, and the new arrangements of the calendar, continued to give some idea of the outlook and values of the great king. But his successor, Tullus Hostilius, reversed Numa's policies and jeered at his virtues and devotion to religion, saying that the latter made men *effeminate*, a shameful and disgraceful state according to most men of antiquity. Thus the belligerent, masculine virtues that had been so popular in the reign of Romulus were revived, and, gradually gathering momentum, resulted in the centuries of fighting, brutality and suffering necessary to the acquisition of the Roman Empire. In his comparison of the rule of Lycurgus and Numa, Plutarch writes of the latter:

> That which was the end and aim of Numa's government, namely the continuance of peace and friendship between Rome and other nations, straightway vanished from the earth with him. . . . "What, then!" some

will say, "was not Rome advanced and bettered by her wars?" That is a question that will need a long answer, if I am to satisfy men who hold that betterment consists in wealth, luxury and empire, rather than in safety, gentleness and that independence which is attended by righteousness.

Even Plutarch, writing in the beginning of the second century when Rome was in her hey-day, evidently felt a nostalgic desire for the return of the rule of the goddess.

CHAPTER V

Plato and the Priestess

It seems possible that Plato had Numa in mind when he nominated the King-Philosopher as the highest form of government.

At the present time when, wherever we look, equality is being demanded and regarded as the Highest Good to which quality must be forever sacrificed, Plato's idea of government by the Highest naturally appears reactionary in the extreme, and is probably one of the chief reasons for his neglect by our modern intelligentsia. But being a man of his times, when the worship of the hosts of heaven was universal, it would have seemed utterly unrealistic to advocate as the best possible any government other than that which had always been associated with the Monarch of the skies.

In Persia and Egypt the earthly king, Pharaoh, or emperor, was always identified with the King of Heaven, and so deified. From this fact came his authority since it was believed that he spoke with the voice of God. To those under such a rule, the idea of government by the people for the people, the illiterate and unevolved masses who were so far removed from the highest wisdom, seemed ludicrous, and Socrates logically placed democracy lowest but one on his scale of governmental systems; the lowest being tyranny, the rule of violence, which became inevitable when the baser elements were given too much power and got out of hand. The degeneration of government, from Kingship to Timocracy, or aristocracy, thence to oligarchy—government by the few— and finally to democracy and tyranny, as outlined by Plato, can be clearly traced in the history of many nations since his time. But the more the *Republic* is studied, the more metaphysical its conception is seen to be. Like the Golden Age of Pythagoras, the Kingdom of Righteousness of the Buddha, and the Kingdom of God of Jesus Christ, Plato's *Republic* was essentially an inward state, and a plea for government by the highest wisdom. It was also a plea for the subordination of the lowest to the highest in man, a plea for sanity and spiritual evolution, Plato's philosophy itself being the natural evolution from the philosophy of Pythagoras to which it owes much more than most modern critics allow.

St Augustine in Book VII, Ch. 4, of *The City of God*, after describing how Plato, not content with the wisdom of Socrates, travelled first to Egypt and then to Italy where the Pythagoreans were so famous, in order to add to his knowledge, writes that "the study of wisdom is either concerning action or contemplation ... the active consisting in the practice of morality in one's life, and the contemplative in penetrating into the abstruse causes of nature, and the nature of divinity. Socrates is said to excel in the active: Pythagoras in the contemplative. But Plato conjoined them into one perfect kind."* We find evidence of this in many of his works.

When present day writers refer to the influence of Pythagoras on Plato, they usually cite *The Timaeus*, thus giving the impression that such influence is exceptional and slight; but, in fact, there is much more and much clearer evidence of it in *The Republic, The Phaedras* and the 9th book of the *Laws*.

These writings show his debt to Pythagoras in their teachings of the immortality of the soul, the unity of Being, the metempsychosis, the transience, impermanence and final unreality of the material, and the permanence, substance and reality of the spiritual; and the concepts of being and becoming. As to the last, we read in the summary found in the Introduction to Jowett's translation of *The Timaeus:*

> First I must distinguish between being which has no becoming and is apprehended by reason and reflection, and endless becoming which has no being, and is conceived by opinion with the help of sense.

This continual becoming, which results from generation in matter, is what we now think of as the theory of evolution. It is true to sense-experience, but it is not the reality of being, and was deplored by the Emperor Julianus when he spoke of "limitlessness" and the necessity for escaping from it to the "defined and uniform", the one Good, unchanging and perfect. For the sense of becoming is always illusory, and seems to be a fact because the senses see life as a series instead of as a whole. In *The Timaeus* we read:

> What is that which is Existent always and has no Becoming? And what is that which is Becoming always and never is Existent? Now the one of these is apprehended by thought with the aid of reasoning, since it is ever uniformly existent; whereas the other is an object of opinion with the aid of unreasoning sensation, since it becomes and perishes and is never really existent. .... As Being is to Becoming so is Truth to belief.

The transmigrating soul, without beginning or end, of Pythagoras, becomes, in the teachings of Plato, not only the essence of man but his only reality.

> For by nature (the physical or animal nature) none of us is immortal, and if any man should come to be so he would not be happy as the vulgar

---

* *The City of God*, by St Augustine, translated by John Helsey. (J. M. Dent & Sons.)

believe; for no evil nor good worthy of account belongs to what is soulless but they befall the soul whether it be united with the body or separated therefrom. But we ought always truly to believe the ancient and holy doctrines that the soul is immortal and that it has judges and pays the greatest penalties whenever a man is released from his body.

In the *Meno* Socrates equates immortality with omniscience, calling to mind the Buddha's definition of Nirvana as "all-knowingness". He says:

The soul then is immortal and has come to life a number of times. It has seen what is here and in the underworld and everything, and there is nothing which it has not come to know. Small wonder it can call to mind what it has previously known about virtue and other things. Inasmuch as the whole of nature is akin, and the Soul has learnt everything, there is nothing to prevent it, once it has recollected one thing—and this men call to learn—from rediscovering everything else, if the man is brave and does not tire of his investigations.*

This argument for immortality based on recollection possesses the ring of truth for those who have ever applied themselves to the thorough investigation of any subject. For when we turn our attention in any one direction with an integrated desire to understand, to learn, and to know, the way the knowledge flows in from innumerable sources has often been described as "miraculous". It is difficult to rationalise this experience in any other way than to say that it seems as though the individual mentality achieves, or realises, unification with a greater and all-knowing Mind upon which it can draw for whatever information it requires by the apparently magnetic application of attention. And since it can manifest this unity whenever it pays enough attention, it must always be in some way connected with that which, in its omniscience, may be conceived as super-human, and, as Mind, may well be thought of as immortal.

Those who have failed to recognise the close relationship of Plato's teachings with those of Pythagoras, and therefore to those of the goddess, may reasonably ask why, if he and Socrates were really in sympathy with the teachings of the older philosopher, they did not teach the necessity for non-violence and a harmless diet, and condemn the evil of war, as he did. The answer is that they *did* teach these things, but so subtly that only the keenest eye can discern them.

The reason for the need of such subtlety lay in the nature of their audience. If his teachings are to be propagated, a philosopher must have

---

* *Five Dialogues*, Plato. The *Meno*, translated by Floyer Sydenham. (J. M. Dent & Sons Ltd., Everyman's Library.)

pupils as the Church must have congregations; therefore neither dare teach things that would offend their audiences to the extent of dispersing them. Socrates taught many highly spiritual truths which conflicted with the popular and political thought of his times, but he was wise enough to know how far he could go. Only at the end of his life did he consider it ethically necessary to go too far, and then it was with full realisation of the penalty he must pay. Until then, he was wide awake to the necessity for discretion. He makes the point clearly in the *Apology*, where he says:

> You know full well, gentlemen, that, if long ago I had tried to engage in politics I should have been executed long ago and of no use to you or to myself. Do not be angry with me for telling you the truth: no man can remain alive who genuinely opposes you or any other crowd and prevents you from doing many wrong and unlawful deeds in the State.

Despite their idealism, both Socrates and Plato were realists, seeing no point in martyrdom since the sole purpose of a philosopher was to live in order to instruct others in the Truth, or in as much as they would receive of the Truth; and this could not be achieved by dying. Therefore, as their audience was necessarily composed of highly sophisticated patriots and libertines, young men of a race that had been deliberately trained into militarism and homosexuality since the time of Lycurgus, they had to teach in terms that such perverted mentalities could comprehend. Even Plato's loftiest conception, *The Republic*, which is essentially a description of how the kingdom of God can be established in a man once he has accepted rule by the Highest, had to be brought down to "earth", or the materialistic outlook of his hearers, and presented as a blue-print for a factual totalitarian State. And as the materialisation of a spiritual concept almost invariably perverts it, *The Republic* appears to contain some of the worst features of that type of State with which we are all too familiar at the present time. Interpreted metaphysically, it contains the teaching of all the Evolved Men: complete and absolute submission to The Good. But only by describing it as an external State that could be established in the visible world, could Plato hope to interest his audience as a whole, and perhaps, at the same time, make it clear to the select few that he was really speaking of a higher internal order by which men, perfectly self-governed, could dispense with any form of external government.

As a true philosopher, he naturally wished to advocate what he himself practised: the continence and purity of thought demanded by the goddess. But to moralise openly to such sensualists and lovers of pleasure would have been at once to lose their patronage.

That both Socrates and Plato wished to outlaw homosexuality and, finally, all lusts of the flesh, is obvious from their persistent advocacy of purity and the philosophical life lived through the mind rather than through the body. Indeed, the octogenarian Plato explicitly condemns homosexual intercourse in the *Laws*. Although Socrates never does this directly, he makes his opinion on the subject abundantly clear, not only in his dialectical advocacy of pure love that he puts in the mouth of Diotima, but by his personal example.

In *The Symposium* this is described by the beautiful but drunken Alcibiades who relates his futile attempts to seduce the philosopher. He admits to having used all his wiles, but Socrates, who desires to possess men's minds rather than their bodies, continues to treat him as a father or a brother would do, remaining quite unmoved though they slept on the same couch.

This is obviously one of the subtle and indirect means of making the philosopher's true attitude to homosexuality known to the public. Although he dared not openly denounce a recognised vice, the living sermon of his personal example was always present for those who cared to be instructed by it. While they consented to listen to his words, there was always the possibility of the seeds of wisdom taking root in the hearts of his young hearers. Attending to his arguments, their thoughts were at least temporarily elevated above matter and physical obsessions to the things of the mind and Spirit. Some, like Plato himself had done after listening to Socrates, might be found willing to leave the lower life of the flesh for the more honourable life of true philosophy.

In the same way, it was hopeless to demand that the Pythagorean diet should be adopted by such self-indulgent hearers. The subject had to be introduced with the utmost discretion. And this Socrates did by pointing out that such a diet was a necessity if peace were to be enjoyed and war avoided. In *The Republic*, when he was describing the manner of life that should be lived by the citizens of the Ideal State, he said:

> For food they will make meal from their barley, and flour from their wheat, and kneading and baking them, they will heap their noble scones and loaves on reeds or fresh leaves and . . . drink wine after their repast . . . and sing hymns to the gods. So they will live with one another in happiness, not begetting children above their means, and guarding against the danger of poverty or war.*

This certainly made no appeal to his audience.

* *The Republic of Plato*, translated by A. D. Lindsay, M.A. (J. M. Dent & Sons Ltd., Everyman's Library.)

"Apparently you give your men dry bread to feed on", Glaucon comments with distaste. Socrates admits that he has forgotten the relish they would have with it.

> They will have salt and olives and cheese, and they will have boiled dishes with onions and such vegetables as one gets in the country. And I expect we may allow them a dessert of figs, and peas and beans, and they will roast myrtle berries and acorns at the fire. . . Leading so peaceful and healthy a life they will naturally attain to a good old age, and at death leave their children to live as they have done.

The implication here is that, having had no wars, there will be children to leave!

But Glaucon is unimpressed, and remarks: "If you had been founding a city of pigs, Socrates, that is just how you would have fattened them." He insists that there must be comforts and luxuries in the Ideal State; whereupon Socrates indicates the inevitable price that will have to be paid for such indulgence. Rich dishes and sweet-meats, and general high living, will lead to the need for more doctors, and also for more cattle. Land extensive enough to support people with simple, vegetarian tastes will not be enough for pasturing herds; it will have to be enlarged by acquiring someone else's territory, and that means warfare.

Socrates does not pursue the subject of war, but he has clearly exposed its origins. It comes, he tells us, from the greed and covetousness and lusts of mankind, when men are not satisfied with pure and simple living— (a diagnosis made centuries later, in the Epistle of James 4:1–3)— and war necessitates the maintenance of a large and expensive army.

He continues from here to build up his Republic on the premises insisted upon by his audience. They have rejected *his* premises, but he has made his point, that peace and harmless living go together, while luxurious living and its demands lead inevitably to war. Had he been personally in favour of, or in agreement with war as a policy, he would obviously never have called attention to the means of avoiding it; nor would he so penetratingly have diagnosed its cause. He had shown them the way, but seeing that they were determined not to accept it, he could only make the best of the situation as it was, and not as it should have been. The alternative to right living must inevitably be tyranny and war, so the only thing in the circumstances was to come to terms with the mammon of unrighteousness, and, by a strengthening of arms and civic discipline, at least try to ensure victory over the enemy rather than submit to being vanquished by him.

We find in *The Republic* that immaculate conception of God which is so notable a feature of the true perennial philosophy of East and West. It is constantly maintained in Platonism, Neo-Platonism, Zoroastrianism and the Gospel of Jesus Christ, even as it is constantly forgotten in the teachings of Judaism and Church-Christianity.

"The Good", says Socrates, "is responsible for the things that are good, but not responsible for the evil. . . We must contend with all our might against the assertion that God, who is good, is the author of evil to any man. . . God is not the author of all things but of the good alone."

God cannot change his character, because, being perfect, if it changed it must be for the worse, not the better, which is unthinkable, for a God cannot be conceived of as lacking any good.

In his views on health, Plato not only forecast the theory of psychosomatic healing in his contention that, for a thorough cure, the whole man must be treated and not just the body or the affected part, but he also strongly hinted at the possibility of the method of spiritual healing that was afterwards such a feature of the New Testament.

In the *Charmides* he imparts to his youthful listener, who has complained of a headache, the secret of the Thracian physicians' success in healing. He says that they cured their patients by charms, or incantations, and explains that these are "words of the right sort" that heal the soul; and once the soul is healed, its lesser part, the body, must follow suit. He quotes a Thracian physician as saying, "Our king who is a god, says that as you ought not to cure eyes without head, or head without body so you should not treat body without soul". And then Socrates goes on to explain the ideas of this doctor more fully:

> And this is the reason why most maladies evade the physicians of Greece— that they neglected the *whole* . . . for if this were out of order it were impossible for the *part* to be in order. For all that was good and evil, he said, in the body and in man altogether was sprung from the soul. . . Wherefore that part was to be treated first and foremost if all was to be well with the head and the rest of the body. And the treatment of the soul, so he said . . . is by means of certain charms, and these charms are words of the right sort: by the use of such words is temperance engendered in our souls, and so soon as it is engendered and present we may easily secure health to the head, and to the rest of the body also.*

The phrase "words of the right sort" in this connection, brings to mind the Sermon on the Mount, and the Gospel of the Kingdom of God, which so strikingly fit this description, as well as references to the healing Word in older Scriptures, such as, "He sent His Word and healed

* *Plato*, Vol. VIII, translated by W. R. M. Lamb. (Wm. Heinemann, Loeb Classical Library.)

them, and delivered them from their destructions". In the *Zend Avesta*, too, there is a passage which declares that healing by the Word is the best kind of healing. Evidently this method was widely known and practised both before and after the days of Plato.

According to the Socratic teachings, virtue and health are inseparable, which again finds echoes in the New Testament in passages such as, "sin no more, lest a worse thing come unto thee". (John 5:14.) And since, according to Socrates, the Pythagorean simple life and harmless diet are more virtuous than luxury and flesh eating, they must necessarily lead to better health.

In the *Timaeus* Socrates shows how thought and emotion produce diseases that can therefore only be cured, or prevented by the control and harmonising of thought. His diagnosis of the cause of catarrh is particularly striking in view of modern medical theories:

> When the soul (mind) engages, in public or in private, in teachings and battles of words carried on with controversy and contention, it makes the body inflamed and shakes it to pieces and induces catarrh.

He advocates dieting rather than drugging for the remedy of physical ills, for "whenever anyone does violence (to the structure of disease) by drugging . . . diseases many and grave in place of few and slight, are wont to occur. Wherefore one ought to control all such diseases, so far as one has the time to spare, by means of dieting rather than irritating a fractious evil by drugging".

In other words, he recommended non-violence even in medicine, advice that might well be heeded by our modern advocates of wonder-drugs and antibiotics, who are continually perplexed by their "side-effects" that are often more fatal than the disease they were supposed to cure. What was essential, according to Plato, was spiritual healing:

> Ought not the doctor who is giving counsel to a sick man who is indulging in a mode of life that is bad for his health to try first of all to change his life, and only proceed with the rest of his advice if the patient is willing to obey?

In the opening chapter of the *Critias*, Timaeus prays that God will grant that medicine which of all medicine is the most perfect and the most good—knowledge. And part of this knowledge, so essential for the health and well-being of mankind, was undoubtedly the teaching of the nature of true Being, such as that of Parmenides, a still earlier exponent of the perennial philosophy, who contended that Being alone is, and that all else—all forms of materiality and limitation—must be considered as non-being, and finally not existent at all.

Matter and the physical world, to the idealistic Greeks, were not only evil in their unlikeness to The Good but essentially unreal since Good was Reality. The Forms of the Good, the invisible perfections of which all things visible were but imperfect images and shadows, were the reality and substance of what was perceived. But since they were invisible, they could only be apprehended by mind, never by sense-perception, which was deceptive and hindered true knowledge.

The eternal verities are known, according to Socrates, to the mind or soul before birth; and when it enters the illusory world of Becoming, it is reminded of these by the sense-images that bear only the faintest resemblance to the perfect models. It is this recognition, or recollection, that constitutes true education. But the materialist believes the imperfect images to be reality, and refuses to believe in anything above or beyond them. Such men, who imagine they are realists, are, in fact, dreamers. As we read in *The Republic* (476):

> As for the man who believes in beautiful things, but does not believe in beauty itself nor is able to follow if one lead him to the understanding of it —do you think his life is real or a dream? Consider: is not to dream just this, whether a man be asleep or awake, to mistake the image for the reality?

And as with Beauty, so with Truth, Goodness and Life itself. The spiritual Form is real; materiality a transient appearance. This line of thought leads logically to the conclusion that disease, which is not even an image of the Form of health or wholeness, but is the reverse of it, belonging wholly to the non-being of matter, is therefore the reverse of Reality. It is, then, for the knowing Mind, unreal, in the same sense that matter has for so long been considered unreal by the more deeply metaphysical philosophies of the East. The soul, or mind, that is aware of this can therefore conquer fear of the appearance of that evil called disease, and replace it by the Form of wholeness, which is the reality behind this particular illusion.

But it was on the subject of chastity, a ticklish one with his particular audience, that Socrates displayed the greatest ingenuity and subtlety. To avoid personal moralising, he represented the teachings of the goddess on this all-important subject, as coming from a woman, who, he said, had once instructed him in the philosophy of love. She, and not he, would, therefore, be to blame if the instructions were not acceptable.

His introduction into the all-male *Symposium* of Diotima, a Mantinean priestess, was a masterly stroke. The Initiate among his listeners would know that he was giving the teaching of the Mysteries; the libertine would, perhaps, be hearing it for the first time. For at Mantinea, as we learn from a footnote in *Herodotus* (Book 1: 67), Minerva Alea, an Arcadian goddess of Wisdom, was worshipped; therefore it would be understood that her priestess was preaching her gospel. And, indeed, the teachings of Diotima on the subject of platonic love are simply a restatement of Cybele's instruction to Attis only to beget in the intellectual realms. For Diotima, turning thought from the love that is of the senses to the love that is of the mind, pointed out that what men really loved was the Good, the Beautiful and the True, and that nothing less would satisfy the soul, since men are by nature lovers of The Good. Procreancy of the body, she urged, does not satisfy this longing, for the flesh has no permanence, "But those whose procreancy is of the spirit rather than of the flesh . . . conceive and bear the things of the Spirit . . . wisdom and all her sister virtues".

Friendship or love, therefore, should be upon this basis, so that it could produce the best of offspring—that of the mind. If a man accepted this higher love, rejecting the lower as unworthy,

> he and his friend will help each other rear the issue of their friendship— and so the bond between them will be more binding, and their communion even more complete than that which comes of bringing up children, because they have created something lovelier and less mortal than human seed. . . . Who would not prefer such fatherhood to mere propagation, if he stopped to think of Homer and Hesiod, and all the greatest of our poets; who would not envy them their immortal progeny?

Diotima then traces the ascension of love from physical attraction to love of the soul, of that which is immortal. The vision of the true lover of the Beautiful, she says, will not be of form or face, or anything fleshly, or of anything that exists in something else, such as a living creature; it will be of Beauty itself. And gazing on that heavenly Beauty, a man becomes like that which he contemplates. "And when he has brought forth and reared this perfect virtue, he shall be called the friend of God: and if it is ever given to man to put on immortality, it shall be given to him." A passage that vividly calls to mind 2 Corinthians 3: 18.

But although Diotima so persuasively argues the relationship of purity to immortality, and points out that it is better to leave beautiful and immortal works behind us as a testament to friendship rather than temporal and perhaps ungrateful children of the flesh, she was certainly not speaking for Plato when she praised Hesiod and Homer. For one of the chief proofs of his hatred of violence and war lies in the fact that the philosopher banished heroic poetry from his Ideal State, saying that by its exaltation of belligerence and brutality, it induced such emotions in its hearers.

In *The Republic* we find the Pythagorean theme of metempsychosis dealt with in the story of Er, son of Alcinous (Rep. 614, *et seq.*). Here Socrates speaks of a man who was believed to have died but who came back to life on his funeral pyre, and told of his experiences in "the next world", where, he said, he saw the Fates weaving patterns of lives for the discarnate souls to choose before they returned to earth.

> And he said it was a sight worth seeing to behold the several souls choose their lives. . . The choice was mostly governed by what they had been accustomed to in their former life.

Some chose the life of birds and animals, some of humans; but only the philosopher, the lover and follower of Truth, could be sure of making the right choice.

> For if any man always steadfastly pursues philosophy whenever he comes to life in this world . . . it appears, from what we are told from Yonder, not only that he will be happy in this life, but that his journey from here to the world beyond and back again to this world will not be along the rough and underground track, but along the smooth and heavenly way.

In the *Phaedo* where we find the most convincing arguments for the immortality of the soul, Socrates points out that philosophers, those who know the truth, despise the body which they perceive is mortal, changeable and transient, and are concerned only with the soul, which, being invisible and immaterial, must be presumed to be immortal, unchangeable and permanent. Throughout his life the true philosopher is, therefore, separating himself as far as possible from the body with its pleasures and pains, so what terror can death, which ends this life-long process, have for him?

We cannot learn wisdom by means of the physical body, for the senses continually mislead us. Neither justice, goodness nor beauty are perceived by the senses but only by the mind. Physical pleasures distract the mind from the search for Truth; diseases impede it. Therefore the less communion man has with his body, the better.

> It has then in reality been demonstrated to us that if we are ever to know anything purely, we must be separated from the body, and contemplate things by themselves by the mere soul . . . For if it is not possible to know things purely in conjunction with the body, one of these two things must follow, either that we can never acquire knowledge, or only after we are

dead; for then the soul will subsist apart from itself, separate from the body. . . And while we live we shall thus, as it seems, approach nearest to knowledge, if we hold no intercourse or communion at all with the body except what absolute necessity requires.

The death of a purified, non-attached man can, therefore, be looked upon as his liberation from the limitation and ignorance that all his life has irked him. Therefore how illogical to grieve when faced by physical death!

But then one of his audience objects that many people believe that when the soul is separated from the body it ceases to exist. In reply Socrates reminds him of the theory that they have already accepted from him, that education is really the evocation of knowledge that the soul has previously known but has forgotten, and that true learning is reminiscence. He argues that this pre-cognition necessarily implies the pre-existence of the soul or mind.

"When did our souls receive this knowledge? Not, surely, since we were born into the world?"

"Assuredly not."

"Before, then?"

"Yes."

"Our souls, therefore Simmias, existed before they were in a human form, separate from bodies, and possessing intelligence."

In the *Meno* Socrates has already dealt with this theory in more detail, therefore his audience in the *Phaedo* is familiar with the argument and readily agrees that pre-existence is proved thereby, but not necessarily existence after death. The philosopher then argues that the very nature of the soul ensures its immortality. There are, he says, two species of things, the tangible and intangible, the visible and invisible, the body belonging to the first category, the soul to the second. He then shows how the soul, coming into contact with things through the body, is confused and misled by changing and transient appearances, and only by turning from the body and retreating into its own nature does it find Wisdom and the permanent things of the Spirit, like Beauty, Goodness and Truth, which proves that its nature is akin to these things while the body is not. He also points out that the soul rules the body, and dominion is a god-like quality, therefore:

The soul is most like that which is divine, immortal, intelligent, uniform, indissoluble, and which always continues in the same state, but . . . the body . . . is most like that which is human, mortal, unintelligent, multiform, dissoluble and which never continues in the same state.

And since the inferior body can be preserved for countless years by means of embalming, how can the superior soul "when separated from the body be immediately dispersed and destroyed as most men assert?"

Socrates therefore maintains that the philosopher who has separated himself from the impeding flesh on earth will find joyful liberation after physical death; while those who have lived for the body and its pleasures, and only understand life through the body, will naturally be drawn back to earth, wandering as phantoms until they are reincarnated as men, or, in worse cases, as the animals their depraved natures resemble. The libertine, having practised no restraint, may reappear in the form of an ass. (This may well be the statement upon which Apuleius, an ardent Platonist, based his book, *The Golden Asse*.) The unjust and the violent may return as carnivorous beasts and birds of prey. The less depraved may be domestic animals or social insects, while the purely human will become men again. But only the lover of Wisdom can hope to avoid any such return to earthly states, and be able to ascend to the gods—to a higher form of existence.

The soul, he goes on to say, is imprisoned by its own desires, and will be freed by the knowledge of the illusory nature of those things which it desires and which hold it captive, learning that everything experienced through the senses is full of deception, evanescent, and finally unreal. Neither delight nor grief will be felt by the true philosopher since what occasions these emotions cannot endure, and pleasure and pains "nail the soul to the body". Therefore the soul, or mind, should steadfastly contemplate what is true and divine so that "when it dies it shall go to a kindred essence, and one like itself, and shall be freed from human ills".

But two of his hearers still remain unconvinced. To one, the soul is to the body as harmony is to the lyre, utterly dependent upon its instrument, being non-existent when the lyre is broken. But the fallacy of this argument is shown when Socrates points out that the lyre must precede the harmony, whereas the soul, according to the belief in its pre-existence to which they all subscribe, precedes the body and is superior to it. If they are agreed that knowledge is reminiscence, something the soul knew before the body existed, then the analogy of harmony and lyre is false, for the harmony is produced last and perishes first. And far from being subservient to the body, the soul is that which throughout life resists the body's demands, desires and passions, and regulates its conduct.

The second objector suggests that although the soul may reincarnate, it is not necessarily immortal. It may wear out many garments but still in the end, perish.

Socrates then describes his early inquiries into natural science, or the history of nature, when he tried to gain knowledge of cause from visible existents, but was always driven back to reason by the sheer impossibility of finding Truth through sense-perception. Finally, he shows that nothing that is can admit its contrary; an odd number cannot become an even, nor can life become death. And the soul animates all it touches, therefore it is life, the contrary of death, and so can the soul, since it is immortal, be anything else than imperishable?"

But the fact that the soul is immortal does not offer an easy way of escape for wrongdoers, for its very immortality ensures the continuance of their suffering in connection with physical life, until they, too, turn to The Good, and become philosophers. Then, after describing the suffering of the evildoers, he speaks of those who, through philosophy and non-attachment, win freedom from physical life: "They who have sufficiently proved themselves by philosophy shall live without bodies throughout all future time."

Then follows a passage so poignant that it is comparable with the scene in the garden of Gethsemane. Socrates, too, was face to face with death, and his disciples also slept the sleep of spiritual dullness and incomprehension. Having marshalled every argument in his armoury in order to convince them of the immortality of the soul, and the necessity, therefore, to cease identifying man with the perishable body, he finds that they have not really understood what he has been telling them, for he is asked by the obtuse Crito: "How shall we bury you?"

This is probably one of the most moving and ironical moments in literature. Socrates has done his utmost, leading his hearers to the very pinnacle of Wisdom, yet they are still confusing him with that which has to perish and be buried. "Just as you please, if only you can catch me, and I do not escape from you," he answers, smiling, in spite of what must have been his desolating sense of spiritual isolation; this full realisation of the soul's essential solitariness. Then he points out that Crito is still believing, after all that has been said, that Socrates who is speaking to them is that which will soon be considered dead. Whereas in Truth, that which thinks and speaks will have escaped to a happier state of existence. He assures them that "he" will neither be burnt nor buried, and so begs them not to be afflicted when such things happen, and not to identify that to which they happen, with Socrates. And then, having theoretically separated soul, or mind, from body, he demonstrates the sincerity of his belief in his courageous and calm acceptance of physical death, his actions being even more convincing than his arguments.

In his book, *The Philosophy of Religion*, Hegel wrote:

(Christ's) history . . . is exactly similar to that of Socrates. Socrates, too, made men conscious of the inwardness of their nature. . . He, too, taught that man must not stop short with obedience to ordinary authority, but must form convictions for himself, and act in accordance with these convictions. These two individualities are similar, and their fates are also similar. The inwardness of Socrates was in direct opposition to the religious belief of his nation, and to the form of government, and consequently he was condemned; he, too, died for the truth.*

When we think of that good, wise and noble man being handed the hemlock cup by his ungrateful State, surrounded by his disobediently sorrowing students, we could wish that Diotima, with her awakened, comprehending mentality, could have been at his side to confirm his faith, and to assure him of the approval of the Mother of the Gods of this, her so loyal son.

* *Lectures on the Philosophy of Religion* by G. W. F. Hegel. Speirs and Sanderson Translation. (Kegan Paul, Trench, Trubner & Co. Ltd.)

CHAPTER VI

The Seed of the Woman

The history of Zoroastrianism is difficult to trace owing to the many phases through which it has passed. We know that as it survives today in the form of Parseeism, it is the result of the reform made of the ancient Persian religion by a prophet known as the Bactrian Zoroaster, who did for it what Gautama did for Brahminism and Jesus for Judaism, purifying a degenerate system. But as in both these other cases, much of the ancient Faith inevitably survived, for good or ill, in the new religion. Both the ancient and modern forms of Zoroastrianism betray their connection with sun-worship in their reverence for fire, which is always the symbol of the heavenly Source. Known as fire-worshippers, they explain that they reverence fire as the purest of the elements, the only one that cannot be polluted and that always purifies—hence its likeness to the One, true God. That the symbol even today still plays a great part in the ritual of Parseeism is evident from the admission by the late Kaikhushru J. Tarachand, a member of the hereditary priesthood of Ancient Persia, who wrote in an article printed in *The Voice Universal*, "The sacred fire which is today burning in the Fire Temple of Udwara near Bombay, is the same fire the Parsees brought with them to India 1,300 years ago that had already been burning in its native home in Persia for at least 1,000 years prior to that date."

Once again we find evidence of the one universal Faith of antiquity, the sacred fire of the priests of Baal, of Solomon, of Aeneas, of Vesta, and of the Torch-bearer of the Mystery Religions—the ubiquitous sign of the sun-god.

Dadabhai Naoroji, a Parsee scholar writing at the end of the last century, spoke of the difficulty his fellow-religionists had had in recovering their old Faith in its purity through its sacred literature, after the adulteration that had taken place in its teachings since the Parsees emigrated to India from Persia after the conquest of the latter country by the Mohammadans. It was really a return to what had once been their homeland, for the Persians were Aryans who had taken from India many of its religious concepts, including that of the God, Mithras, who was first mentioned in the Vedic hymns, and whose cult was later to play such an outstanding part in the Roman world, when they and the Medes entered what is now Persia in the ninth century B.C. It was then that they came into contact with the Assyrians and the great Babylonian civilisation founded by Nimrod and Semiramis, or Rhea and Nin; and this is when the religion must have come to be formed that was afterwards *re*-formed by the Bactrian Zoroaster.

The Parsees are often referred to as the Jews of India, and there is no doubt whatever that Judaism was tremendously influenced by the Persian religion at the time of the Captivity under Cyrus. As Gibbon put it (*The Decline and Fall of the Roman Empire*, Vol. I):

> The doctrine of the immortality of the soul is omitted in the law of Moses... The hopes as well as the fears of the Jews seem to have been confined within the narrow compass of the present life. After Cyrus had permitted the exiled nation to return into the promised land, and after Ezra had restored the ancient records of their religion, two celebrated sects, the Sadducees and the Pharisees added that of tradition, and they accepted ... several speculative tenets from the philosophy or religion of the eastern nations... The immortality of the soul became the prevailing sentiment of the synagogue under the reign of the Asmonaean princes and pontiffs ...

It was certainly through the teachings of the Pharisees that the angelology and eschatology of the Persian Religion seeped into Judaism, although already the roots of both religions had been firmly intertwined many centuries before, in the soil of the primitive Babylonian religion which so mightily influenced the Aryans nine-hundred years before Christ, during what seems to have been the first great merging of Eastern and Middle-Eastern religious thought.

By the time of the Bactrian Zoroaster, however, this synthesis had evidently degenerated into some base form of nature or sunworship. Like the Jewish reformers, he substituted the idea of a God uncreated, invisible and omnipotent to whom even the revered hosts of heaven were subservient. His system seems to have flourished until the conquest of Persia by Alexander, and then, as Naoroji tells us, "the national religion did not occupy its predominant position, but when the Persian dynasty was re-established by Ardeshir Babezan, a great council of the learned priests was called, and the religion was re-established and proclaimed as the national religion".*

This lasted until the overthrow of the Persian rule by the Mohammadans, and only a remnant of the Faithful, known as the Parsees, or Parsis —a name derived from Persians—escaped from the Islamic yoke. They were accepted into India on the condition that they should lay down their arms, change their style of dress, and abstain from killing the cow.

* *The Parsi Religion*, by Dadabhai Naoroji, "Religious Systems of the World". (Sonnenschien.)

These compromises were later followed by more "accommodations" both with Hindus and Mohammadans, and the Parsees lost touch with their old religion as it had been originally taught, remembering only that there was but one God, and that they must remain monogamous.

Under British rule, however, they were more free from local restrictions, and, curiously enough, it was the attacks made on the Parsee Faith by the Christian missionaries that goaded them to make vigorous enquiries into the nature of that Faith, and eventually to revive it. Since when, translations of their Scriptures, the *Zend Avesta*, have made it possible for the West to study what Plato considered the purest of all religious systems.

But before we can understand a reformed religion, we must know something of the religion it has reformed, and in this case we are provided with a clue in the name of Zoroaster. Here, Dr. Hislop is most helpful when, referring to Semiramis, he writes:

> When she was worshipped with her child in Babylon, that child was called ZERO-ASHTAR, "the seed of the woman".

This would explain the theory that has so often been advanced, namely, that there were many Zoroasters. The name would have meant that those who assumed it were followers of the Babylonian religious system founded by Semiramis and Nimrod, the chief of the fire-worshippers, the God of which was Baal, so detested by the Israelites. It would also explain why, after the reform, the name Zoroaster was replaced by that of Zarathustra, the extremely masculine prophet so popular with the mad Nietzsche, since his teachings seemed to support the idea of the virile super-man, the conquering Aryan that so greatly, and most dangerously for the the peace of the world, influenced Hitler. For the new name symbolised the casting out of the influence of the Woman. Dr. Hislop writes:

> The modern system of Parseeism which dates from the reform of the old fire-worship in the time of Darius Hystaspes, having rejected the worship of the Goddess-Mother, cast out also from the name of their Zoroaster the name of the "woman", and therefore in the Zend, the sacred language of the Parsees, the name of their great reformer is Zarathustra (the delivering seed.)

This name, Dr. Hislop points out, is the equivalent of Phoroneus, "The Emancipator or Deliverer", which was a title given to Nimrod. He writes:

> The exploits of Nimrod . . . in hunting down the wild beasts of the field and ridding the world of monsters, must have gained for him the character

of a pre-eminent benefactor of his race. . . But not content with delivering men from the fear of wild beasts, he set to work also to emancipate them from that fear of the Lord which is the beginning of wisdom. For this very thing, he seems to have gained, as one of the titles by which men delighted to honour him, the title of the Emancipator, or Deliverer = Phoroneus. The era of Phoroneus is exactly the era of Nimrod. . . He is said to have been the first that gathered mankind into communities (*Pausanias*, lib 2, *Corinthiaca*, cap. 15, p. 145), the first of mortals that reigned (*Higinius*, Fab. 143, p. 114), and the first that offered idolatrous sacrifices (Lutatius Placidus in *Stat. Theb.* lin. 4:5, Apud *Bryant*, Vol. III, p. 65) This character can agree with none but the name of Nimrod.

By the time of the advent of the Bactrian Zoroaster the ancient fire-worship would doubtless have suffered the usual degeneration of exoteric religions. We know that it would have been polytheistic in the deceptive sense that the worship of the hosts of heaven was always apparently polytheistic, and that the fire worshipped was merely the earthly emblem of the supreme sun-god. That it included image-worship is obvious from a passage in *More Nevochim*, p. 426, by Maimonides who writes of Thammuz—yet another name for the sun-god that was the seed of the woman:

> When the false prophet named Thammuz preached to a certain king that he should worship the seven stars and the twelve signs of the Zodiac, the king ordered him to be put to a terrible death. On the night of his death all the images assembled from the ends of the earth into the temple of Babylon, to that great golden image of the Sun, which was suspended between heaven and earth. That image prostrated itself in the midst of the Temple, and so did all the images around it, while it related to them all that had happened to Thammuz. The images wept and lamented all the night long, and then in the morning they flew away each to his own temple again to the ends of the earth. And hence arose the custom every year, on the first of the month Thammuz, to weep for Thammuz.

This appears to be a description of a very early Jewish rejection of sun-worship with its images, for we read of women mourning for Thammuz in Ezekiel 8:14. At that time the Queen of Heaven had doubtless become the Alma Mater, or virgin Mother, pictured with Thammuz in her arms. Therefore, what seems to have confronted the Bactrian Zoroaster was a sort of ancient Catholicism to which he reacted like a protestant reformer. Images were banished from his monotheistic system that acknowledged but one supreme, invisible God, Ahura Mazda, or Ormuzd, the God of Light, or Enlightenment, often described as the Good Mind. This is the first instance in religious history of God being explicitly defined as Mind, the Perfect or Divine Mind that was, from time immemorial, the highest Good of the idealistic Greek philosophers. Hence, doubtless, Plato's warm approval of Zoroastrianism. The sun, moon, and all the hosts of heaven were but creations of this Mind, which was responsible for all the good that was in the world, but for nothing that was evil. Evil in all its forms was attributed to Ahriman, the Bad Mind, the Father of Lies, who, envying his brother, Ormuzd, had fallen from heaven. For him and his angels was prepared the Lake of Fire that afterwards became, via Judaism, the hell of the Christians. Through the same medium such teachings as the Last Judgment, heaven, hell, and the resurrection of the body, found their way into the Christian faith. Like the early Christians, Zoroaster seemed to think that the end of the world was imminent. He prophesied that it was to be destroyed by fire and streams of molten metal, thus confirming the predictions of the Sibyl of Cumae.

One of the great virtues of Zoroastrianism was the high value it placed upon truth and honesty, and on what today would be called "right-thinking". In fact the way of salvation for the followers of Zoroaster was by means of good thoughts, good words and good acts, for then the aspirant became like his deity, the Good Mind. The individual was a free agent, and the fate of the world depended upon his choice between good and evil, for life was nothing but a perpetual struggle between good and evil, and the supreme Zoroastrian commandment was: To fight for good against evil. This entailed being kind to good things but to destroy every form of evil, and as enemies of one's country are always considered evil, this rule evidently accounted for the Persians' ruthlessness in war.

Although rewards and punishments are meted out after death, the paradise of a man's soul, according to Zoroastrianism, is his good conscience and, "The high priest is he who is learned in the religion, and whose whole life is devoted to the promotion of righteousness in the world". (Ha. 19.)

All the creations of God have their angels, which seem to have been something of the same nature as Plato's Good Forms, and it is to these intelligent beings, the Fravashis, that the Zoroastrians address their prayers, not to the visible elements. Thus, although fire is on the altar, it is to the angel of fire that prayer is addressed. In fact, the gods have become angels, or spirits, devas or Djinns, all subsidiary to the one and only God, Ormuzd. "He who knows God through his works reaches him". (Ha. 30.)

Zoroastrianism, like Judaism and Islam, is a world-affirming Faith. The world is good because God created it, and God can be known and loved through his creation. There is a heaven for those whose minds are like the Good Mind, but meanwhile the earthly life is to be enjoyed to the full within the law of morality.

In Zoroastrianism there is no despisal of matter or the physical world such as we find in Plato, the Mysteries, and other exponents of the Wisdom of the goddess. To do good and be good seems to be the Zoroastrian's simple aim, which might be adequate if a clear and authoritative definition could be given of what to do good and to be good involve. As it is, we know that Xerxes, a devoted follower of Ormuzd, cruelly and wantonly devasted the Western world with his ravening hordes, the justification for which could be found in a religion that demands the fighting of evil, since all war propaganda includes the pious affirmation of the evil nature of the foe. The cruelty of the Persians was notorious; with them compassion was far from being a moral absolute, and, as we have seen, even the Parsees who are now pacific enough, did not lay down their arms until compelled to do so as a condition on which they entered peace-loving India. From some of their modern literature, it is obvious that the Parsees—now too small a community to be aggressive in any case—have imbibed the pacific nature of their hosts. But that non-violence was no part of the Persian religion either before or after the reform, must be assumed from that country's history in which no trace can be found of the policy of the goddess regarding bloodshed.

Nor do we anywhere find insistence on the need for celibacy in the leading of the spiritual life. As with the Jews, the begetting of children was a duty. Monogamous marriage was as far as Zoroaster went in restraining the sexual urge, and we find none of the demands for sexual purification in the teachings of Zoroaster that are to be found in the Mystery Religions or the systems influenced by them.

For all its apparent moral excellence, the reformed religion was a revolt not only against the idolatry of the sun-worshippers but against the influence of the Woman while still paying lip-service to her demand for self-purification by its emphasis on the necessity for good thoughts, good words and good deeds. But to see how far practice fell beneath theory, we have only to study the history of the Persians whose empire followed that of the Babylonians.

Although the Zoroastrian reform is said to have taken place during the reign of Darius, it is obvious from the history of Herodotus that the old religion and its rites lingered on for a considerable time after that period. Xerxes, the son of Darius, for all his devotion to Ormuzd, constantly sacrificed to any gods likely to favour him. When a number of his troops were killed by a thunderstorm as they encamped under Mount Ida, which was dedicated to the Mother of the Gods, Herodotus tells us that Xerxes "made an offering of a thousand oxen to the Trojan Minerva", i.e. Cybele.

The cruelty of Xerxes is well known. One of the worst examples of this is found in the story of Pythius, the Lydian, an elderly man whose five sons were accompanying Xerxes to the wars; and the father, having been warned in a dream of the fate of Xerxes' legions, begged him to leave one of his sons behind. Whereupon Xerxes took the eldest, cut his body in two, and placed the halves on either side of the great road so that the army might march out between them.

Although Ormuzd is spoken of as "chief of the gods" in the inscriptions left by the armies of Xerxes, the worship of the hosts of heaven was far from being a thing of the past for them. Herodotus quotes Xerxes as saying before going into battle: "And now let us offer prayers to the gods who watch over the welfare of Persia". And then he goes on to say:

> They burnt all kinds of spices upon the bridges, and strewed the way with myrtle boughs while they watched anxiously for the sun which they hoped to see as he rose. And now the sun appeared; and Xerxes took a golden goblet and poured from it a libation into the sea, praying the while with his face turned to the sun, "that no misfortune might befall him such as to hinder his conquest of Europe, until he had penetrated to its uttermost boundaries".

This habit of calling for God's blessing on the massacre of their fellow men has, of course, been the way of the militarists, whatever their religion, from the beginning of history. Persians, Jews, Greeks, Romans, Germans, Gauls, Britons have all, in their turn, implored whatever deity they claimed as theirs to "confound their enemies", so that it would be manifestly unfair to judge Zoroastrianism by the behaviour of its rulers and warriors. But it is curious that the Emperor, and therefore the head of what was said to have been a *reformed* religion should still have been openly sacrificing to the gods banished by the reformer. That the reform had already taken place is obvious from Herodotus (131), where he writes:

> The Persians have no images of the gods, no temples, no altars, and consider the use of them a sign of folly. This comes ... from their not believing the gods to have been the same nature with men as the Greeks imagine.

Of their love of Truth he says:

> Their sons are carefully instructed from their fifth to twentieth year, in three things alone,—to ride, to draw the bow, and to speak the truth. (135). . . . The most disgraceful thing in the world, they think, is to tell a lie; the next worst to owe a debt. . . (139).

Referring to the Magi, or holy men of the Persians, he writes:

> The Magi are a very peculiar race, different entirely from the Egyptian priests, and indeed from all other men whatsoever. The Egyptian priests make it a point of religion not to kill any live animals except those which they offer in sacrifice. The Magi, on the contrary, kill animals of all kinds with their own hands, excepting dogs and men. They even seem to take a delight in the employment.

Herodotus must have gained this impression from the lowest grade of Magi; although, as we have seen, the dualism in the Zoroastrian system might justify such cruelty, for it demands kindness to what are considered to be the creatures of Ahura Mazda, such as cattle, sheep, otters, cocks and dogs, but ruthlessness towards the creatures said to have been made by the evil spirit, Ahriman, such as wolves, scorpions, hyenas, snakes and disease-carrying insects.

A probably better informed description of the Magi and their practices is found in Porphyry's *De Abstinentia*, IV:16, where he tells us that

> The Magi were divided into three grades, according to the assertion of Eubulus who wrote the history of Mithraism in many books. Of these the highest and most learned neither kill nor eat any living thing, but practise the long-established abstinence from animal food. The second use such food but do not kill any tame beasts. And following their example not even the third permit themselves the use of all.

Apart from this evidence, we know that the doctrine of the metempsychosis was a teaching of Mithraism, so we must assume that it was also somewhere to be found in the parent religion, if only in its Reserve, or esoteric teachings. The difference in the reports of Herodotus and Porphyry might be explained by the fact, either that the Magi referred to by the former were of the lowest degree, or else that between his days and those of Eubulus, from whom Porphyry quoted, the merciful wisdom of the goddess had been reintroduced into the Zoroastrian religion, despite all the efforts of the reforming Prophet.

Whatever the theoretical virtues of the Persian religion, its practical fruits, inasmuch as they affected the ancient world and the history of mankind, have been particularly bitter. The Persian kings took over the empire-building policy of Nimrod, together with his religion, and continually plagued the rest of the world with their invasions. Owing to their long and successful dominance of the Western world, they served as a pattern for all the succeeding kings, rulers and power-addicts: Greeks, Romans, Germans, Gauls, who in turn emulated those first triumphant invaders of the West.

It is significant that the Roman Empire owed much to Ormuzd's great aide, Mithras, the sun-god, who was a direct behest from Persia to Rome, and whose militaristic cult accounted for some of the best disciplined and most courageous troops among the Roman Legions. By these conquerors and power-lovers, the peaceable goddess and her wisdom were despised and rejected, and the sun-god's votaries, making and unmaking empires, continued to drench the battle-fields, first of Greece and then of Europe, with their fellow-men's blood.

In our times, the masculine influence of Zarathustra was sufficiently powerful to affect the twisted minds of Nietzsche and Hitler, so that Nazi Germany's ideal became the Soldier of Mithras, the blond beast, the super-man who was really only a super-animal that, strangely enough, betrayed its origin by loudly proclaiming its Aryan blood.

Hitler, who was no student of Comparative Religion, spoke perhaps more truly than he knew. Nazi-ism was certainly the total rejection of the wisdom of the goddess. Women, under Hitler's rule, were banished to the kitchen, the outward woman sharing the debasement of the deity. The revolt of the seed of the woman from the Divine Mother devastated Europe, causing moral degeneration, an almost total departure from spirituality, and a reign of materialism that has resulted in the devolution of the human race referred to by those unaware of the cause of these things, in such inadequate terms as "delinquency", "increase of crime", and "scientific irresponsibility".

CHAPTER VII

The Fatal Divorce

If Zoroastrianism was a revolt from the divine Woman, exoteric Judaism was the complete rejection of her and her wisdom. But accent must be laid on the qualifying adjective "exoteric", for Judaism, like all other religions of antiquity, had, as we shall see, its esoteric Mysteries in which the wisdom of the goddess is invariably found, and of which we learn much from Philo Judaeus.

This great Alexandrian philosopher, writer and diplomat was so ardent a Platonist that men of his time were apt to say, "either Plato Philonises or Philo Platonises". That he belonged to the highest social circles of his era is suggested by the fact that his son, Tiberius Alexander, married Berenice, the daughter of King Agrippa. The date of his birth is unknown, but that it must have been before, or very early in the first century A.D. follows from the fact that in the Treatise in which he gives an account of his embassy to Rome, and which was written in the reign of Claudius who succeeded Caligula (A.D. 41), he speaks of himself as an old man. He was evidently a contemporary of Josephus, but the historian refers to him in his ambassadorial capacity as "the elder Philo".

For all his love of Hellenism, and such evident knowledge of the teachings of the Mysteries that it seems certain that he was an initiate, Philo was first and foremost a Jew whose chief aim was to make the primitive Scriptures of his Faith acceptable to the cultured Greek or Roman, who, having been familiar with the theories, and the exalted concept of The Good, of Socrates, would hardly be likely to be attracted to the character of the Jewish Jehovah as portrayed by Moses and the more materialistic writers of the Old Testament. Therefore, Philo allegorised the cruder portions of the Hebrew Scriptures in the light of his own esoteric knowledge and Hellenistic wisdom, thus bringing Judaism to the highest state of development that it ever reached. "Philonised", it was not only compatible with the advanced, eclectic pagan thought of his day, but—though this was a consequence he could certainly not have foreseen as he had no knowledge of Jesus Christ—it made a perfect framework for the Catholic theology evolved by the Alexandrian Fathers of the Early Church.

As Denis writes in *De la Philosophie d'Origene*, "All the elements of Christian theology were already prepared in the religious and philosophical eclecticism of Philo and other Jewish Hellenists".

This was a godsend to the Christian theologians who, having made the prophecies of the Hebrew Scriptures the test of Jesus' discipleship, were faced with the formidable task of persuading Gentile congregations to hold these in as much reverence as they were held by the Jews. As R. B. Tollinton, D.D., observes in his *Selections From the Commentaries and Homilies of Origen*:

> Allegory saved the Scriptures for the Church. Taken literally the Old Testament could not have been shown as against Jewish controversialists to be Christian literature, nor could either Testament have been defended against the criticism of educated Greeks.

But while the Church undoubtedly benefited from Philo's heroic attempt to reconcile the irreconcilable, the original Creed of Christ suffered grievous harm in the process. For Philo's allegorisations, added to Paul's assiduous eclecticism, made it possible for the Judaism that Jesus had sought to purify and replace with a more perfect faith, to survive under the cloak of Christianity. These men, in fact, ensured that the Scriptures of the Jews would go down to posterity as the revealed Word of God from which, according to the Fundamentalists, nothing can be added nor anything taken away. This attitude has perpetuated the errors that should long ago have been eradicated by the substitution of Christian Truth.

But if Philo glorified the Old Testament, he also played a considerable part in influencing the New. In *The Christian Platonists of Alexandria* (Bampton Lectures, 1886), Dr Biggs says "It is probable that Philonism colours the New Testament, and it is certain that it largely affected the after development of Christian doctrine". He quotes Siegfried as saying: "It is universally acknowledged that John borrowed from Philo the name of LOGOS to express the manifestation of God". And in a footnote he makes the interesting observation that "Logos" may always be used for "Sophia", or Wisdom; and then quotes Siegfried as having pointed out "that Sophia is sometimes spoken of as the higher principle, the Fountain, or Mother of the Logos. The differing gender of the two words in the Greek, the one being feminine and the other masculine, was a difficulty".

Here, again, we find the distinct suggestion that the Word was believed at some time to have proceeded from the Mother of the Gods. But in only one passage in the entire works of Philo, can we find anything approaching such an idea; for Philo remains a Jew in his complete masculinity and his suppression and denigration of the Woman.

Biggs writes: "To Philo religion is the emancipation of the intelligence from the domain of sense". But this was the aim of all esoteric religion, both of East and West. In Philo's case, however, he perpetually identifies man with intelligence and woman with the external senses; therefore, to him, salvation depended on the latter's negation. Nevertheless, because he was a true philosopher, his instincts inevitably led him to the wisdom of the Woman, though it probably reached him through the Essenes and such teachers as Pythagoras and Plato, enabling him to disregard any previous, feminine source; and he was—most curiously in a man of his race—a humanitarian. With Pythagoras he pleads for a merciful and harmless diet. After mentioning the fish, birds, and terrestial animals that men unnecessarily feed upon, he says:

> It was not necessary that the animal which of all others is most akin to wisdom, namely man, should . . . change his nature into something resembling the ferocity of wild beasts; on which account . . . those who have any regard for temperance entirely abstain from such things, eating only vegetables and herbs, and the fruits of trees, as the most delicious and wholesome food.

Like the Platonists, he despises the flesh and glorifies the mind:

> While the soul of the wise man . . . comes down upon and enters a mortal, and is sown in the field of the body, it is truly sojourning in a land which is not his own. Since the earthly body is wholly alien from pure intellect, and tends . . . to drag it downwards into slavery, bringing every kind of affliction upon it, until the sorrow, bringing the attractive multitude of vices to Judgment, condemns them . . . then the mind is released from its mischievous colleague, departing out of the body and being transferred not only with freedom but also with much substance. . . .

Here we find Philo preaching the Gospel of the Mother of the Gods, deploring the descent to matter, applauding the re-ascent; but refusing to give her credit as its source. Philo's great failing throughout is the failing of Judaism itself: his fatal divorce of the female from the male aspect of God.

In primitive Judaism the revolt from the Queen of Heaven and her wisdom was open and aggressive. The seed of the woman was completely rejected and replaced by the idea of the seed of Abraham becoming "established as the stars of heaven and as the sand which is upon the sea-shore". (Genesis 22:16, 17.) Here we have an entire reversal of the demand of Wisdom for transcendence of physical life. On the contrary, it must be perpetuated to the uttermost by the Children of Israel. Castration, whether symbolic or factual, becomes a crime. According to Mosaic law, a mutilated or physically imperfect man, however spiritually minded, cannot be admitted into the priesthood (Deuteronomy 23:1), which, far from being celibate, had, apparently, to set the example of obedience to the demand of Jehovah to increase and multiply (Genesis 1 : 28).

What has been totally ignored by both Jews and Christians throughout the ages is that this directive was issued to a perfect man—the image and likeness of the parent mind, or Spirit. It most obviously did not refer to the world we see about us, where life is painfully sustained on other forms of life. It referred to a *very good* creation such as one might expect to be conceived by a supremely intelligent and perfect Mind. The provision of a harmless diet for both man and beast, is specifically stated in Genesis 1 :29, 30. The demand to increase and multiply related, therefore, to a perfect creation, a god-like man, and certainly not to a race of predatory, bellicose, carnivorous, animal-sacrificing human beings whose history we find recorded in the Old Testament. Philo Judaeus at least made this fact plain to an unheeding world when in *The Creation of the World*, XLVI, he wrote that Moses,

> shows most clearly that there is a vast difference between man as generated now, and the first man who was made according to the image of God. For man as formed now is perceptible to the external senses, partaking of qualities, consisting of body and soul, man or woman, by nature mortal. But man made according to the image of God was an idea . . . perceptible only to the intellect, neither male nor female, imperishable by nature.

This concept had long since been held by the Greeks and the philosophers of the Far East, but it never seems to have entered the thought of the orthodox Jews who, refusing to distinguish between good and evil evidently supposed their physical bodies to be good and worthy of perpetuation. And the Christians, instead of heeding Philo's argument in this instance, unfortunately accepted the Jewish idea, despite the celibacy of their Exemplar. Thus the misreading of the first chapter of Genesis may be said to be the basis of that philosophic confusion that has brought mankind to its present condition, the cause of the perpetuation of all human woes, and a state of affairs that could never conceivably have been the will or work of a good God.

The fact is that the first chapter of Genesis contains the wisdom of the goddess, and does not appear to belong to the rest of the Old Testament, or indeed to the exoteric Hebrew religion at all. It relates rather to those Mysteries, closely guarded by the Essenes in secret and Apocryphal writings, from which many of the teachings of Jesus came. It would have been much more suitably placed had it directly preceded the New Testament, for it certainly confirms the idea of God and his relation to man, held by Jesus Christ: the perfect Father and perfect Son enjoying the invisible Kingdom of Heaven of peace, love and harmony that is their true habitation. As it is, in the vast area of Jewish history, secular and spiritual, that lies between these two compatible concepts, we are given only brief glimpses of a good and beneficent God, in an occasional Psalm, or the declamations of some of the more spiritually minded Prophets, who were, in many cases, also considerable mystics; or in the experiences of such a rare and exalted character as Joseph. But most of the time we are presented with a wrathful, vengeful, angry, bellicose deity who is very obviously the image and likeness of the patriarchs, prophets and lawgiver who describe Him.

Writing of Abraham, who seems to have been the first to have had this idea of an insatiable Creator-God, Philo refers to him as "the most ancient person of the Jewish nation", and tells us that he was a Chaldean by birth,

> born of a father who was very skilful in astronomy, and famous among those men who look upon the stars as gods, and worship the whole heaven and the whole world; thinking that from them do all good and all evil proceed to every individual among men; as they do not conceive that there is any cause whatever, except such as are included among the objects of the outer senses. Now what can be more horrible than this?

As we have already seen, this is far from being the truth about the esoteric teachings of the Mysteries that originated in Chaldea, or the philosophy based on them; but Abraham may never have come in contact with the deeper teachings of the ancient religion. Philo *had*, however, so that this passage reads suspiciously like intentional misrepresentation. He goes on to say:

> This man having formed a proper conception of him (God) in his mind, and being under the influence of inspiration, left his country and his family and his father's house, well knowing that if he remained among them, the deceitful fancies of the polytheistic doctrine abiding there . . . must render his mind incapable of arriving at the proper discovery of the one true God, who is the only everlasting God and the Father of all things, whether appreciable only by the intellect or perceptible by the outer senses; on the other hand, he saw that if he rose up and quitted his native land deceit would also depart from his mind, changing his false opinions into true belief. . . . And thus he went forth . . . to the investigation of the one God. And he never desisted from this investigation till he arrived at a more distinct perception, not indeed of His essence, for that is impossible, but of his existence, and of His overall providence as far as it can be allowed to man to attain to such; for which reason he is the first person who is said to have *believed in God* (Genesis 15:16), since he was the first who had an unswerving and firm comprehension of Him . . .

To suggest that Abraham was the first man to have believed in God is manifestly absurd. Both the Babylonian and Egyptian religions were thriving long before his time, and it was said to have been Noah's belief and trust in God that saved him from the deluge.

A rather more realistic account than Philo's is found in the *Antiquities* of Josephus (Book I, Ch. 7), where we read:

> Abraham was the first to publish this notion, that there was but one God, the creator of the universe . . . for which doctrines when the Chaldeans and other people of Mesopotamia raised a tumult against him, he thought fit to leave that country. . . . Abraham reigned at Damascus, being a foreigner who came with an army out of the land above Babylon, called the land of the Chaldeans. . . But after a long time he . . . removed from that country . . . and went into the land then called the land of Canaan, but now the land of Judea.

Abraham's idea of God, which included the very unpleasant notion that human sacrifices were acceptable to Him, might well have been extremely distasteful to the more advanced Babylonians of his day, and his opposition to the established religion would have appeared both impertinent and offensive since he had so little to offer as an alternative. For that he had no very clear notion at that time as to the true nature of God is admitted by Josephus in a citation from Chapter 8, which runs:

> When a famine had invaded the Land of Canaan, and Abram had discovered that the Egyptians were in a flourishing condition, he was disposed to go down to them, both to partake of the plenty they enjoyed, and to become an auditor of their priests, and to know what they said concerning the gods, designing either to follow them if they had better notions than he, or to convert them into a better way, if his own notions proved the truest. . . . He communicated to them arithmetic, and delivered to them the science of astronomy; for before Abram came into Egypt they were unacquainted with those parts of learning; for that science came from the Chaldeans into Egypt, and from thence to the Greeks also.

We must deduce from this that when the Father of the Jewish nation descended on the Egyptians, long after he had parted from his nephew, Lot, his idea of God was still but a notion, and very uncertain. He was, in fact, a seeker for truth, and open to conviction. How unstable his concept of the nature of deity was had already been demonstrated in his first imagining that God could wish him to slay his son, Isaac, and then, when common sense and fatherly love had triumphed over a primitive superstition, he had substituted an animal, thus establishing the horrible practice of animal sacrifice, which continued in the race he "fathered" from his time until the final destruction of the Temple, despite all that Isaiah and Jesus could do to put a stop to this merciless custom.

Abraham could have learnt little from the priests of Isis that he had not heard from the priests of Baal and Rhea; but one thing he does seem to have adopted from the Egyptians was their habit of circumcision.

As we know, the need for chastity in the aspirant to the spiritual life, which was symbolised by the castration of the priests under the rule of the goddess, was basic to the world-transcending outlook of the Mysteries. Men must return from the realm of matter to the Kingdom of Mind, which could only be done by overcoming the lust of the flesh. Such an idea was completely foreign to the world-affirming Abraham, whose God, like the unrestrained sun-god, demanded constant multiplication of the physical man. Because of this, the Egyptian habit of circumcision evidently appealed to him as having exactly the reverse effect to that of castration.

It has been generally supposed that this Jewish custom was adopted for merely hygienic purposes, but Philo let the cat out of the bag when he wrote (On Circumcision):

> The ordinance of circumcision on the parts of generation is ridiculed though it is an act which is practised to no slight degree among other nations, also, and more especially by the Egyptians who appear to me to to be *the most populous of all nations.*

And a little further on he remarks that "those nations which practise circumcision are the most prolific and the most populous". This, then, is extremely likely to have been the Patriarch's chief reason for adopting, and insisting upon, this custom for the new race.

The desire for procreation and the hatred of celibacy is also clearly shown in one of the laws that Moses left at his death, quoted by Philo:

> Let those who have made themselves eunuchs be had in detestation; and do you avoid any conversation with them who have deprived themselves of their manhood, and of that fruit of generation which God has given to men for the increase of their kind . . . nor is it lawful to geld either man or any other animals.

Here we have the limitlessness of the sun-god perpetuated in the Patriarchal determination to increase and multiply at all costs, not the good and harmless creation of a perfect God, but the animal kingdom of violence and cruelty observable by the senses. This outlook, wedded as it was to the visible world and matter, reversed the wisdom of the goddess, which was thenceforth regarded as *un*wisdom, and Woman was no longer accepted as the Symbol of Sophia. A new Trinity was evolved, in which the Woman, far from being represented as the Mother of the Gods, became the dupe of the knowledgeable serpent, and the temptress of the god-like man, who was portrayed as being as superior to Woman as God was to him. Equating man with mind, the likeness of the divine Mind that is God, Philo equates Woman with the external senses. In *The Allegories of the Sacred Laws*, he writes:

> Immediately after the creation of the mind it was necessary that the external senses should be created as an assistant and ally of the mind. . . . How . . . was this second thing created? When the mind was gone to sleep; for in real fact, the external senses come forward when the mind is asleep. And again when the mind is awake the outward sense is extinguished. . . . The mind . . . departing from the intense consideration of objects perceptible to the intellect, is brought down to the passions . . . yielding to the necessities of the body . . . and so we become enslaved. . . . Therefore the awakening of the outward senses is the sleep of the mind; and the awakening of the mind is the discharge of the outward senses from all occupation.

This is, of course, a very great metaphysical statement, the truth of which must be apparent to any practising philosopher or mystic. But as Philo was clearly aware of the position of the Mother of the Gods in the Wisdom religion, it was manifestly unfair of him to degrade woman to the status of external sense. His awareness is proved in a passage which reads:

> On account of the external sensation, the mind, when it has become enslaved to it, shall leave both the Father, the God of the Universe, and the mother of all things, *the virtue and wisdom of God*, and cleave to and become united to the external sensation, and is dissolved into external sensation, so that the two become one flesh. . . .

Here, once again, we have a description of the abandonment of the Mother of the Gods, and the descent to the nymph in the cave of matter.

The primitive Abraham was, of course, incapable of the subtle allegorising of the cultured Philo; but from the moment he appears on the scene with his new-born idea of an all-male Lord God, the Motherhood of God disappears as completely as though the androgynous, divine Parent had been cut in half, and the female portion destroyed. And with the disappearance of the goddess went all the feminine qualities, such as compassion, tenderness, protectiveness and non-violence. Nowhere in the Law of Moses do we read of a deific request for unbloody sacrifices; the slaughter of animals keeps pace with the slaughter of men, until

Woman once more speaks through the lips of Isaiah, deploring the rule of violence:

> I delight not in the blood of bullocks, or of lambs, or of the goats. . .
> And when ye spread forth your hands, I will hide mine eyes from you;
> yea, when ye make many prayers, I will not hear: your hands are full of
> blood.

Here, indeed, the goddess speaks, but was ignored by a violent, stiff-necked people. And meanwhile the Woman became subordinated not only philosophically, but in fact. Females were treated like herds, as mere possessions for procreative purposes, and considered as Philo even at his late date so persistently represented her, as a lesser creation who must submit to her lord and master, man. Deity thus became completely unbalanced. In Judaism, the divine equipoise, which constituted the divine perfection, or wholeness, was utterly lost, masculinity totally outweighing the feminine values.

The following passages from Philo's *Questions and Solutions* accurately describe the Jewish attitude to woman from the days of Abraham to those of Paul:

> The question is, why, according to the report in the second chapter of Genesis, the woman was not made out of the earth like man and the animals, but out of a rib? The answer follows: "This was in order that the woman might not be of equal dignity with the man".

Then it is asked why the woman touched the tree of good and evil first, and the man afterwards, the reply being:

> It was suitable that immortality and every good thing should be under the power of the man, and death and every evil thing under that of the woman. . . . The woman being imperfect and depraved by nature, made the beginning of sinning and prevaricating; but the man, as being the more excellent and perfect creature, was the first to set the example of blushing and of being ashamed (Genesis 3 : 8), and indeed of every good feeling and action.

Philo was no exception to the rule among his race of having illusions of *grandeur* about his sex! But why the stronger, nobler and more god-like should fall such an easy prey to the weaker, the inferior and the ignoble, he does not attempt to explain. Adam blamed the woman, and the Jewish race seem to have followed his example throughout history, and to have resisted and deplored the worship of the Queen of Heaven whenever it approached anywhere near the devotees of the patriarchal and all too masculine Jehovah.

They were not, however, so successful nor so rigorous in their exclusion of the sun-god. The claim that their religion was a unique revelation, and that neither it nor their God were in any way related to the older religion was as foolish as it was untrue. For the Truth to be true must be one and universal, the best proof of the validity of any teaching being that it has been arrived at by independent thinkers in widely separated parts of the earth and in different eras; and all Faiths have inevitably owed much to their precursors.

In reading the history of the Jews from the time of Abraham to the final sacking of their Temple by the Romans, and onward to their persecution and butchery by Hitler, it is impossible to escape the conclusion that their exclusiveness, so infuriating to cultured men of other Faiths, and their stubborn refusal to allow their idea of a partial and imperfect God to evolve, account for much of their constant and severe suffering. Their unwillingness to admit any fault in their obviously man-made God —an idea born in the mind of Abraham—and their clinging to his obsolete and primitive rulings, have made them a devolutionary element in a world destined for evolution or extinction. Their opportunity to share in this evolutionary movement, and, indeed, to take a major part in it, was lost on Calvary, where they violently rejected a higher ethic. And so tenacious was, and is, their prejudiced loyalty to their predatory and primitive Jehovah that even those who accepted the Gospel of Jesus Christ, have, as we shall see, retarded rather than helped the progress of the new Faith.

As with the Greeks, so with the Jews, Truth never seems to have been a moral absolute until the advent of Jesus Christ who made it clear that, without Truth, there could be no freedom. But if the truth as to the origins of Judaism had ever been faced, it would have been impossible to maintain the myth of its uniqueness, since from the first it had, in fact, been constantly infiltrated by sun-worship.

It is true that Abraham made a very definite break with the worship of the gods of his fathers, and replaced the radiant sun and fire god with a benevolent super-Patriarch made in his own image and likeness, possessing great power and a very partial love for his devotee. A friendly god who advised, tested and supported him in war, and in plans for enriching himself by means of the admirers of his beautiful wife. A companionable god with Whom he could converse, and even try to influence, as we see from the way he pleaded for the men of Sodom to be spared. In a word, a primitive anthropomorphic God conceived on the assumption that physical man was made in His likeness, and therefore that God must be like man, writ large.

We see little, if any, change in this idea of God as we study the histories of Isaac and Jacob. On the whole, and despite their armies, these three patriarchs seem to have been a peace-loving Trinity, who—at least in the case of Abraham and Jacob—were willing to agree to the concubinage of their wives rather than to start a war. But apart from this reasonable expediency, these patriarchs do not seem to have created any elevated ethical system. Jacob's treatment of Esau was flagrantly dishonest, and his sons, with the exceptions of Benjamin and Joseph, were capable of fratricide and untruthfulness. From whence, then, came the extremely moral and likeable character of Joseph?

Throughout, there is something extremely puzzling about the story of Joseph. In an age of primitives, he seems like someone belonging to a much later period, and to an infinitely more advanced culture. We not only admire him but feel kinship with him. We can understand and respect him as we would a man of outstanding Christian character of our own times. He was intelligent, unresentful, patient; psychic in the matter of pre-cognitive dreams, but essentially practical; a magnificent organiser, highly moral, completely reliable and trustworthy, and most loving and forgiving. His reunion with his unworthy brethren—who seem like creatures from another world—is intensely moving, even after many readings. How did Joseph become like that? Certainly not through anything the patriarchs had to teach. The answer may well be: the training and instruction given him by his mother, Rachel.

It is noteworthy that Abraham, for all his devotion to his new God, sent to his old home, to his relations who were still worshipping the hosts of heaven, for a wife for his elder son. And when *her* son, Jacob, was of marrying age, she insisted that he, too, should select a wife from her family; and Rachel not only became Jacob's wife, but also brought back with her to Canaan her father's gods, the images so odious to Abraham, as we find in Genesis 31 : 19, 30–35. This passage is particularly illuminating, for when Laban asks his nephew why he has stolen his gods, Jacob replies: "Because I was afraid: for I said peradventure thou wouldst take by force thy daughters from me." An answer which betrayed a belief that the pagan gods gave power to their possessors, and showed that he had not wholly cast off his faith in the deities rejected by his grandfather.

Rachel, Joseph's mother, a devotee of the old religion, may, then, have instilled into her son the outlook, and some of the Wisdom of the goddess. Furthermore, he was but a youth of seventeen when he was sold into slavery in Egypt, where he would have found a familiar echo of his mother's religion in the worship of Isis and Osiris. From the first, his relationship with his master, and all those he met, seems to have been excellent, which it could not have been had he betrayed any antipathy to the prevailing culture. From the biblical account he seems to have found it far from alien, and with the exception of the treacherous wife of Potiphar, he made no enemies, felt no enmity, and fitted into the strange land to which he had been brought as though he had been born into it. All of which may well have been the result of his mother's influence and teaching. Certainly his ability to interpret dreams which led to his acquisition of fame and fortune, although outstanding, was a familiar phenomenon at the court of Pharaoh, and among the priesthood which owed so much to the culture that had produced Joseph's maternal ancestry.

In fact the story of Joseph, who, to all intents and purposes, became a peaceful Egyptian, is the first of the many Jewish contacts with the worship of the sun-god recorded in the Old Testament. Pharaoh was, as we know, worshipped as the earthly counterpart of the sun. We have descriptions of his Toilet Ceremonies that were performed each morning in front of his courtiers, to symbolise the rising of the King of Heaven. We know that, after his elevation, Joseph was second in the land of Egypt only to Pharaoh himself, and would necessarily have shared in the honours paid to the sun-god. As Prime Minister, it is quite impossible that he should have remained unaware of and unaffected by the customs and religion of the hospitable land of his adoption. In the years of famine, his distribution of grain earned him one of the titles of the sun-god—the Sustainer of Life. His wife, the daughter of the Priest of On, i.e. of Heliopolis, the City of the Sun, would have been a highly cultured devotee of the Egyptian religion.

It is safe to assume from all this that Joseph had a very definite knowledge of the Wisdom of the goddess, and that his demonstration of that wisdom, in his forgiveness, helpfulness, tenderness, foresight, and lovingkindness to his one-time enemies, must have impressed his family, even if he said nothing in words about the inadequacy of their patriarchal Faith. And since they, too, with Jacob, came to inhabit the land of Egypt, we may assume that certain elements of the Egyptian Faith—and not always the highest elements after Joseph died and the Israelites were enslaved—would have permeated the patriarchal system during the Israelites' long sojourn in this country.

It is equally certain that despite his fanatical opposition to idolatry and his jealous devotion to Jehovah, many features of sun-worship entered the new Faith through Moses.

As the adopted son of Pharaoh's daughter, he seems to have been given what was the equivalent of a university education in that age. Philo writes of him that "he had all kinds of masters . . . some coming . . . from the neighbouring countries and the different districts of Egypt, and some being even procured from Greece by the temptation of large presents. . . . And the philosophers from the adjacent countries taught him Assyrian literature and the knowledge of the heavenly bodies so much studied by the Chaldeans . . . ".

Possessing this extensive knowledge, Moses would have been aware that the simple patriarchal system existing among his people, now slaves in Egypt, was simply not enough. Not only must they be rescued from slavery, but they must be given a religion advanced and comprehensive enough to regulate their lives and conduct; and when he had brought them out of Egypt, it was to the task of building up such a system that he devoted so much of his life.

The prejudiced Philo describes Moses as "the greatest and most perfect man that ever lived", and tells us that he was a genius who easily surpassed his teachers, and that his education all seemed to be recollection rather than learning. This, of course, hints at the doctrine of pre-existence taught by the priests and philosophers of the goddess, but which was not a feature of the patriarchal Faith. Comparing Philo's description of the great lawgiver with the portrait in the Old Testament of a rather slow-witted, slow-speaking, and, on the whole, simple man, we can only suppose that a myth of Moses had evolved in the course of the centuries as afterwards the Pauline myth was to take the place of the historical Jesus. Nevertheless, the myth is of interest, suggesting, as it does, the close connection of Moses with the worship of the Hosts of Heaven.

A most curious passage is found in *Antiquities*, Book I:26 (*Against Apion*), where Josephus reports that:

> Manetho, after describing the invasion of Egypt by the Jews and the disgraceful manner in which they behaved, killing the sacred animals, ejecting the priests and prophets naked out of the country, writes: "It is also reported that the priest who ordained their polity and their laws was by birth of Heliopolis; and his name Osarsiph from Osiris who was the God of Heliopolis; but that when he was gone over to these people, his name was changed, and he was called Moses."

As we know, the high priests of the Mysteries were named after the god of their cult, and if this report of Manetho is true—and Josephus would hardly have reported it if it were not, as the first part of it does not redound to the credit of the Jews—it proves that Moses was a high priest of the pagan Faith, as he might well have been if he were regarded as Pharaoh's grandson. Further confirmation of this is found in *Against Apion*, Book III, where we read:

> I have heard of the ancient men of Egypt that Moses was of Heliopolis, and that he thought himself obliged to follow the custom of his forefathers, and offered his prayers towards sun-rising, which was agreeable to the situation of Heliopolis.

This suggests that Moses was compromising between the two religions. Of Heliopolis Philo writes:

> ON is said to be a hill, and it means, symbolically the mind; for all reasonings are stored up in the mind; and the law-giver himself is a witness of this, calling ON, Heliopolis, the city of the Sun. For as the sun when he rises shows visibly the things which have been hidden by night, so also the mind, sending forth its own proper light, causes all bodies and all things to be seen visibly at a distance. On which account, a man would not be wrong who called our minds the sun of our composition.

This passage not only implies that Philo considered the Sun to be the symbol of the highest man can know, but also that Moses was aware of, and taught, this truth as a priest of Heliopolis, or the mind.

When we remember that Moses did not kill the Egyptian overseer and fly for his life into Median until he reached the age of forty, we must conclude that he was, by that time, steeped not only in the available secular learning of his time but also in the teaching of the Egyptian religion. Moreover, he married Zipporah, the daughter of the priest of Median, and of the good and intimate terms that prevailed between him and his pagan father-in-law we can read in Exodus Ch. 18. It is quite impossible that all these religious influences should have left no mark on his concept of God, and, indeed, except that his deity was, in theory, as Philo put it, "superior to all mortal conceptions; invisible to the senses, known to us by His power, yet unknown to us as to His essence", in practice he was, in many ways, extremely like the sun-god with which Moses had for so long been familiar. In fact, in the burning bush episode, he seems to have assumed the appearance of the solar deity.

A god of power, the creator of all things, visible and invisible, honouring the sun and moon so highly that He gave them to the heathen as objects of worship (Deuteronomy 4:19–21, Moffatt's Translation), only allowing the Israelites to know that there was something still higher, i.e., the God of the Jews, Jehovah, as he is represented in the Old Testament, has all the worst features of the King of Heaven, except for his weakness for women. Those Jehovah studiously ignores, although Miriam, the sister of Moses, was tolerated as a priestess until she had the temerity to complain when her brother married a black woman. Then the Lord God, who evidently approved of the match, or objected to the implied colour-prejudice, struck her down with leprosy.

There was also a female judge, or prophetess, called Deborah, a name that, most curiously, means "a Bee", like that of Mylitta or Melissa, the female counterpart of Mithras. The Bee played a prominent part in the Mystery Religions from the time of their inception. Porphyry writes in *De Antro Nympharum*, Ch. 18.

> Our ancestors used to call the priestesses of Demeter . . . mystic bees, and the maiden herself honied: to the moon also . . . they gave the name of Bee.

The name Deborah therefore suggests that, her wisdom being evident, this Judge of the Israelites was acknowledged to be a priestess of the Queen of Heaven. The honey, or Wisdom, issuing from the bee was believed to preserve as well as to purify, an idea which seems to have been current among the ancient Jews as it was among the Soldiers of Mithras in the days of the Roman Empire, who had honey placed on their tongues at the time of their initiation.

The God of Moses was certainly patriarchal, like that of Abraham, but His character had not improved in the course of the ages. Calling Himself just, he behaved with the greatest possible injustice to the enemies of the Children of Israel. One of his most memorable portraits, painted apparently by Moses, appears in Deuteronomy 7:1–6, and runs:

> When the Lord thy God shall bring thee into the land whither thou goest to possess it . . . and hath cast out many nations before thee . . . thou shalt smite them and utterly destroy them; thou shalt make no covenant with them, nor show mercy unto them: neither shalt thou make marriages with them . . . for they will turn away thy sons from following me, that they may serve other gods. . . . But thus shall ye deal with them; ye shall destroy their altars, and break down their images, and cut down their groves, and burn their graven images with fire. For thou art an holy people unto the Lord thy God: the Lord thy God hath chosen thee to be a special people unto himself above all people that are upon the face of the earth.

Here is Jehovah in all his brutality, exclusiveness, power, anger, treachery and injustice. From such instructions we may gather why the Jews became so detested by other nations. What was wrong with them was their God, i.e. their highest sense of what was good. That they willingly obeyed his instructions to the letter, we have seen from the passage quoted from Manetho by Josephus, as well as from Biblical evidence. How could they, who talked so much about justice and of men reaping what they sowed, have hoped to have escaped the Nemesis of such actions?

The Hebrew Scriptures present us with such a fantastic reversal of the outlook and wisdom of the goddess as to suggest that the revolt from her was as intentional and deliberate as it was in the case of Zoroastrianism. The first chapter of Genesis constitutes, according to Philo's elucidation, a statement of the Wisdom philosophy, presenting man as having been made in the image and likeness of Mind, and remaining in the intellectual realm, in obedience to the divine Mother, in the form of Mind, neither male nor female but having the attributes of both. Here, also, we have the harmless creation of Wisdom, a world based on the idea of unbloody sacrifices, with all things living in unity, amity and peace, being of the "very good" nature of their Source.

But in an instant, all this is reversed. The first chapter is set aside as though it had never been written, and, in the second, instead of unity, we have the unholy trinity of a fleshly man, woman and serpent, this creature being no longer a god, as at Delphi, inspiring the woman with wisdom, but her tempter who makes her an advocate of the knowledge of something besides good—evil. She still delivers the Word of the serpent to mankind, but it is a Word that ruins instead of aiding him. Woman, whom the earlier religion represented as the educator and elevator of mankind, striving to keep him from the evil of matter and physical life, now drags him down and becomes responsible for all the woes of mankind. She is still equated with knowledge, but a false sort of knowledge that is not wisdom, for it is dualistic, containing evil as well as good.

It was this dualism that was condemned by the Lord God. And here we have a very significant idea which has unfortunately never been followed up by the theologians. The first chapter of Genesis portrayed a perfect creation where only good was known, a state that can be sustained by focussing attention on good only. Woman is accused of a straying of attention, a downward, dualistic look, and as wanting something other than good, i.e., a change. This is a reversal indeed of the concept of the Mother of the Gods who steadfastly demanded that consciousness should remain pure and only beget in the spiritual realm. But just as the Jews lusted after the power that they, as a small, nomadic tribe, envied in their wealthier neighbours, and so invested their God with the power that they lacked, hoping to come at it through him, so they were in constant search for a scapegoat—hence their unceasing sacrifice of animals. Aware of their imperfections, they must mollify a demanding god with their gifts. But when it came to the question of the *beginning* of evil, the fall of man which was all too evident, the blame for that must be shifted to the woman; the physically weaker vessel must be the scapegoat. This was the Jewish version of the fall of consciousness to matter taught by the pagans. As a theory, it was not nearly so plausible, but the primitive Jews, like the Zoroastrians, were not prepared to allow that matter and the physical sense of life were evil. Such an idea was only found among their mystics, in the sect of the Essenes, or among the Kabbalists. It never appears in the canonical Jewish Scriptures.

A most curious thing about the total rejection of the compassion of the Mother-Goddess was the insensitive savagery attributed to Jehovah in his demand for the sacrifice of only good and harmless creatures, more particularly in the case of the pigeon and the dove. Was it only coincidence that the latter had always been the symbol of the Woman, the holy spirit of God? According to Moses, only these two gentle, harmless birds were to be sacrificed and eaten. Philo writes (On Animals Fit For Sacrifice):

> Of birds God chose only two classes out of them all, the turtle-dove and the pigeon; because the pigeon is by nature the most gentle of all those birds which are domesticated and gregarious, and the turtle-dove the most gentle of those who love solitude. Also ... of land animals ... he selected those specially as the best—the oxen, the sheep, the goats; for these are the most gentle and most manageable of all animals. ... And the victims must be whole and entire, without any blemish on any part of their bodies, unmutilated, perfect in every part, and without spot or defect of any kind.

The gentle, the perfect, the harmless, the good—only these would satisfy their blood-thirsty deity. The connection of this command with the tragedy on Calvary is significant, since it was to the same brutal, demanding Jehovah that the human sacrifice was offered. A man who met all the requirements for the sacrificial rite was the victim chosen by the hate-god of the Jews, who ordained that the good and the perfect must always suffer and die.

Philo does, in fact, comment on the apparent injustice of this decree of the lawmaker, saying, "One might suppose it to be just that those beasts which feed upon human flesh should receive at the hands of men similar treatment to that which they inflict on man", and therefore that man should eat them rather than the trustful, harmless animals. But he seems to think that Moses imagined that men grew like what they fed upon, and so might become brutalised by eating, for instance, a man-eating tiger. It does not appear to have occurred either to Philo or his lawmaker that to prey on herbivorous animals was to share the lion's eating habits. However, the more practical reason for this strange stipulation eventually appears in the prosaic statement that Moses "has forbidden with all his might all animals . . . which are most fleshy and fat . . . well knowing that such . . . produces insatiability . . . for insatiability produces indigestion, which is the origin and source of all diseases and weaknesses".

With the divorce of the female from the male in the idea of divinity, all sensitivity to the suffering of others, all compassion, tenderness, love and mercy disappeared from the religion of the Hebrews as moral absolutes. It was in vain that the worshippers sang: "Holy, holy, holy, Lord God Almighty"; mighty he may have been, but very far from whole. Depicted as an unbalanced, entirely male god, without his female or better, half, he stood revealed as little less than a monster in his attitude both to animals and men. His alleged instructions for animal sacrifice in Leviticus, and his demands for the utter extermination of the Canaanites, are examples of this, while he reversed the will of the good God described in the first chapter of Genesis by the orders found in Genesis 9:1–3.

In fact, Jehovah, though superior to the sun-god according to his devotees, demanded precisely the same sacrifices of innocent life, whether of beast upon the altar or of the enemy in war. And it was obvious that Moses did not intend his deity to lack any of the glories of ceremonial worship that had been accorded to the god of Egypt. There would not be images, but there would be a magnificent Tabernacle, containing many features of the Sun-Temple. He demanded the fine linen that was compulsory for the priests of Isis, but disregarded their humane reason for its use. He introduced the purple, blue, scarlet and gold veils, which represented the rainbow of the natural world, and, as we have discovered from recent excavations, were hung over the seven doors of the Mithraeum. The incense and the seven lamps, representing the seven spirits of the god of Mithraism, also reappeared in the Mosaic system; and the golden candlestick mentioned in Exodus 25:31–37 is of particular interest. It was recognised as a symbol of the sun-worshippers by Philo, who writes in *On Who Is the Heir of All Things*, XII, 5, *et seq.:*

> The sacred candlestick . . . was made having six branches, three on each side, and the main candlestick in the middle made the seventh. The sacred candlestick and the seven lights upon it are an imitation of the wandering of the seven planets through the heaven . . . and brilliant beyond them all is he who is the centre one of the seven, the sun. Those persons appear to me to form the best conjectures on such subjects, who, having assigned the central position to the sun, say that there is an equal number of planets,

namely those above him and below him. Those above him being Saturn, Jupiter and Mars; then comes the sun himself, and next to him Mercury, Venus and the Moon...

Moses was evidently loth to abandon all traces of the ceremonial of his former high priesthood, so the candlestick remained as a reminder to the observant that the most "unique" religions owe something to those that have preceded them.

Perhaps if the great law-giver had not been so pre-occupied with designing a sanctuary for Jehovah as magnificent as that of Osiris, he would not have found the Israelites sacrificing to the Egyptian gods when he returned to them with the deific commandments. His rage and his extermination of the idolators were just what might have been expected from a devotee of the jealous Hebrew God; but no one seemed to notice that the sixth of the commandments that the law-giver had compiled at the deity's request was *Thou shalt not kill*. Since he both literally and in spirit broke all ten of them in his most ungodlike fury, we can only suppose that the law-giver still thought of them in terms of theory rather than of practice.

The Decalogue is Moses' most notable legacy to mankind, and Western civilisation, such as it is, was founded upon it. Had these commandments been fully obeyed by the majority of the people, the world would undoubtedly be a much better place, for they were good and necessary. But we are apt to forget that there have been other lawmakers, and that the greatest part of humanity has managed to survive under their jurisdiction. Nor must it be forgotten that it was those who at least nominally accepted the legislation of Moses who have twice plunged humanity into a world-war during the present century. Furthermore, it was not until the advent of Jesus Christ that the West was presented with the Golden Rule which had long since been included in all the other major world-faiths.

What, in reference to a perfect God, was Moses' greatest contribution to the thought of mankind—the inspired commandment to love God with all the heart, soul, mind and strength, which is the basis for all true morality and spiritual living—was marred by the glaring imperfection of his God. We become like that which we love with all our heart, and, regarding Jehovah through the medium of the Old Testament, we cannot wonder that his devotees became what they did.

His eclecticism suggests that Solomon, the wisest of Israel's kings, was aware of this stumbling-block. It was certainly a proof of his dissatisfaction with the patriarchal system; and undoubtedly the greatest infiltration of the worship of the hosts of heaven was made through him.

Four opinions of this remarkable man may seem at first sight to be contradictory: (1) that he was the wisest king the Jews ever had; (2) that he was mad about women; (3) that he worshipped Ashtoreth, the Queen of Heaven; and (4) that he alone was considered worthy to build a temple to Jehovah.

That he worshipped Ashtoreth was a great scandal in his day, and to all the Jewish historians who recorded it. But what wise man does not worship Wisdom? As for his madness about women, he certainly is reputed to have had a great number of wives, many of them foreigners, but this might well have been the result of his desire for knowledge. Like Louis XIV, he might have liked "good conversation", and it is quite obvious that he learned a great deal of what we now call Comparative Religion from his womenfolk. In 1 Kings 2, 11:4 we read: "His wives turned away his heart after other gods." And we know that he married the daughter of the reigning Pharaoh with whom he had "made affinity".

The reason why he was permitted to build the Temple seems a strange one in connection with Jehovah, for, as we read in 1 Chronicles 22:7, 8:

> David said to Solomon, "My son, as for me, it was in my mind to build a house unto the name of the Lord my God: but the word of the Lord came to me, saying, 'Thou hast shed blood abundantly, and hast made great wars: thou shalt not build a house unto my name, because thou hast shed much blood upon the earth. . . . Behold, a son shall be born to thee, who shall be a man of rest . . . for his name shall be Solomon, and I will give peace and quietness unto Israel in his days. He shall build an house for my name'."

This, from Jehovah, who, from first to last, encouraged and aided the Israelites in their wars with the heathen, and approved of blood-letting on a large scale, seems a little inconsistent. But, from the evidence of some of the Psalms, the idea of God in the mind of David was evolving to something nearer to the God of the New Testament. Certain it is that Solomon was believed to have received the honour of building the house of the Lord because he was a man of peace; and he was a man of peace because, when offered the choice of anything in existence, he asked for Wisdom, which he prized as the greatest good, and which was therefore his god—or goddess. Perhaps the oddest thing about this episode is that what Solomon actually built, according to the description given in the Bible, and by Philo and Josephus, was undoubtedly a Sun-Temple.

It faced East, which was ever the way of those temples that awaited the rising of their god. The walls and doors were enclosed with boards of cedar covered with sculptured golden plates, "so that", as Josephus tells us, "the whole temple shined, and dazzled the eyes of such as entered, (Solomon) left no part of the temple, neither internal nor external, but what was covered with gold".

The wise king may well have imagined that this was what Moses, as the former high priest at Heliopolis, had intended, for he would have recognised the origin and symbolism of the Sacred Candlestick, of which he had 10,000 copies made, one of which was to burn perpetually in the Temple, even as the fire of Vesta and of the Zoroastrians. He also had the Mithraic rainbow veils of purple, blue and scarlet.

The description of the brazen sea, or immense bath, that he designed also belonged to the sacrificial worship of the heathen religion. "This brazen vessel was called a sea for its largeness," writes Josephus, "for the laver was ten feet in diameter. This sea contained 3,000 baths." Of its design, he says, "There stood about it twelve oxen that looked to the four winds of heaven, three to each wind."

What are these but the Twelve Oxen of the Sun, such familiar features of the worship of the hosts of heaven? The Sea was for "washing the hands and feet of the priests when they entered the Temple, but the lavers to clean the entrails of the beasts with their feet also". . . . Then follows a description of the engravings on the lavers, one of a lion, another of a bull, another of an eagle, all of which figure prominently in Mithraism and other sun-cults. The description of a golden table with loaves upon it conjures up the picture of the Mithraic fresco illustrated in Cumont's book, of the sun-god's Eucharist, with its loaves, or bouns on a golden tripod.

The amount of golden censers in which fire was carried from the outer to the inner Temple, was said to be 50,000, which suggests that fire played a large part in the ritual; while the censers for carrying incense to the altar numbered 20,000. As Josephus writes (*Antiquities*, Ch. 4:1):

> The king himself, and all the people and the Levites, went before rendering the ground moist with sacrifices and drink offerings, and the blood of a great number of oblations, and burning an immense quantity of incense; and this till the very air was so full of these odours that it met . . . people at a great distance, and was an indication of God's presence.

But the God who was present, and desired—most understandably— a thick cloud of perfume to disguise the slaughter-house atmosphere of his Temple, was so akin to Baal by nature as to be indistinguishable from that bloodthirsty deity. Josephus writes (*Antiquities*, Ch. 4:4):

> Solomon brought sacrifices to the altar, and when he had filled it with unblemished victims, he most evidently discovered that God had with

pleasure accepted of all that he had sacrificed to him, for there came a fire running out of the air, and rushed with violence upon the altar, in the sight of all, and caught hold of and consumed the sacrifices.

This hideous picture of a flesh-hungry god clearly identifies the god of Solomon with the solar deity. But where, now, is the good God, and His harmless, united creation described in the first chapter of Genesis? and where are the mercy and wisdom of the blood-forbidding goddess?

In the holy of holies there reposed the Ark containing the two tables of stone upon which the commandments of Moses were written. This seems to have been the only difference between the temple built to Jehovah and that of the sun-god. But the presence of the Mosaic law did nothing to prevent the primitive, repellent and cruel ceremonial of animal sacrifice always demanded by the solar deity.

A further identification with sun-worship is found in Philo's description of the High Priest's mantle, which he admits is a representation of heaven itself. He tells us that it is "of hyacinth colour, purple and scarlet, with embroideries of gold thread and studded with jewels", and writes (Book III:12):

> The two emeralds on the shoulder blades . . . are in the opinions of some persons who have studied the subject, emblems of those stars which are the rulers of night and day, namely, the sun and the moon. . . . Six names are engraved on each of the stones, because each of the hemispheres cuts the Zodiac in two parts, and in this way comprehends within itself six animals. Then the twelve stones on the breast, which are not like one another in colour and which are divided into four rows of three stones in each, what else can they be emblems of, except of the circle of the Zodiac?

The priest in his glittering garments so like those which were afterwards to be worn by the Pontifex Maximus of the heathen Faith in Rome, who bequeathed them to their papal successors, wore on his head "a gold leaf wrought like a crown . . . and in it there was a mitre, in order that the leaf might not touch the head". The mitre is also mentioned as having been worn by the Mithraic priests, and appears on the heads of dignitaries of the Catholic Church to this day.

With all these adaptations from the ancient religion, it is not surprising that when the Christian Bishops of the Early Church began to look into the ritual and customs of the heathen religion, they were amazed and horrified at its likeness to their own, which had been taken over from Judaism. Unable otherwise to explain the similarity, they blamed the devil for having inspired the sun-worshippers centuries before the birth of Jesus Christ to adopt ritual and give out teachings that were afterwards to be repeated by the Christians. Unable to trace the perpetual infiltration of Paganism into Judaism, as we can, this seemed to be the only explanation for a startling and utterly perplexing discovery.

But Solomon was not only responsible for the perpetuation of the exoteric features of sun-worship. Josephus tells us that he left four thousand and five books of his own composition. And if this is an oriental exaggeration, such books as he did leave, containing, as they did, the knowledge of a great eclectic, have undoubtedly influenced religious thought mightily through the ages. *The Wisdom of Solomon* was one of the sacred books of the Essenes; and that the wisdom of Solomon is the basis of the Kabbalic teachings is known to all students of the occult. Those modern descendants of the Mysteries, the Freemasons, built on the ground-plan of Solomon's Temple. In fact, it seems obvious that it was through Solomon and his writings that the ancient religion, at its best and worst, was preserved: its worst being its blood-baths, its superstition, its astrology; its best being the Wisdom of the Mother of the Gods, which was perpetuated by the Essenes.

One branch of this sect, known as the *Therapeutae*, practised spiritual healing, and this may also have been an inheritance from Solomon; for in *Antiquities*, Book VIII, Ch. 2 and 5, Josephus writes of him:

> God enabled him to learn the skill which expels demons, which is a science useful and sanitive to man. He composed such incantations also by which distempers are alleviated.

In this passage we recognise the method advocated by Plato who reminded us that "incantations" meant the right sort of words, or good teaching. Josephus goes on to say of Solomon:

> He left behind him that manner of using exorcisms, by which they drive away demons, so that they never return: and this method of cure is of great force unto this day; for I have seen a certain man of my own country, whose name was Eleazer, releasing people that were demoniacal in the presence of Vespasian and his sons. . . .

That a practical, non-Christian historian of the first century should have written this should cause those who insist that the only certain things about the miracles of Jesus was that they never happened, to retract such a sweeping statement.

The sun-worship instituted by Solomon evidently long survived him according to the statement in *Antiquities*, Ch. 5:5, that Josiah, a direct descendent of the wisest of kings, "took away the chariots (of the Sun) that were set up in his royal palace, which his predecessors had framed".

A footnote explains that "there were certain chariots with their horses dedicated to the idol of the Sun, or to Moloch".

We know, too, from 1 Kings 16: 30–32, that Ahab, King of Israel, was a worshipper of Baal, and built a temple for him; and that he married Jezebel, the daughter of Ethbaal, king of the Sidonians and Tyrians, and, as Josephus tells us, Jezebel "built a temple to the god of the Tyrians which they call Belus, and planted a grove of all sorts of trees". Ahab also made golden heifers and worshipped them.

Nevertheless, whenever any infiltration of the heathen religion was recognised by the prophets of Jehovah, it was bitterly denounced, as though such worship lacked any redeeming feature. From first to last, the book of Ezekiel is a diatribe against this adulteration, or whoredom, as he puts it. The people of Jerusalem and Samaria had forsaken Jehovah, who had done so much for them, and gone over to the gods of Assyria, Babylon and Egypt (Ezekiel 16). It never seems to have occurred to this prophet that the witting or unwitting eclecticism of priests and leaders had been largely responsible for this desertion. In Ezekiel Jehovah is shown at his most jealous, possessive, devilish and repellent, and no one can wonder at his having been deserted. His equally unpleasant-minded prophet reports him as saying:

> Because thou hast defiled my sanctuary with all thy detestable things and with all thine abominations ... neither will I have any pity. A third part of thee shall die with the pestilence, and with famine shall they be consumed in the midst of thee: and a third part shall fall by the sword round about thee. . . So will I send upon you famine and evil beasts, and they shall bereave thee; and pestilence and blood shall pass through thee. I the Lord have spoken it. (Ezekiel 5:11, 12, 17).

In blind fury he gave his directions for destroying those who had dared to look towards other gods:

> Slay utterly old and young, both maids and little children and women ... fill the courts with the slain.

The Christian heretics were undoubtedly correct when they insisted that the God of the Old Testament was not the God of the New.

Ezekiel's god seems to have been particularly prejudiced against Pharaoh, the Egyptian king, notorious for his disinclination for war. He much preferred the belligerent Babylonian king (Ezekiel 30:25). Nor, apparently, did his prophet see any connection between Daniel's behaviour during the Captivity, and the increased interest in the heathen gods among the Israelites, for he speaks with reverence of the great

Magian whom he associates with Noah and Job as men approved of God (Ezekiel 14:14). Yet undoubtedly Daniel had become very involved with the pagans and their customs, vying with their magicians in the interpretation of dreams, accepting the position of chief magician to the sun-worshipping king, not rebuking Nebuchadnezzar when he affirmed that in him (Daniel) was "the spirit of the holy gods", and allowing himself to be worshipped as Belteshazzar, the representative of the sun-god, Bel. As Josephus writes (*Antiquities*, Ch. 10:2):

> When Nebuchadnezzar heard (Daniel's interpretation) . . . he fell upon his face and saluted Daniel in the manner that men worship God, and gave command that he should be sacrificed to as a god. And . . . also imposed the name of his own god upon him (Baltaser).

He was also involved with the Persian conquerors, Darius and Cyrus, who made him chief president of the conquered kingdom. And though it is said that Darius (a worshipper of Ormuzd and Mithras) acknowledged Daniel's god as the only living god (Daniel 6:26), we read of no such conversion in the works of non-Jewish historians.

It is quite obvious from his behaviour that, consciously or unconsciously, Daniel had absorbed much of the Wisdom of the Goddess, including the Pythagorean diet upon which he and the other three sons of King Zedekiah insisted. Also, from the vision described in Daniel 7, *et seq.*, it is clear that the prophet's mind was highly coloured by sun-symbolism and imagery which led to a literary style of Apocalyptic writing that not only affected Ezekiel but was afterwards revived in the Revelation of John which the Fathers of the Early Church were—most understandably—so reluctant to include in the canonical Christian writings.

But the influence that the Captivity had on Judaism is now so generally acknowledged that it is unnecessary to labour the point. Ezekiel and his god might well be appalled, but it was only the culmination of a process that had been continuing steadily throughout the ages. Unfortunately Judaism had all too often embraced the worst elements of alien Faiths; the better, those that came from the Wisdom of the Goddess, being ignored.

We find, however, echoes of that Wisdom in some of the Psalms written by the father of Solomon, and in the Proverbs of that wise king who extols the goddess so magnificently in Proverbs Ch. 8, alluding always to Wisdom in the feminine gender, which would be readily understood by the heathen, but was probably thought to be an idiosyncrasy of this woman-mad king, by his Jewish recorders. We find it also in the

God-realisation of many of the devout mystics in the Old Testament, and most vehemently in the exhortations of Isaiah, who, unlike his contemporaries, was aware that the creation of God was harmless and good, and that no other view of creation should be tolerated. Reverence for life was to be universal. Even the ideas of God conceived of as insects would be non-injurious:

> The suckling child shall play on the hole of the asp, and the weaned child shall put his hand on the cockatrices' den. . . . They shall not hurt nor destroy in all my holy mountain: for (and this is the sole condition by which such a state can come about) the earth shall be full of the knowledge of the Lord as the waters cover the sea.

Through the Wisdom of God mankind will recognise the nature of God as wholly good, and know that there is none else. Worshipping the Good Mind, they will not propagate or perpetuate evil. The nightmare world of ignorance will vanish, and the true kingdom of God will be seen as already established. The Golden Age, of Pythagoras, the kingdom of Heaven, of Jesus, will be found to have come "on earth as it is in heaven".

The actual existence of this kingdom, and the present operation of its laws, were revealed in the life and teachings of Jesus the Nazarene. The bridge between exoteric Judaism and the Gospel of Jesus Christ appears to have been built by the Essenes.

CHAPTER VIII

The Secret of the Essenes

On the evidence provided by Philo and Josephus, it would seem to be established that the secret teachings of the Essenes constituted the Gnosis, or the Mysteries, of the Jews; that esoteric knowledge found in all the great world-faiths, which we have named, the Wisdom of the Goddess.

Since the discovery of what have come to be known as the Dead Sea Scrolls in the caves of Qumran, we have further proof that the philosophy of this strange sect came from teachings other than those found in the orthodox Hebrew Scriptures, and that much of it was contained in the apocryphal works forbidden to the orthodox Jews. Philo writes of the Essenes that "they have also writings of ancient men who having been founders of one sect or another have left behind them many memorials of the allegorical system of writing and explanation, whom they take as a kind of model".* Pliny writes that the Essenes "possessed secret, holy writings of their own, which they guarded with special care". And Josephus tells us that among other things the would-be initiate has to vow before he is allowed to partake of the common food, and so become one of the Order, is that "he will preserve the books belonging to the sect".

It is these books, or scrolls, apparently, that have recently come to light. In his book, *The Scrolls from the Dead Sea*, Edmund Wilson tells us that "four apochryphal Old Testament books have close connection with the literature of the Essenes: *The Book of Jubilees;* the *Book of Enoch; The Testaments of the Twelve Patriarchs:* and *The Assumption of Moses*".

Their policy of non-violence can certainly be traced to the influence of *The Book of Enoch*, even in the abridged and mutilated form that it has come down to us, for, in that, the two paths open to men are described as the Path of Righteousness, and—its antithesis—the Path of Violence. For the writer of *The Book of Enoch*, violence is the great sin. The test of the Righteous is that "no manner of violence is found in them". He has evidently taken to heart the passage in Genesis 6:11-13, in which it is twice stressed that violence was the sin so unforgiveable that it was punished by the Flood, for he traces the Fall of man from the time

---

* Brucker (*Hist. Philosoph. Tom*, ii, p. 787) proved that the Therapeutae gave preference to the philosophy of Plato.

when Azazel, the fallen angel, taught mankind to make armaments with the metals of the earth.

> Then said the Most High: "The whole earth has been corrupted through the works that were taught by Azazel: to him ascribe all sin."*

And in this book occurs a description of the end of those who have followed the path of violence, which reads astonishingly like a prophecy of nuclear warfare:

> In the fire shall they burn. . . . And I saw there something like an invisible cloud; for by reason of its depth I could not look over, and I saw a flame of fire blazing brightly and things like shining mountains circling and sweeping to and fro. And I asked one of the holy angels who was with me. . . . What is this shining thing? for it is not heaven, but only the flame of a blazing fire, and the voice of weeping, and crying and lamentation and strong pain.

This was obviously not the Mazdean Lake of Fire, for it was located in the heavens, and certainly reads most uncomfortably like a precognitive vision of modern aerial combat.

The Essenes appear to have taken these warnings from their sacred books deeply to heart, for they not only practised non-violence by refraining from warfare, but were strict vegetarians, neither eating flesh nor drinking wine. Josephus, who had made a study of their teachings, writes:

> Their doctrine is this: that bodies are corruptible, and that the matter they are made of is not permanent; but that souls are immortal and continue forever; and that they . . . are united to their bodies as to prisons, into which they are drawn by a certain natural enticement; but that when they are set free from the bonds of the flesh, they then, as released from a long bondage, rejoice and mount upward.

If we had no other, this would be sufficient evidence to show that they propagated the doctrine of the other Mysteries. That they taught the Wisdom of the goddess not only as regards non-violence but also in the matter of sexuality, is evident from Pliny's description of them as an entirely celibate Order who yet managed to survive for thousands of years owing to the many recruits they made from people disgusted with the natural world. He writes of them:

> A solitary race and wonderful above all others on the globe; without women, renouncing all usual enjoyment, without money. . . . From day to day they are recruited by the flocks of newcomers whom the world

---

* *The Book of Enoch*, translated by R. H. Charles, D.Litt. (S.P.C.K. 1952.)

drives from itself, all tempest-tossed by the way of fortune. In this way, incredible to tell, the race wherein no birth ever takes place, has endured for thousands of years, so useful for recruiting their numbers is the disgust of other men with the world.

Yet the very basis of their faith was their belief in the unchangeable goodness of God. Philo speaks of their firm assurance "that God is the source of all good, but of nothing evil". Of their customs he writes:

> The Essenes have organised communities which are grouped around a centre, where they come together for meals and to which they are always responsible. They hold all their goods in common. New members must surrender their property to the Order; and all must contribute to it their earnings. In return they get everything they need. . . . Even the clothing is common property. . . . There is no buying or selling among them, and anyone can take anything for nothing from his "brother".

It should be noted that, as in the case of the Early Christians, this communal life was only lived, and indeed was only possible, among the tried and trusted members of the Order, those who had served a long probation and of whose good character the other members were assured. Otherwise it would have been quite unrealistic owing to the exploitation that would inevitably have taken place by the admittance of unregenerate mankind. Even when all possible care had been taken, we know that this did happen in the case of the Early Christians, when Ananias and Sapphira defected. This is ignored by those who argue that modern Communism finds authority in true Christianity. Lovers of God being lovers of Wisdom would never be so unrealistic as to attempt communal life, as the materialists have done, with unethical members. The ideal of Communism, which has still to be attained—"to each according to his need"—was practised from the first by this Order as a result of the spiritual love that based it. Josephus writes:

> The sick are supported if they cannot work; the old people are cared for. . . . Most of them live to be over a hundred. . . . They will not make instruments of war. They will not engage in commerce. They maintain a fraternal equality believing that human brotherhood is the natural relationship of men, which has only been destroyed in society by the competition of the covetous.

There is something Brahmanical about their manner of feeding. Josephus tells us that "when they have clothed themselves in white veils, they then bathe their bodies in cold water". He refers several times to this habit of covering themselves when washing or performing the natural functions. In the latter case he explains this rather curiously by saying that they do it "that they may not affront the divine rays of light". This notion has persisted in the Catholic Church, for early in this century, pupils at certain Continental convents were still obliged to bath under a sheet, in deference to their "guardian angels", who were presumably of the male sex!

The passage from Josephus continues:

> And after this purification is over, they everyone meet together in an apartment of their own, into which it is not permitted to any of another sect to enter... The baker lays them loaves in order; the cook also brings a single plate of one sort of food... a priest says grace before meat; and it is unlawful for anyone to taste of the food before grace be said.

This is a very early instance of the saying of grace which has persisted through the centuries. In a footnote, the editor of the *Antiquities* remarks that the first instance of this custom, as far as he could ascertain, was recorded when the seventy-two priests assembled before Ptolemy for the translation of the Holy Scriptures, and the king asked the chief of them to say grace; which suggests that the habit originally came from Egypt. Josephus writes of the Essenes:

> The same priest says grace again after meat; and when they begin and when they end they praise God, as he bestows their food upon them; after which they lay aside their white garments and betake themselves to their labours again till the evening.

In describing a festival of the *Therapeutae* which takes place at the end of every seven weeks, Philo seems to have forecast the idea of the Christian's heaven, held for centuries by simple minds. He speaks of the gathering together of the Order in their white garments offering up prayers to God that the entertainment may be acceptable, before sitting down to meat at a table "which bears nothing which has blood". But before the feast is consumed, there are allegorical explanations made of the Holy Scriptures, and the secret meaning explained. Applause and rejoicing follow this, and then a hymn is sung by one of the members. After the feast they "celebrate the sacred festival during the whole night". Male and female choruses sing together,

> moving their hands and dancing in corresponding harmony....Then when each chorus of the men and each chorus of the women has feasted separately by itself, like persons in the bacchanalian revels, drinking the pure wine of the love of God, they join together and the two become one chorus, in imitation of that one which... was established by the Red Sea....Moses the prophet leading the men, and Miriam the prophetess leading the women....Therefore being intoxicated all night till the morning with

this beautiful intoxication, without feeling their heads heavy or closing their eyes for sleep ... and standing there till morning, when they saw the sun rising they raised their hands to heaven, imploring tranquility and truth and acuteness of understanding.

There is no doubt that the harmless, God-obsessed and compassionate life lived by the Essenes bore a remarkable resemblance to that lived by Jesus and his disciples, so it is not surprising that the idea should have arisen that Jesus was an Essene, and that Philo was referring to the Early Christians when he wrote of the *Therapeutae.**

The earliest statement of this theory seems to have been made by Eusebius in his *Ecclesiastical History* (Book II, Ch. 17), where, referring to the branch of the Essenes known as Therapeutae, or Healers, he writes:

> These ancient Therapeutae were Christians, and their writings are our Gospels and Epistles.

This startling and extraordinary statement about a pre-Christian sect seems recently to have received confirmation in the discovery of the Dead Sea Scrolls. Nevertheless, the arguments against it are as strong as those for it and it will perhaps be as well to examine both before offering an alternative that would reconcile the two hypotheses. But first we must consider the suggestion even more frequently made, that John the Baptist was an Essene, owing to his emphasis on baptism which was such a feature of this sect. This theory is not popular with humanitarians who point out that no member of an Order that was so humane that it would neither sacrifice nor eat animals, would appear in "camel's hair, with a girdle of skin about his loins". And this is certainly not the garb designed by the goddess. But, oddly enough, we find Philo writing of the Essenes that "their raiment is of the most ordinary description, just stout enough to ward off cold and heat, being a cloak of *some shaggy hide* for winter, and a thin mantle or linen shawl in the summer". Either they were as inconsistent on this point as the ladies complained of by Bernard Shaw, who attended an anti-vivisection meeting wearing furs and feathers, or they may have assimilated the Zoroastrian idea of two kinds of animals, which permitted them to kill and wear the skins of the creation of Ahriman.

But there is one very strong argument against John the Baptist being an Essene in the statement that he lived on locusts and wild honey. For there seems to be no doubt whatever that the Essenes were strictly vegetarian, refusing to eat anything that had sentient life. The argument often put forward that locusts might be rendered "locust-beans" must be

---

* This notion is found in *Schurer* (II, ii, p. 218: iii, p. 358), who argues that Philo's *Contemplative Life* is spurious, and that the Therapeutae were Christian monks.

ruled out, for the word used undoubtedly means the living locust, and Herodotus tells us that these creatures were eaten in his day by people called Nasamonians, of whom he writes:

> They ... chase the locusts, and, when caught, dry them in the sun, after which they grind them to powder, and, sprinkling this upon their milk, so drink it. (Book IV, 174.)

This, again, has Zoroastrian echoes, for locusts and scorpions were on the list of Ahriman's creatures.

It is, of course, possible that John the Baptist may have belonged to a branch of the Essenes who were not so strict on the subject of diet; for there seems to have been at least one other branch beside the Therapeutae, that differed from the others on one very fundamental point, in that it did not wholly renounce marriage. Josephus says that this branch considered it a duty to procreate in order to ensure posterity, and of all three witnesses he is, perhaps, the most reliable, having, as he tells us, for a time "made a trial of their Order", so that his knowledge was first hand. He writes:

> When I was about sixteen years old, I had a mind to make trial of the several sects that were amongst us: Pharisees, Sadducees, Essenes ... for I thought that by this means I might choose the best. ... So I contented myself with hard fare ... and went through them all.

His final choice was made at the age of nineteen when, he says, "I began to conduct myself according to the rules of the sect of the Stoics." But from his evident and uncritical admiration of the Essenes, it is obvious that there was nothing in their philosophy with which a Pharisee could find fault. Therefore, in the light of what he and Philo tell us of this sect, we may examine the arguments for and against the Essenes having been the pre-Pauline Christians.

Probably the strongest argument for this assumption is that neither Josephus nor Philo, writing as they did in the first century, mention the Christians. The two obvious interpolations referring to the Christ in *Antiquities*, Books XVIII and XX, have long since been dismissed by scholars as spurious. Origen in the *contra Celsum* does not mention them, although they would have been most pertinent to his argument with the pagan. On the other hand, he does quote the passage referring to John the Baptist, which shows he was acquainted with the *Antiquities*. No Christian writer refers to the two paragraphs before Eusebius, who was not to be trusted. The paragraph in Book XVIII was missing in the copies of Josephus seen by Photius in the ninth century. How was it possible that two such well-informed and prominent Jews as Philo and Josephus should apparently know nothing of that heresy that so infuriated their co-religionist, Saul of Tarsus—a Pharisee, like Josephus—that he could hound and persecute the Christians wherever he found them? Surely some details of the exemplary life lived by these people, so like that of the admired Essenes, should have come to their hearing? But there is no mention in the works of either of them of the Leader of this heresy, nor of his many wonderful acts that would surely have caused something more than merely local interest.

But although the Christians are never mentioned, the Essenes *are*, and with considerable respect, by both writers. And what they say of them seems, in the main, to illustrate the sort of life that the Early Christians would be living if they were carrying out the teachings of Jesus Christ.

Josephus, having described the Essenes as being Jews by birth, says that they have a greater affection for one another than the other two sects (Pharisees and Sadducees). He tells us that they "reject pleasure as an evil, but esteem continence and the conquest over the passions to be virtue"; that they despise riches and have everything in common. And this, as we know, was the rule with the first Christians, not only from the statement in Acts 4:32, but from *The Didache*, section 4, where we read:

> Thou shalt share all things with thy brother, and shall not say that they are thine own; for if ye are fellow partakers in that which is immortal, how much more in things that are mortal?

Of their hospitality Josephus writes:

> They have no one certain city, but many of them dwell in every city; and if any of their sect come from other places, what they have lies open for them, just as if it were their own; and they go into such as they never knew before, as if they had been ever so long acquainted with them, for which reason they carry nothing at all with them when they travel into remote parts.

This would certainly explain Jesus' instructions to the disciples in Mark 6:8–10, and how he and they managed to live during the years of his ministry, with no settled headquarters.

When we consider the innumerable physical healings attributed to Jesus and his disciples by the writers of the Gospel, the following passage from Philo assumes significance:

> Having mentioned the Essenes... I will now proceed ... to speak of those who have embraced the speculative life. They are called Therapeutae, and Therapeutrides*... They profess an art of medicine more excellent than that in general use in the cities, for that only heals bodies, but the other heals souls.

* From the Greek; to heal.

According to Philo, these men were mystics and seers, taught to "see" without interruption.

> I am not speaking of the sight of the body but of that of the soul....They always retain an imperishable recollection of God, so that not even in their dreams is any other object ever presented to their eyes except the beauty of the divine virtues and of the divine powers.

This might well be a description of the single-minded obsession with God and His Kingdom at all times manifested by Jesus. Philo describes the criteria of the Essenes as the love of God, and the love of virtue, and the love of mankind; and speaks of their strict adherence "to the principle of looking on the deity as the cause of everything that is good and of nothing which is evil"; a teaching found stated explicitly in James 1 : 17, and 3 : 11,12, as well as implicitly in every word and act of Jesus Christ.

In reference to animal sacrifice, which, as we know from John 2:14–16, was so displeasing to Jesus, Philo writes that the Essenes "are above all men devoted to the service of God, not sacrificing living animals, but studying rather to preserve their own minds in a state of holiness and purity". Of their pacifism he says that "among these men you will find no ... makers of arms ... no one attending to any employment whatever connected with war". Of their devotion to truth he tells us that they look upon truth and falsehood "as standing in the light of fountains, for from falsehood proceeds every variety of evil and wickedness, and from truth there flows every imagineable abundance of good things both human and divine".

Their relationship with their fellows is of the spiritual character described in Mark 3:31–35, the young people regarding the old as their true parents and "like legitimate sons with affectionate rivalry minister to their fathers and mothers, thinking their common parents more closely connected with them than those who are related by blood, since ... to men of right principles there is nothing more nearly akin than virtue".

As we know, they were celibate, and, according to Josephus, ensured the continuance of their Order by adopting other people's children, and forming them "according to their own manners", this evidently being a second means of recruiting new members, for we have already been told by Pliny that disgust for the world accounted for a great number. "The women", Josephus tells us, "are virgin in respect of their purity out of love of wisdom with which they are desirous to pass their lives, on account of which they are indifferent to the pleasures of the body, desiring not a mortal but an immortal offspring, which the soul that is attached to God is alone able to produce by itself and from itself."

The Essenes were non-attached in the sense indicated in Mark 10: 28–30. Philo writes, "They flee without ever turning their heads back again, deserting their numerous families, their native lands." There were prophets among them; and Josephus refers to one who made a prophecy about Antigonus. He remarks that they "seldom miss their predictions". We know from *The Didache*, or *The Teaching of the Twelve Apostles*, that the early Christians were instructed by travelling or resident prophets. In sections XI–XIII (Respecting Prophets), we read:

> Whoever cometh and teacheth you all these things spoken above, receive him. . . . Every genuine prophet who wishes to settle among you is worthy of his support. . . . All the first-fruits . . . thou shalt take and give to the prophets; for they are your chief priests.*

This was written before the establishment of Bishops, and would agree with the custom of the Essenes.

They obeyed the injunction in Matthew 5:34–36, to "swear not at all". Josephus writes that "swearing is avoided by them, and they esteem it worse than perjury; for they say he that cannot be believed without swearing by God, is already condemned".

In all this the similarity with the teachings of the Gospel is so striking that there would seem to be an excellent case for assuming that these virtuous people were indeed the first Christians were it not for the objections that can be brought up against it, among them being : (1) that Pliny who greatly admired the Essenes, regarded the Christian religion, as it had become in his day, as infatuation and madness; (2) the extreme respect that Philo and Josephus evince for this sect. Josephus was a Pharisee, like Saul of Tarsus; why, then, should Saul and other men of the synagogue, have such a bitter, fanatical hatred of a sect so strongly approved of by two of the most notable of his co-religionists? We know that this hatred was originally evoked in the orthodox Jews by the violation of the strict Sabbatarian law (Mark 3:26). It was when Jesus healed the man with the withered hand on the Sabbath day that the Pharisees determined to destroy him. And we know that the Essenes were most punctilious about the Sabbath. Josephus writes:

> They are stricter than any other of the Jews in resting from their labours on the Sabbath Day, for they not only get their food ready the day before, that they may not be obliged to kindle a fire on that day, but they will not remove any vessel out of its place, nor go to stool thereon. . . .

---

* *The Teaching of the Twelve Apostles*, a translation with notes by Canon Spence, M.A. (James Nisbet & Co.)

This is precisely the concept of keeping the Sabbath that Jesus opposed. That the early Christians were convinced that their Master had cancelled observance of the Sabbath is not only clearly stated by Irenaeus in *Against Heresies*, but attention is constantly called to the fact by the Fathers of the Early Church. Justin admits to Trypho that the Christians do not keep the Sabbath as the Jews do, for "the new law wishes you to keep Sabbath all the time". In his *Answer to Jews* Tertullian says that "to Christians Sabbaths are unknown". In the *contra Celsum* Origen defines the higher concept of the Sabbath entertained by the Christians when he writes (Book VIII, 22): "The perfect man who is always engaged in the words, works and thoughts of the divine Logos . . . is continually observing the Lord's Day." The Jews keep a Sabbath once a week; the Christian's life must be a perpetual Sabbath.

At their feasts, as we have seen, the Essenes indulged in choral singing and dancing. Although in the Gospels we read of prayers and occasional hymns, there is never any mention of dancing. This belongs to the sun-cults, of which circular dancing is a feature. Miriam may well have been instructed in it by her brother Moses, the priest of On; but it would have seemed most inappropriate to the men of the New Testament.

The holding of all things in common was obviously a long-established and successful practice of the Essenes, but, as we find in the Acts of the Apostles, the attempt at communal living by the Early Christians did not survive the defections of Ananias and Sapphira.

The Essenes wore white garments, which is not recorded of the disciples and early Christians. In fact, at the Transfiguration, Jesus' garments were said to have been "transformed" into a "glistering white".

Josephus tells us that anyone wishing to join the sect of the Essenes had to have a year of probation. The Christian demand was that men should *immediately* leave all and follow the way of Christ. At the same time it is true that the Christians did not admit anyone to their Love-Feast who had not been baptised, and as baptism was only supposed to be performed after perfect inward purification, there must have been a period of probation of uncertain length. It is curious and worthy of note that both Christians and Essenes had to pass the test of purification before being admitted to the common meal.

On the other hand, the Essenes seem to have had stringent dietetical laws which are not recorded of the Christians. Josephus speaks of the plight of a member of the Order, who, for heinous sin, is cast out of the sect, and says that he often dies, for "he is not at liberty to partake of the food that he meets with elsewhere, and is forced to eat grass". This seems a far cry from the instruction to "eat what is set before you for conscience sake".

The Essenes were a secret society with teachings that must never be revealed outside the Order. Josephus writes of them that they "will neither conceal anything from those of his own sect, nor discover any of their doctrines to others . . . though one should compel him to do so at the hazard of his life". Such an attitude is nowhere found in the Gospel records or in Pauline Christianity.

According to both Philo and Josephus, the Essenes were never persecuted, but were, in fact, in favour with the authorities owing to their virtuous way of life. Philo writes that they achieved

> a freedom which can never be enslaved. And as a proof of this is that, though at times a great number of chiefs . . . have occupied their country . . . no one . . . not even . . . the more treacherous and hypocritical oppressors was ever able to bring any real accusation against the multitude of those called Essenes, or Holy.

In *Antiquities*, Book V, Josephus writes that "Herod had those Essenes in honour, and thought higher of them than their mortal natures required".

The equality among them referred to by both Philo and Josephus, seems to have been confined to practical matters, for, according to Philo, they had a caste system among themselves which was far from egalitarian. He says that "after the time of their preparatory trial is over, they are parted into four classes; and so far are the juniors inferior to the seniors, that if the seniors should be touched by the juniors, they must wash themselves, as if they had intermixed themselves with the company of a foreigner". Few customs could be more uncharacteristic of the Mind of Christ as we know it than this, which has a strong Brahmanical or Pharisaical flavour.

Finally, and most conclusively if we are to believe both Josephus and Philo, the perfect man of the Essenes, like that of most other good Jews, was Moses. The former writes: "What they most of all honour after God himself is the name of their Legislator; whom if anyone blasphemes, he is punished capitally."

This last statement, if true, would in itself constitute an impassable gulf between the Christian doctrine and that of the Essenes; for, as Origen assures us in the *contra Celsum*, Jesus "did not consider it compatible with his inspired legislation to allow the taking of human life *in any form at all*". His protection of the Magdalene from the legal penalty for her crime was yet another instance of his opposition to the letter of the Mosaic law. Yet it is obvious from the account given by Philo, that the Essenes considered that the Law of Moses was divinely inspired, and that they esteemed it beyond all things. He writes:

> They devote all their attention to the moral part of philosophy, using as instructors the laws of their country which it would have been impossible for the human mind to devise without divine inspiration.

The great gulf dividing the Jews from Christians has always been the vast difference in their concept of what constitutes the perfect man, which is basically the difference between their ideas of God. For the Jew, the perfect man was the virile, earthly, animal-sacrificing, stern law-giver, Moses. For the Christian, the perfect man is the non-violent, healing, compassionate and chaste Jesus Christ. To Philo, one of the most cultured men of his race and times, Moses was something more than an inspired law-giver, High Priest, prophet and Friend of God. On more than one occasion he actually speaks of him *as* God, as Christians were later to do of Jesus. He writes:

> Moses means gain. . . . To be able to procure good for others belongs to a greater and more perfect soul, and is the profession of one who is really inspired by God, which he who has attained to may reasonably be called God.*

And in *On the Virtuous Being Also the Free*, he states even more forthrightly: "The man who is wholly possessed with the love of God and who serves the living God alone, is no longer man but actually God . . . the God of man."

This appears to have been Philo's truest conception of Moses. From his approval of the Essenes, and his description of their great reverence for the Law, it is plain that they must have shared his views of the great Law-giver. But while Jesus respected the Law, and often referred to it, there was no adulation in his attitude towards the Lawmaker, and, as we find in the Gospels, he frequently opposed the letter of some of the Mosaic laws. This was directly opposed to the attitude of Philo, the Pharisees, and, as far as can be judged, of the Essenes.

But here again we find a puzzling contradiction. Although Philo writes of the devotion of the Essenes to Moses as the perfect man, we know that they, like Jesus, often acted contrary to his rules. Their abstention from animal sacrifice which excluded them from the common court of the Temple, and their abstinence from flesh food and from propagation, were all violations of the known laws of Moses. Which brings us to the possibility that he, like the Alexandrian Fathers, had a doctrine of "Reserve", or one set of rules for the masses and another for the Elect, the esoteric doctrines being given only to initiates. As we know, Philo

* *On the Change of Scripture Names*, XXII.

refers to the Mysteries of Moses, as though esoteric Judaism was just another form of the Hellenic Mysteries, with its secret teachings enshrined in books not available to the multitude. If this were so, it would account for the deviation of the Essenes from Orthodox practices.

However this may be, there is no doubt that Jesus expected men to follow *him* rather than Moses. As the Messiah, he had superseded Moses. The Law and even the prophets must give place to the Son of God. This change of authority was symbolised by the experience known as the Transfiguration, at the end of which the figures of Moses and Elias vanished, and Jesus was left alone, the divine Voice declaring: "This is my beloved son, hear HIM." The new testimony had come: the old must be relinquished. This would have been the wildest heresy to the Essenes, as described by Philo and Josephus.

But although these objections seem to rule out the possibility of the Therapeutae having been the Early Christians, it by no means rules out the possibility of Jesus having originally been a member of this Order. As we know from Josephus, children were adopted by the Essenes to replace older members. It is therefore possible that the interest evinced by Jesus as a child of twelve in the things of the Spirit, when he questioned the doctors in the Temple (Luke 2:46), may have been noted by an Essene who recognised in the unusual spiritual development of so young a boy, a likely candidate for his Order. The silent years between that episode and the beginning of his ministry may well have been spent studying under the Essenes, serving their probation period, and, when his amazing capacity for healing became apparent, being admitted into the Therapeutic branch.

Among the sacred books in the keeping of his instructors, he would have found *The Book of Enoch*, which contains certain teachings and phrases that have a familiar sound to the student of the New Testament. And we may well imagine the ardent young mystic and God-lover, Jesus, poring over such writings, eagerly memorising them; and perhaps, at times, applying them to himself.

During his ministry he referred to the "many mansions" in his Father's house. In *The Book of Enoch* he would have read, "And after that I saw the mansions of the elect and the mansions of the holy. . . ." Enoch also tells of how he questioned an angel as to who and whence was the Son of Man. To which he received the reply:

> This is the Son of Man who hath righteousness
> With whom dwelleth righteousness,
> And who revealeth all the treasures of that which is hidden,
> Because the Lord of Spirits hath chosen him.

The constant reference Jesus made to himself as the Son of Man, often so puzzling to Bible students, would have been clearly comprehensible to those among his listeners who had read *The Book of Enoch*. In a further verse referring to the Son of Man, we find what may well have been the source of the statement, "Before Abraham was, I am", which so shocked the Jews:

> Yes, before the sun and signs were created,
> Before the stars of heaven were made,
> His name was named before the Lord of Spirits.

Jesus' self-identification with the Son of Man would also doubtless have caused him to ponder the prophecy:

> And those who practice righteousness shall die
> on account of the deeds of men,
> And be taken away on account of the doings of the godless.

What we now know, without shadow of doubt, is that this integrated lover of God chose the Path of Righteousness, whatever it might entail, no matter by what means the idea was presented to him. But what could be more likely than that it came from a sacred book preserved by the holy men of his day?

We have already noted the likeness of Philo's concept of Judaism to that of the Essenes. We also know that his works contained some of the highest metaphysical teachings of his times, and that, as far as can be ascertained, he and Jesus were contemporaries. Therefore, it is safe to assume that the ideas found in Philo were those already in currency among the Pharisees and Essenes when Jesus walked the earth; and that they represented the climate of thought in which he lived. It is because of this that Philo's Works must be of intense interest to any student of the evolution of religion. As a definition of man as God's likeness, or "Son", he wrote:

> The human mind is made as a copy of the mind of God, having been created after the archetypal model, the most sublime reasoning.

And of the chief aim of life:

> What can be a greater good than for mortal man to imitate the everlasting God?

Elaborating this statement by:

> Absolutely never to do anything wrong at all is a peculiar attribute of God, and perhaps one may also say of a god-like man.

These two last passages might well have been written of Jesus Christ of whose existence Philo obviously knew nothing. But they prove that they were ideas current in his time and which obviously so influenced Jesus that he applied them to himself. The former might indeed be a comment on John 5:19, and on the man who never ceased to "imitate God".

Philo's words: "The extremity of happiness is to rest unchangeably and immoveably on God alone," would explain the joy referred to in John 15:11: "That my joy might remain in you, and that your joy might be full."

The materialisation of the Eucharist which took place after the Catholic Church had accommodated itself to the usages of its pagan congregations has blinded most people to the meaning it had in the thought of Jesus, Paul and Philo, who writes of Exodus 16:15:

> You see now what kind of thing the food of the Lord is, it is the continued work of the Lord. . . .This is the bread, the food which God hath given for the soul. . . .

And he goes on to explain: "For this bread which he has given us to eat is the word of life."

Philo would have perfectly understood Jesus' reference to himself as the Bread of Life which came down from heaven. It was the soul-Wisdom, symbolised by the Dove, which *can* only come from "heaven"—a perfectly purified consciousness.

If we are to accept, therefore, the overwhelming proof that the Gospel of Jesus was influenced by Essenic teachings, we have to square this assumption with the undoubted fact that, by the time of his public ministry, he was opposed to some of the basic teachings and practices of the Essenic Order. The simple explanation may well be that he had, by that time, evolved beyond the gate through which he had attained to Wisdom. This is a common experience of the mystic. Such an ardent seeker for Truth who, even from childhood, seems to have realised his sonship with God, may well have progressed beyond his preceptors. Like Gautama the Buddha, his compassion would have flowed out to the whole of suffering mankind who so urgently needed the saving truth that the Essenes reserved for the initiated. He may well have disagreed with their exclusive policy, and so have become a heretic. The fact that his ministry was, from the first, a public one proves that, if he ever were an Essene, he must have broken with a sect that kept its teachings and ministrations among its own members. In this case, the explanation of the incident recorded in Mark 3:21,31,32, may well be that Jesus' family feared the retribution of the Order through the power of the sympathetic Pharisees who would also strongly object to the secret doctrines being given to the multitude, and to healing being bestowed indiscriminately upon the worthy and the unworthy. Worst of all, the strict Sabbatarian law had been deliberately broken (Mark 3 : 1–6). To the Pharisee such an act merited death. Even to the more merciful Essenes, it would have called for the strongest disciplinary measures. And, finally—the most unforgiveable sin in the eyes of both sects—this new Teacher was saying: "Follow me", instead of "Follow Moses". Their sacred Moses was being relegated to the status of a mere legislator, and this upstart was claiming to be the Exemplar, the perfect man. We can imagine what horror would have filled the hearts of even the peaceable Essenes at such heresy in one of their members, so we cannot wonder at the retribution meted out to the perpetrator by the power-loving, merciless churchmen of his day.

Yet is is just through these unorthodox acts of his that we can follow the processes of Jesus' thought when he found himself, as a member of even such an excellent Order as the Essenes, in what with his expanding thought of the universal nature of God, would have seemed to him a sectarian cage, bound to exclusiveness and secrecy. His integrated love of God, the perfect, compassionate Parent of all mankind, and his at-one-ment with this idea of the Good, demanded a universal ministry. The great love with which he was united could not be canalised. He must give all he knew, all he had, to the ignorant and the suffering. He must use his God-bestowed gift of healing, as well as his knowledge, to aid his fellow men. He must have followers who could be trained into this ministry. It was not enough to remain in a sheltered sect ministering to the few, however devout.

Besides, there were his intellectual reservations. He could no longer honestly acknowledge Moses as the perfect man. Even the men among whom he lived were more perfect in their gentleness, chastity and loving-kindness than Moses had been. The law-giver, for instance, had explicitly ordained the animal sacrifices that the Essenes refused to make. To Jesus, it may well have seemed illogical to repudiate such sacrifices and yet continue to honour one who had so explicitly ordained them; and he may have regretted that its rejection by the Order had done nothing to eliminate a practice that had been condemned by the inspired prophet, Isaiah, at least 800 years previously. Was it not the undue reverence in which Moses was held that ensured the survival of policies that should long since have been outgrown?

As a young and ardent enthusiast, concerned solely with doing the will of his all-loving Father, such obstructions caused by Tradition must have seemed intolerable. They must go. All that checked the outflowing of the will of the Good must go. But the Traditionalists with their vested interests were just as determined that they should remain. Animal sacrifice was essential to the revenues of the Temple, as were the fines due for the violation of the Sabbatarian law; and these flowed in steadily, owing to the near-impossibility of keeping the all too many and stringent rules made by the Churchmen.

In other words, Jesus, like the mystics of all Faiths, may eventually have reached the point where no one sect could contain him and his expanded vision. The Essenes, through the Wisdom of the goddess, had progressed far on the evolutionary path. An equality between men and women seems to have been practised among them. The Miriam and Moses chorus indicates that they had grasped the idea of the divine male-female equipoise. But in Jesus the idea had become actual fact: the Word was made flesh. He had, in his own person, achieved the perfect balance of male-female qualities. In him the Wisdom of the Goddess perfectly controlled the power of the God. In fact, he had taken the next step in spiritual evolution, and stood revealed as the image and likeness of the common Parent of all: the Father-Mother God.

CHAPTER IX

The Perfected Man

> And it came to pass ... that Jesus ... was baptised of John in Jordan. And straightway coming out of the water, he saw the heavens opened, and the Spirit like a dove descending upon him: and there came a voice from heaven saying, Thou art my beloved Son, in whom I am well pleased. (Mark 1: 9-11.)

This passage is obviously related to the words of Jesus that so puzzled Nicodemus: "Except a man be born of water and of the Spirit, he cannot enter into the kingdom of God." John 3:5.

The baptism of John was the outward and visible sign of inward purification. When this has taken place in a man, the Wisdom of God, symbolised, as we have seen, throughout the ages, by a dove, enters into him, and he becomes the Word of God.

The Ebionites, or Nazarenes, the original Jewish Christians, believed that Jesus was manifested as the Son of God at the time of his baptism, not at his physical birth. Dr Biggs writes (Bampton Lectures, 1886):

> Theodotus belonged to the Ebionite school and taught that "Jesus was a man born of a virgin according to the will of the Father, who having lived the life of other men, but in perfect piety, afterwards at the baptism of the Jordan received the Christ, who came down from above in the likeness of a dove!" Hence the miraculous powers did not work in him until the Spirit which Theodotus calls Christ came down and was manifested in him.

This belief persisted in the Churches until as late as the fifth century A.D. when Pope Leo, in his 18th Epistle to the Bishops of Sicily, is found rebuking the idea that Jesus was "born of the Holy Ghost at the time of his baptism". By that time the Nativity stories introduced into Christianity after the days of Paul, had shifted the emphasis from this all-important act of purification that must necessarily take place before a man manifests his son-of-Godhood, to the birth of the infant Jesus, the date of which was unknown. But, as it seemed advisable to celebrate the event, the 25th of December was fixed upon during the lifetime of Chrysostom, who died in 407 A.D., and stated that this date was deliberately chosen as being the day on which the heathen commemorated the birth of the sun-god, so that "while the heathen were busied with their own profane ceremonies the Christians might perform their holy rites without molestation".

That the modern idea of Christmas, with its rejoicing at the birth of a child, was quite alien to Christian thought in the days of Origen is evident from the following extracts from his *Commentaries and Homilies*:

> Good men do not celebrate their birthdays. . . . It is only sinners who have joy in this kind of birth.... The saints not only do not hold festival on their birthdays, but even in the fulness of the Holy Spirit curse the day of birth.... Listen to David when he says, I was conceived in iniquity and in sin my mother hath borne me (Psalms 51:5), proving that every soul which is born in flesh is tainted with the stain of iniquity and sin.*

It was evidently in order to conform with the ideas of their pagan congregations that the Christmas celebrations were introduced, containing, as they did, the age-old familiar figures of Mother and Child, with Joseph as the third member of the Trinity. They also introduced the Zoroastrian theme of the wise men following a star, found in the Zend Avesta, where the Prophet foretells:

> You, my children, shall be the first honoured by the manifestation of that divine person who is to appear in the world: a Star shall go before you to conduct you to the place of his nativity; and when you shall find him, present to him your oblations and sacrifices; for he is indeed your lord and everlasting king.

While such an innovation would have been popular with the pagan converts, it was spiritually disastrous inasmuch as the beautiful and true teaching of regeneration by means of total purification with the consequent influx of the divine Wisdom of God, was replaced by an age-old myth of a God visiting a physical woman who gives birth to a phenomenal child, or demi-god, who redeems mankind from its sins. In a word, a wholly unnecessary miracle was substituted for the universal experience of the mystic, or evolving man, which Jesus described in John 3:5 as being the only means of attaining to that state of reality which he called the Kingdom of God. He was describing not only his own experience, but that which could and should be the experience, or rebirth, of every man who sought release from the cage of mortal life.

The Essenes were as familiar with this idea as were all initiates of the Mysteries, the whole aim of which was to bring man to perfection. Jesus had fully attained to this goal, and so had taken the next step in the evolution of man. From this spiritual baptism he had emerged as a whole man, the image and likeness of the whole God; a man in whom the power

---

* *Selections from the Commentaries and Homilies of Origin*, R. B. Tollinton, D.D. (Macmillan) S.P.C.K., 1929.

of God was perfectly balanced and controlled by the Wisdom and compassion of the Goddess. His experience in the wilderness was a demonstration of the control of power by Wisdom. When, one by one, the suggestions of the carnal mind had been rejected, he knew that this power must be used only to glorify God, to testify to His rule, and to bless humanity.

The four Gospels present us with a picture of a God-obsessed man to whom a Supreme Being, and His invisible and perfect Kingdom were more real than anything observable by the senses. They were so real to him that he was able to bring the law of harmony, of which he was so keenly inwardly aware, to bear upon the affairs of mankind. God was good and omnipresent, therefore, despite the evidence of the external senses, the troubles and ills of mankind could not exist as realities. They were shadows of a dream that must be dispersed by the light of Truth. As Augustine was afterwards to put it, "Where God is, there the evil one is not."

With Jesus this had ceased to be a theory, as it was with so many other teachers, and was a living reality which he "brought to earth" by healing his fellow men and harmonising their lives.

E. W. Barnes, one-time Bishop of Birmingham, observed in his book, *The Rise of Christianity*, in which he casts doubts on the occurrence of the miracles of Jesus, that "they proved nothing but themselves". This opinion could only result from a deliberate refusal to face the prominence that the healing works are given in the Gospel records, and the evident fact that, from first to last, for Jesus himself, these works were all-important. As a divine Scientist, they were his demonstration, without which he could not, and did not, hope to be believed. They were the guarantee of the truth of his teachings, the proof of his Messiahship, or, as it may better be described in modern terms, the conclusive evidence of his evolution to a higher state of being. Peter, one of his nearest disciples, thoroughly understood the importance of the works as affording proof of his Master's at-one-ment with the Deity. In Acts 2:22 he is reported to have declared:

> Jesus of Nazareth, a man approved of God among you by miracles and wonders and signs.

Peter had, of course, been present when Jesus himself had offered these credentials as evidence of his Messiahship to the disciples of John the Baptist who came to ask whether he was the Messiah, or Saviour, that should come. Peter must have duly noted that, instead of answering yes or no, his Master had indicated his works as providing the most substantial and convincing proof of his at-one-ment with the all-powerful Father, and so of his genuine son-of-Godhood:

> Go and shew John again those things which ye do hear and see: the blind receive their sight, and the lame walk, the lepers are cleansed, and the deaf hear, the dead are raised up, and the poor have the gospel preached to them.

This test of his Messiahship was given at the very commencement of his ministry. Unlike other teachers, he did not expect to be judged on his teachings alone—after all he was making a very great claim on their credulity by asserting that God and His Kingdom were actually "at hand", as ever-present realities—but on his acts. If these revealed the operation of a power beyond the human, surely, on the strength of them, he might be believed? Hence, he was constantly drawing attention to his works.

> If I cast out devils by the Spirit of God, then the Kingdom of God is come unto you.

This was the supreme value of his healings: not that a single individual might be made whole for a few brief years of physical life, but that God's presence and beneficent will might be proved to exist at precisely the point where pain and suffering had seemed to be. Such a demonstration was obviously the hope of the world.

With the utmost urgency he impressed on friend and foe alike that they should judge him by his works. In Solomon's porch, when he was asked by the Jews to tell them plainly if he was the Christ, he replied:

> I told you, and ye believed not: the works that I do in my Father's name, they bear witness of me.

As "name" may be rendered as either "character", or "nature", what Jesus implied was that the healing, blessing works revealed the all-beneficent nature of his God, which was obviously a very different nature from that of Jehovah, the God of his interrogators. This conclusive proof of superhuman power naturally enraged them, for it left them without argument. They could hardly maintain that good works were of the devil, but if they admitted that Jesus was revealing the nature of the true God, they would have to admit the imperfections of their own. So that when he urged them to accept his test: "If I do not the works of my Father, believe me not. But if I do, though you believe not me, believe the works: that ye may know and believe that the Father is in me and I in him", they "sought to take him: but he escaped out of their hand".

The Editors of the 1930 edition of Cruden's *Complete Concordance to the Old and New Testaments*, in the first part of their definition of *Christ*, write as follows:

> Christ. The anointed one.... The expected King and deliverer of the Jews, who expected a strong and gloriously earthly King to deliver them from oppressors and form again a great independent kingdom of the Jews.

This Messiah had been looked and longed for since the time of the Captivity, and when Jesus Christ was proclaimed as being this Messiah, it was utterly impossible for those holding the above concept of their deliverer to recognise him in the pacific and gentle healer of the sick, sinning and sorrowful; utterly impossible to equate their vision of a conquering, powerful, all-male God with the tender, maternal yearning evinced by the new Teacher in the words:

> O Jerusalem, Jerusalem, thou that killest the prophets, and stonest them which are sent unto thee, how often would I have gathered thy children together, even as a hen gathereth her chickens under her wings, and ye would not! (Mark 23:37).

What use had they for one who sorrowed over Jerusalem when he should, with his undoubted power, have been liberating it? They rejected the Messiah because they could not see him: they could only see their own concept of what a Messiah should be. His vision of an inward liberation was incomprehensible to their literal mentalities. They could not understand that what was needed was not liberation from the Roman rule, but from themselves, from their own base, unevolved natures. He knew that human nature in its contemporary state of evolution could only be manifested in the sort of world men saw around them. He did not make the mistake of the reformers, ancient and modern, of blaming the material, visible conditions, and trying to improve them. He knew they were only the effects of an underlying cause, and, being a true prophet, he was concerned entirely with the cause: the unregenerate state of human consciousness. He knew that if this were thoroughly purified, external conditions would automatically improve, and that until this purification was achieved, there would always be tyrants and victims, war and suffering, injustice and domination. If Caesar were removed from the throne, it would only be occupied by another tyrant until the concept of tyranny was eliminated from the consciousness of humanity, and replaced by submission to the government of God, and the spirit of fraternity, co-operation and love.

It is significant that the title given to both the great World-Teachers,

Gautama the Buddha and Jesus the Christ, was "Lord of Compassion". This designation most clearly indicates the nature of the deity that both these Saviours worshipped: the Spirit of compassionate Love, manifested in the harmlessness and peaceableness of the Buddha, and the mercy and dynamic love of Jesus Christ, expressed in the healing of the sick, sinning and sorrowful, and the harmonising of discordant human situations.

Continually faced with unmistakeable evidence of this power, it must have been most frustrating to the Jews to find that it was not to be used to free them from the Roman rule, which seemed to them the greatest good. But the Master was adamant on this point. His Kingdom was not of this world. He had come to establish quite another kingdom—in the consciousness of mankind: the kingdom of God *within*. And the Monarch of such a kingdom must be a God of peace, and not the Lord of Hosts.

That the heretics were right who maintained that the God of the Old Testament was not the God of Jesus Christ is obvious throughout the records of the Gospel; but a single instance will suffice to show the complete dissimilarity of the two God-concepts.

In Genesis 19:24, we are given a picture of Jehovah and His will in the words: "Then the Lord rained upon Sodom and Gomorrah brimstone and fire from the Lord out of Heaven"; but in Luke 9:53–56, we find Jesus rebuking such an interpretation of the will of God when his disciples, finding that the Samaritans would not receive their Master, asked: "Lord, wilt thou that we command fire to come down from heaven, and consume them, even as Elias did?" But he turned and rebuked them, and said, "Ye know not what manner of spirit ye are of. For the son of man is not come to destroy men's lives, but to save them." As a pendant to this he says (John 5:19): "The Son can do nothing of himself, but what he seeth the Father do: for what things soever he doeth, these also doeth the Son likewise." And since the Son's acts were all of non-violence, compassion, healing and peace, these were, to him, the will of his God. So that by both the acts and character of the new Teacher, the Jehovah-concept of the Old Testament was openly rejected.

Only once did Jesus explicitly describe the nature of the God, or Father, that he worshipped, and that was when he said to the woman of Samaria: "God is Spirit" (Moffatt's Translation). But as he insisted that he came to do the will of the Father, no one could come to any other conclusion than that reached by the writer of the Epistle of John who affirmed that God was Love (1 John 4:18).

Jesus believed this all-loving Spirit to be the universal Parent of all, and taught that it was through man's likeness to Him that he became a true brother to his fellow-men. Such relationship was not that of flesh and blood. It lay in the spiritual unity of those who worshipped the same wholly good and loving God, and manifested His will and nature:

> Whosoever shall do the will of God, the same is my brother, and my sister, and mother. (Mark 3:35.)

He did not, therefore, as modern religionists seem to believe, teach the brotherhood of man *per se*, but only as the result of men ratifying their primal union with the common Parent-Mind. This fact tends to be entirely overlooked by our reformers who harp constantly on the brotherhood of man without reference to the Fatherhood of God. They refer to Jesus as having been the founder of this brotherhood, as though that had been his entire mission, whereas it was secondary to, and dependent upon, his chief object, which was to reveal the nature of God to man, and by doing so to draw all men unto Him. Unity with Cause would naturally involve unity with effect. The acceptance of the universal Fatherhood of God would inevitably result in a brotherhood of man.

For Jesus the spiritual life was based squarely on the commandment which both he and the orthodox Jews were agreed upon was the greatest of all: "Thou shalt love the Lord thy God with all thy heart, and with all thy soul, and with all thy strength, and with all thy mind." (Luke 10:27.)

For some reason the small but essential word "all" is overlooked by those who pay lip-service to the demand. But without taking it into account, it is impossible to obey the spirit of the commandment, which is one of total surrender, total love. And without obedience to the first commandment it is impossible really to obey the second: Thou shalt love thy neighbour as thyself. For the God man is asked to love with everything that is within him, is, according to Jesus, the Spirit of all-compassionate Love. And when a man loves this Spirit with all his being, his one desire is to be inseparable from it. As Plotinus was afterwards to describe this mystic experience:

> We must endeavour to embrace God with all our being, and to leave no part of ourselves which is not in contact with Him.

This is precisely what Jesus meant when he made the demand: Be ye therefore perfect even as the Father which is in heaven is perfect (Matthew 5:48); for he knew that only when we are entirely and unconditionally one with compassionate Love can we be trusted in all circumstances to love and bless our fellow men; because then Love has become our very nature, and we can no more cease to love than the sun can cease to shine. This indeed is the sole basis for true morality, the only morality that will stand the test of temptation when there is no external power to enforce it. Only the man who obeys the greatest of all commandments can be relied upon at all times to obey the Decalogue, since obedience to the moral law stems naturally from the love of the Highest Good, and the only penalty the lover of God dreads is any sense of separation from the Beloved and His attributes.

It was, therefore to this integrated love of God, which he himself possessed in such full measure, that Jesus sought to draw mankind, for only by means of it could they be perfected. He knew that Love cannot be imposed, but only evoked; and he constantly strove to evoke it by revealing, through his own words and acts, the character of a God so wholly loving, beautiful and adorable as to be irresistible.

From the Gospel records it is evident that for Jesus there was nothing else in life worth thinking or talking about; nothing else worth living for, other than God and His will. He was obsessed, not as modern religionists would have us believe, with humanity, although he invariably blessed and healed all who came his way, but with the thought of God and His Kingdom. And it was just this single-minded obsession that gave him the power to heal and transform his fellow men; for his absolute devotion made him one with the supreme power of Love.

In the Epistle of John we read:

> We have seen and do testify that the Father sent the Son to be the saviour of the world. (1 John 4:14.)

In the sense that the sun sends forth a ray, and by this means reveals its nature, warmth and light to the inhabitants of the world, so the impersonal Spirit of Life, Truth, harmony, wisdom and Love was manifested to mankind in the character of Jesus of Nazareth, which showed what all men have it in them to be. It was in this sense that he was the saviour of mankind, saving it from its imperfect evolutionary state by demonstrating in word and act the whole, or perfected man which each man might, by his own integrated effort and desire, become.

> He came unto his own and his own received him not. But as many as received him to them he gave power to become the sons of God, even to them that believe on his name.

Those who recognised his nature as being the kind that a perfect God would have, could emulate him, seek to manifest the same Spirit, and so become themselves recognisable "Sons" of the Eternal.

> Philip said unto him, Lord, show us the Father, and it sufficeth us. Jesus saith unto him, Have I been so long time with you, and yet hast thou not

known me, Philip? He that hath seen me hath seen the Father; and how sayest thou, then, Shew us the Father? Believest thou not that I am in the Father, and the Father in me? The words I speak unto you, I speak not of myself: but the Father that dwelleth in me, he doeth the works. Believe me that I am in the Father, and the Father in me: or else believe me for the very works sake. (1 John 14:8-12.)

This is the eternal realisation of the mystic of all creeds: that the seer and the Seen are one. It is the greatest spiritual attainment known to man. Philip was evidently not a mystic, but Jesus was surprised that he could not recognise the nature of God, if not in the character of the Son, then in the nature of the works; in the power that made these works possible. Surely they proved that he was factually in possession of a higher power than any known to man, a power that could over-rule so-called "natural" laws, the laws of sin and death? Philip had seen these works being performed yet still he asked to be given evidence of the presence of God, as though these miraculous works had not proved to him either the presence of God's power or the nature of His will as unchangeably good and beneficent. It was as though a mother had been asked by a child: "What is Love? Show me what Love is like." and the mother had replied: "Have not my acts shown you what Love is like? All my care and thought for you, feeding and clothing you, these are all acts of Love. Through them you know what Love is. You experience Love. You cannot see Love as an object, but you can see and be blessed by its effects."

As was inevitable for one who could transform in a moment a withered limb into a whole one, banish leprosy and give light to sightless eyes, Jesus had no illusions about the reality of matter. His whole attitude on the subject was summed up in one brief sentence: "The Spirit quickeneth; the flesh profiteth nothing."

It was this realisation that enabled him to teach that life—the spiritual life of man—was eternal, and that those in whom God-realisation had risen were thereby possessed of eternal life. For the understanding of life eternal came from knowledge of the true nature of God and man; from knowing this nature to be spiritual and eternal, and therefore not subject to the laws of matter, the "law of sin and death". Those who accepted this Truth knew that their essential life was eternal.

After the theologians had deified Jesus Christ they indulged in heated arguments as to whether he had conceived himself through the womb of Mary or whether he was the result of the Father's visitation to the Virgin. What could truly and rationally be said is that Jesus was the outcome of his own perfect conception of God. Many religionists before him had loved, and been devotedly obedient to, what they conceived of as God; but their God had never been good enough. Many great philosophers had theorised about a perfectly good God, but had seldom attempted to behave like his image and likeness, two notable exceptions being Pythagoras and Socrates. Jesus loved the Highest with all his heart, soul, mind and strength, and became like that which he so ardently loved. Having in thought a perfect evolutionary model, he was able to evolve to the status of a Perfect Man. The whole aim and meaning of the Creed of Christ was the reinstatement of the concept of a perfect, whole, or holy God, and the actual attainment of the example man to perfect, whole, or holy manhood.

The Wisdom of the Goddess had imbued the Mysteries with the aim of self-perfectioning. Jesus had achieved that aim. In him the so long divorced God and Goddess were reunited, and the true nature of divinity in its perfect equipoise was revealed. But the orthodox Jews who had ever hated the Goddess with her gentle attributes that he embodied, and whose outraged God, discredited and superseded by this embodiment, was well known to be addicted to the sacrifice of the perfect, the whole and unblemished, made their supreme offering to Him on Calvary.

CHAPTER X

The Mind of Paul

In his book, *The Uses of the Past* (A Mentor Book, 1954), Herbert J. Miller writes of Paul:

> He sacrificed the historic Jesus. He knew Jesus only by hearsay and rarely referred to his human life.

And also:

> Paul preached a Gospel about Jesus that was not taught by the Jesus of the Synoptic Gospels.

Both these statements are undeniably true as I have already shown in my previous book, *Mithras: The Fellow in the Cap*. The two most fatal mistakes made by the theologians of the Early Church were, first, the substitution of Pauline Christianity, which represented Jesus as yet another manifestation of the familiar sun-god, for the original teachings of Jesus which were those of a supreme mystic; and, secondly, the setting aside of Jesus' own test of his Messiahship, which, as we have seen in the last chapter, was that of his healing works, and substituting that of the prophecies contained in the Old Testament. In his *Das Wesen Des Christenthums*, Harnack wrote:

> What is the answer that Jesus sends to John the Baptist? "The blind see, and the lame walk, the lepers are cleansed, and the deaf hear, the dead rise up, and the gospel is preached to the poor." That is "the coming of the kingdom", or rather in these saving works the kingdom is already there. By the overcoming and removal of misery, of need, of sickness, by these actual effects John is to see that the new time has arrived! The casting out of devils is only part of this work of redemption, but Jesus points to that *as the sense and seal of his mission*.

Not only did Jesus insist time and time again that his works were what constituted the proof of his Messiahship, but, as we read in John 5 : 33–37, he definitely disapproved of making the witness of man, even the greatest among them, the authority for confirming his genuineness. "Ye sent unto John", he told the Jews, "and he bare witness unto the truth. But I receive not testimony from man. . . . I have greater witness than that of John: for the works which the Father hath given me to finish, the same works that I do bear witness of me that the Father hath sent me. And the Father himself which hath sent me, hath borne witness of me."

Deliberately to set aside this divine testimony, as the theologians did, and do, not only constitutes flagrant disobedience to the ordinance of Jesus, but had the fatal result of making it necessary to persuade the Gentile world to hold the Hebrew Scriptures in as much indiscriminate veneration as they were held by the Jews, and to believe that the God of the Old Testament and that of the New were one. This induced such split-mindedness among Christians that a gentle saint like St Francis of Assissi and a warrior like General Gordon who was said to go to battle with a Bible under one arm and a rifle under the other, could both claim to be Christians without fear of official contradiction.

The fact was, as heretics like the Marcionites, Manichees, Catharis and Albigenses insisted despite the terrible persecution it brought upon them, that the God of compassionate Love who was the Father of Jesus Christ, was the very antithesis of the vengeful, jealous, belligerent Jehovah pictured for the most part in the Old Testament. But if the words of His prophets were to be the chief tests of the genuineness of Jesus' claim to have been the son of God, then they and the God that inspired them must forever be held in veneration by Christians. In this way, primitive Judaism attached itself to the new Faith like an Old Man of the Sea, and was carried about wherever it went, most of the barbarous errors that Jesus had tried to eliminate going with it.

This eventuality was clearly foreseen by Marcion who was denounced as a heretic for his pains. In his book, *Christian Ethics and Modern Problems*, W. R. Inge, after referring to Marcion as wishing "to discard the Old Testament and begin with Christ", argues that the Church had to possess the authority of the sacred book of the Jews, "for a religion can never proclaim itself *new*. . . . The Church could not afford to give up the support of an ancient dispensation. Therewith came in the fatal error of claiming a continuity between the Jewish priesthood and the Christian ministry. Historically, the claim is ridiculous."

But what was a good deal worse was the infiltration of the old pagan and Jewish ideas into the pure Gospel that had been intended to replace them; and one of the most pernicious and immoral of these was the idea of vicarious atonement.

Nothing could have been more alien to the thought of Jesus who taught explicitly that the consequences of sinning could only be averted by ceasing to sin (John 5:14), and that salvation depended upon following in his footsteps, sharing his spiritual baptism of total purification, keeping the vision single-mindedly on God, and totally surrendering to His will. He never taught, nor could he as a manifestation of divine Wisdom ever have believed, that men could be saved by the sacrificial death of one of their kind. Such a theory denied both the justice and love of God. He knew, as did the founders of the Mysteries, that each man must be brought to perfection, and that this could only be effected by a one-pointed attention to the things of the Spirit, and by basing his thought and actions on the perfect model. Inasmuch as the God-obsessed Jesus had become the image and likeness of That which he so persistently contemplated, doing only what he saw the Father do, he had provided this model in his life, thus "saving" mankind from its lower, animalistic sense of manhood.

His submission to crucifixion rather than allow his followers to employ violence, was to demonstrate that the perfect man would rather lose his human sense of life than relinquish his hold on the Principle of compassionate Love and non-violence which constituted his eternal life. The God of Jesus could not use violence, therefore his son could not use it either, even to escape from the inhumanity of his fellow men. Had he done so he would have lost his divine life in trying to conserve his physical sense of existence, which, as a perfected man, it was in any case necessary for him to lose. "My kingdom is not of this world." (John 18:36.)

To change the sublime meaning of the crucifixion into, on the one hand, and according to Jewish thought, a vicarious sacrifice by which men might evade the consequences of their sins—a thoroughly immoral idea—and, on the other, through the transformation effected by Paul and the writer of the Book of Revelation, into yet another representation of a suffering, dying and resurrecting sun-god, like Thammuz, Dionysus or Osiris, was to lose the redeeming idea of the Example Man, the practical pattern that must be followed by every man who wishes to outgrow his animalism and violence and so evolve to a higher species. It was also to dishonour the God of Love to the utmost. Even young children have been shocked by the idea of a God who could allow his most perfect Son to be cruelly slaughtered in order to atone to Him for the sins of other men.

To make the death of the Saviour the focus of attention rather than the life; to substitute the fiendish God of Judaism for the God of unchanging love of Jesus Christ; to concentrate on suffering, cruelty, sorrow and guilt instead of on the joy and liberation that spring spontaneously from the knowledge that man is the son of a perfect God, is wholly to pervert and entirely to misrepresent the Creed of Christ.

On the other hand, Pauline Christianity, with its revelation of the deeper teachings of the Mysteries, contained much that was necessary for the full understanding of the Mind of Christ.

To understand the mind of Paul we cannot do better than refer to the writings of Philo that must greatly have influenced it. Both men were Pharisees; both were Gnostics, Hellenists and great eclectics. Above all, both were primarily Jews desperately concerned to ensure that their ancient Faith should survive in the civilised world of their time. They both recognised the need for eclecticism if Judaism were ever to find favour with, or even to maintain a footing among, the educated Gentiles of that period. Accordingly Philo, as we have seen, allegorised the Old Testament in the light of Hellenistic philosophy, and Paul preached the universal Christ that had already appeared as an idea in the works of Philo and other Hellenists, as it was afterwards to appear in the Gospel of John, as the Logos, or Word. This, in itself, was legitimate, for undoubtedly Jesus understood his divine nature to be that of the universal Christ; but Paul failed to understand Jesus' individual interpretation of the divine nature.

From Philo's works it is obvious that Judaism had reached the point when it seemed inevitable that a new Teacher must arise to teach the reformed, or evolved Judaism, his mind filled with the teachings of the greatest theologians of his times. Both Jesus and Paul met this requirement, but the difference of their interpretation of those teachings lay in the difference of their characters and state of evolution.

Philo was not teaching anything new, but merely recording a system that had evolved within Judaism in the course of the centuries. And in the works of a man who had apparently never heard of the Master, we find not only echoes of the teachings of Jesus but descriptions of his character, as we saw in Chapter VIII.

Philo's philosophical statements, in many cases, serve to elucidate what sometimes seem to be cryptic sayings in the New Testament. For instance, in *The Allegories of the Sacred Laws*, LXXX, he describes the nature of God in the words: "The Mind is our Father", a conviction evidently shared by Paul when he said, "Let this Mind be in you which was also in Christ Jesus." And, again, in *Migration of Abraham*, I, Philo writes: "Speech is the abode of the Father, because our Father is the Mind." This is the concept behind the Greek idea of the Logos, or Word, being the "son" or "daughter" of God. When Jesus walked the earth, this idea was familiar to the theologians of his race and time. When he spoke of the Father, therefore, it was not necessary to explain that this was the Parent Mind. Again, a passage on relationship in *On Those Who Offer Sacrifices*, XI, illumines the sometimes adversely criticised episode recorded in Mark 3:31–35:

> We should acknowledge only one relationship and one bond of friendship, a mutual zeal for the service of God. And these bonds which are called

relationships of the blood, being derived from one's ancestors . . . must all be renounced if they do not all hasten to the same end, namely the honour of God which is the one indissoluble bond of all united good will. For such men will lay claim to a more venerable and sacred kind of relationship.

This, as we know, was the point of view of both Essenes and Nazarenes, and was not, as Western readers of the New Testament have supposed, an attitude peculiar to Jesus.

Philo was also an advocate of spiritual healing. In *On Rewards and Punishments*, he writes:

The Lawgiver says . . . that a perfect freedom from disease in every respect, both privately and generally, shall be allotted to those persons who labour in the service of virtue and who make the sacred laws the guides of all their speeches and actions.

And in *The Allegories of the Sacred Laws*, LXXX, he says:

Behold the reasoning of the physician: "I will purge the sick man, I will nourish him, I will heal him with medicines and with diet. I will extirpate his diseased parts, I will cauterize him. . . . " But very often nature has healed the man without these remedies; and very often, too, has suffered him to die although they were applied; so that the reasonings of the physician have been utterly found out to be dreams, full of indistinctness and of riddles.

And in *Shepherds and Kings*, XIX, he writes:

Men . . . when anything unexpected befalls them . . . take refuge in the assistance of created things, of physicians, of herbs, of the composition of drugs, in a carefully considered plan of life, and in any other aid which may be derived from mortal man. And if anyone were to say to them, "Flee to him who is the only physician for the diseases of the soul, and discard all this falsely called assistance which ye are seeking to find in the creature who is subject to the same sufferings as yourselves", they would . . . ridicule him. . . . But when it is found that there is no relief from man . . . they renounce all ideas of assistance from other quarters . . . and reluctantly and tardily flee to the only saviour, God.

And then he tells us:

If a thought of God enters the mind, it immediately blesses it and heals all its diseases.

These passages show how natural the thought of spiritual healing was to initiates in the days of Jesus and Paul. It was not a special Christian phenomenon, but was practised more fully and perfectly by Jesus than by any other man of whom we have historical record. The last citation gives a clue to the method whereby it was brought about.

Philo had the truly Essenic, or Christian, attitude to violence, writing in *The Incorruptibility of the World*, XI: "Of all bonds that is the worst which is forged by violence." Unlike Paul, he advocated vegetarianism and praised the Essenes for their abstinence from flesh-eating.

Paul's assertion in Galations 5:17, that the flesh and the Spirit are forever at war, is clarified by Philo's statement that "During the banquet of the outward senses, the mind is labouring under a famine, as, on the contrary, when the outward senses are fasting, the mind is feasting." (*Migration of Abraham*, XXXVII.)

Philo's: "All places are filled at once by God, who surrounds them all and is not surrounded by any of them, to whom alone it is possible to be everywhere and also nowhere. . . . The divine being, both invisible and incomprehensible, is indeed everywhere, but still, in truth, he is nowhere visible or comprehensible" (Confusion of Languages, XXVII) is echoed by Paul's, "In Him we live and move and have our being." (Acts 17:28.)

But it is in the concept of the Word and Son of God that Philo so perfectly made the framework to enshrine the chief character of the New Testament; and, if we accept the evidence of the Gospel of John, it was undoubtedly this concept of his Christhood, his divine and eternal nature, that Jesus himself held.

In *Confusion of Languages*, XXVIII, occurs a passage, with distinct Mithraic overtones, that gives a very clear idea of the Hellenistic view of the Logos, the first line revealing clearly Philo's ignorance of Jesus' existence, as well as his realisation of the need for such an Exemplar:

> Even if there be not as yet anyone who is worthy to be called a Son of God, nevertheless let him labour earnestly to be adorned according to His first-born Word, the eldest of His angels, as the great archangel of many names, for he is called the Authority, the name of God, and the Word, and man according to God's image. . . If we are not yet suitable to be called sons of God, still we may deserve to be called the children of his eternal image, of his most sacred Word.

It was obviously with this contemporary concept that both Paul and John identified Jesus Christ. The idea preceded its manifestation, and the manifestation was recognised on account of the pre-existing idea. And that the idea of his deific nature, his eternal selfhood, was in the mind of Jesus himself is proved by such utterances as: "Before Abraham was, I am," (John 8:58). Unfortunately Paul did not stop there.

Much has been said and written about the momentous vision that he had on the Road to Damascus, but out of the various and conflicting accounts given of it, emerges one clear fact—that Paul believed he had "seen" Jesus Christ. This might mean either that he had seen him visually, or that he had mentally recognised him for what he essentially was, or what Paul imagined he was, for his Epistles undoubtedly describe a very different individual from the central character of the Gospels.

As the accounts of the experience given in Acts and Galatians differ, it would seem wiser to accept the evidence of the latter since it was written by Paul himself. In Acts 9 : 3–5, we are told that,

> As he journeyed, he came near Damascus: and suddenly there shined round him a light from heaven: and he fell to the earth, and heard a voice saying unto him, Saul, Saul, why persecutest thou me? And he said, Who art thou, Lord? And the Lord said, I am Jesus whom thou persecutest: it is hard for thee to kick against the pricks.

In Galations 1, writing more metaphysically, Paul says that God had revealed His son in him "that I might preach him among the heathen". This certainly suggests that what he received was a *mental* impression of the character of Jesus Christ, and subsequent events confirm this explanation, for the idea Paul conceived of Jesus, the Christ, was undoubtedly one that could most successfully be preached "among the heathen", although it was very unlike the historical Jesus.

It is significant that immediately after his vision, Saul of Tarsus adopted his Roman name, Paul,* as though he had determined there and then to take his personal concept of the new Teacher to the Gentiles. Before this experience he had, as a Pharisee, been bitterly opposed to what he saw as a dangerous Jewish heresy. He had met none of the disciples to discuss the matter with them, or to learn from them the true character of Jesus; but as a trained theologian he would undoubtedly have gained a certain theoretical knowledge of what the Master had taught, and would have noted any likeness to the secret teaching of the Essenes, and would have been as shocked at its divulgence as by Jesus' open divergence from the letter of the Mosaic law. This he would certainly have considered as deserving of the death penalty.

As he proceeded on his journey to Damascus, he may well have been thinking how extraordinary it was that even after the shameful crucifixion Jesus' followers should still have acknowledged this heretic as the saviour, a line of thought which may have led to the sudden illumination, or startling idea, that brought him up short.

* W. L. Wilmshurst in *Contemplations*, wrote; "'Saul' implies gross ignorance of Divine things, while 'Paul', the latinised form of the Greek divinity, Apollo, is the Light-bringer."

Did this crucified Teacher not provide what had for long been so much needed—a Jewish version of the suffering sun-god, or son-of-God with which the whole pagan world was familiar, and could so readily understand? Was not this the very figure that he and other Jewish eclectics had been seeking in order to make Judaism acceptable and comprehensible to the pagan world? Was he not persecuting the very sect that could be the means of preserving the wisdom of the Jews in an alien civilisation?

This Nazarene that he had been persecuting had been promulgating the highest truths known to Judaism, the secrets of the Mysteries, including the ability to heal, which had never been intended for the multitude but only for the elect.

But supposing that he had been wiser than them all? Suppose he had realised that the time had come for which Israel had so long prayed, to spread Judaism throughout all the world that it might be the universal religion, and all men be united under the rule of the One, true God? In order to achieve this it would be necessary to teach esoteric Judaism, the forbidden teachings, because they contained the universal Truth that could be understood by the initiates of all the religions. Might this Teacher not have deliberately broken the rule of the Order enjoining secrecy, so that the Truth might be universalised? And, if so, might he not indeed prove to have been the Messiah and saviour, the human representative of that divine Wisdom that was the Logos or Word of God? Was he not in fact, or could he not be made to appear, an incarnation of the idea of a High Priest current among Jewish theologians, and described by Philo in the words:

> The law designs that he should be the partaker of a nature superior to that of man; inasmuch as he approaches more nearly to that of the deity; being . . . on the borders between the two, in order that men may propitiate God by some Mediator, and that God may have some subordinate minister by whom he may offer and give his mercies and kindnesses to mankind. (*A Treatise on the Life of Moses*, Vol. III.)

Might not this man be represented to the Gentiles as this Mediator, a role so well known to them in the forms of Mithras, Dionysus, Bacchus, and the like? Would they not welcome him as the very latest embodiment of the sun-god, a modern Aesculapius, a figure so much more appealing to them than the primitive Moses whose acts, teachings and belligerence were often so adversely criticised by the cultured pagans?

Since it seemed impossible to win the Gentiles to Judaism while Moses was represented as its Perfect Man, why should not this new Teacher replace the ancient Lawgiver as the image of God? What was essential was that the Mosaic Law and Jewish culture should be perpetuated. If this could be ensured, the price of relegating Moses to a secondary position might not be too high. Jesus had apparently been as God-obsessed as Moses, but his concept of God as the universal Father, the beneficent Parent Mind, was so much more acceptable to the Gentile world than the God of Hosts of Moses. If, as the result of the spiritual evolution of mankind, Moses had been outmoded as the Perfect Man, the wise thing was to face the fact, and to replace him with a son of God—Jesus Christ.

Paul may well have had confidence in his ability to interpret the Mind of Christ. Since both of them must have had access to the Wisdom of the Essenes, he and Jesus would have been of much the same mind on many subjects. But Jesus, passing beyond the closed sect, had made his own most considerable contribution to the Wisdom religion of his day. It was this particular contribution that Paul never understood because he was unacquainted with the personal Jesus.

From the first he seems to have resisted any such understanding. For one who had experienced such a wonderful revelation from the Master of the sect he was persecuting, he showed a peculiar lack of interest in the subject. In the circumstances, the most natural step would surely have been to have sought out the nearest disciples of the Teacher in order to find out more about him. But this was just what Paul was determined not to do. Instead, he writes that after his vision:

> I conferred not with flesh and blood: neither went I up to Jerusalem to them which were apostles before me, but I went into Arabia, and returned again unto Damascus.

It is obvious that he was completely satisfied with his own conception of Jesus Christ the Saviour. He believed that it had been revealed to him by God, and he did not wish this perfect concept to be in any way marred by reports of the human Master that might be given to him by men. For him, and for the audience he had in view, it was not enough that Jesus should be a mystic, or even an evolved man, he must also be the recognisable equivalent of Thammuz and Bacchus and Mithras. It evidently took him three years to consolidate this idea and adapt it to the esoteric knowledge of Judaism such as we find in the works of Philo. Then he tells us, "after three years I went up to Jerusalem to see Peter and abode with him fifteen days. But other of the disciples saw I none, save James, the Lord's brother".

Significantly, nothing is said about their reactions to Paul's idea of Jesus Christ, but it may well be imagined that the simple, uncultured students of Jesus, who had often been particularly obtuse even when their Master was making the simplest spiritual statements, were as dazed by Paul's metaphysical flights as a Plymouth Brother might be when confronted with the teachings of Plotinus. Paul simply was not speaking in their, or the Master's idiom. It is well known that the contact between Peter and Paul was brief, and ended in an open quarrel, which was not surprising. Those who had spoken, eaten and lived with the Master, receiving his teachings from his own lips, might well have expected a little humility in this new, self-proclaimed convert in his approach to them. But humility was not Paul's outstanding characteristic. He evidently learned nothing of importance, or that he wanted to learn, from the associates of Jesus. The fact seems to be that he wished to keep what he believed was his divinely inspired concept of the Messiah intact, therefore anything that in any way conflicted with it would be more of an embarrassment than a help. He probably impressed on Peter and James that he was going to propagate the Creed of Christ as strongly as he had at one time persecuted it, but they may well have wondered whether it would indeed be their Master's creed that this zealous newcomer would present to the world.

But even if he had conferred long and often with the followers of Jesus, it is doubtful whether Paul could ever fully have understood the nature of the Master, since it was so fundamentally different from his own. The all-male Paul who could watch unmoved the stoning of the gentle Stephen and demand that the flesh must suffer in order to save the soul, could never comprehend the protective, maternal love in Jesus' nature that sorrowed over Jerusalem, safeguarded the Magdalene from the legal penalty incurred by her crime, and, with persistent, divine compassion, healed the sick. Paul had, in fact, never attained to the deific male-female equipoise of the Master. There was that in him that still fiercely resented the Woman, the Goddess. He could not, or would not recognise her qualities in the nature of his Master who remained for him the all-male figure of a sun-god, like Mithras. There was something in his psychological make-up which demanded that this should be so. As a fanatical Jew there was in him the age-old hatred of his race for the Queen of Heaven. In his Epistles this was betrayed in his attitude to women. Even though, as a teacher of Wisdom, he had to admit that "neither is the man without the woman, neither the woman without the man, in the Lord" (1 Corinthians 11:11), he still, as a man and a Jew, had to forbid women to speak in the churches, and to remind her that the female, as a lesser creature, must be in subjection to the male. Had he ever understood the mind and character of Jesus, he would not have been able to maintain this fallacy, for in the nature of Jesus, the "Woman", unchanging, compassionate Love, was always in control of the power of the "Man". This was a concept of which Paul was incapable.

Even the few physical healings ascribed to him were of quite a different nature to those of Jesus which always stemmed from his outflowing, unfailing compassion, and followed logically from his insistence on the immanence of the Kingdom of God. Those ascribed to Paul seem to have been in the same category as those performed by the Old Testament prophets. In the healing of Eutychus, for example, it is recorded that he was believed to have been dead but that "Paul fell on him, and embracing him said, Trouble not yourselves; for his life is in him". (Acts 20:10.) Jesus is never reported to have used such a method; but it is similar to that employed by the prophet Elisha, who, in recalling the Shunnamite woman's son from death "lay upon the child, and put his mouth upon his mouth, and his eyes upon his eyes, and his hands upon his hands: and he stretched himself upon the child; and the flesh of the child waxed warm".

These were the healings of occultists and magians, not those of Jesus whose method had nothing in it of personal force, for he could heal those afar off as easily as those in his presence, owing to his recognition of the omnipresence of God's kingdom of harmony. "If I cast out devils by the Spirit of God, then the kingdom of God is come unto you", (Matthew 12:28), which might be rendered: "then you have been given a glimpse of reality instead of the imperfect state of things as seen through the external senses".

We find no such persistent emphasis on the immediate fact of the Kingdom of God in Paul. Indeed, in 11 Corinthians 12:2-4, we find him expressing a concept of heaven very like that of Mithraism with its seven heavens, and most unlike the kingdom of heaven within which was the teaching of Jesus, as of all the great Masters. The Pauline concept is found in the Apochryphal books, such as *The Testament of the Twelve Patriarchs* (109–106 B.C.), *The Secrets of Enoch*, and *The Ascension of Isaiah*, which refer to the coming of the Messiah from the seventh heaven, all these works having obviously been influenced by the teachings of the Persian religion.

This localisation of heaven was a very serious deviation from Jesus' teachings, and led to the acceptance of the sun-worshippers' idea of heaven "up there", to be obtained only through physical death, a state that was always future, and never immediately realisable. This was obviously a mistake on Paul's part, owing to his insatiable eclecticism, for that he was aware of the truth is evident from his statement: "Now is the accepted time; behold now is the day of salvation" (2 Corinthians 6:2). But those who had still to build up the theology of the new Faith became increasingly liable, when there was a choice of teachings, to seize upon the lower that would appeal to the greatest number, especially to converts from the pagan Faith. For just as Paul took from the Master that which accorded with his own pre-conceived opinions, so the theologians who came after him accepted those of his teachings which most accorded with their own notions and inclinations; so that there was a continual process of deviation from the original simple, saving teachings of Jesus Christ; and the purity and clarity of his evolved vision was gradually obscured by the confused and carnal mentalities of those who sought to interpret his Gospel through the mind of Paul and the Old Testament.

Paul was also responsible for the pagan innovation of the Eucharist. From 1 Corinthians 11:23-25, it is obvious that it was through his instructions that the original Love-Feast of the Early Christians, the simple, communal thanksgiving meal of which we read in *The Didache*, when both before and after the feast they thanked God for the saving Truth that had come down from heaven in the teachings of Jesus Christ, was replaced by a ceremony having many features in common with the age-old Eucharist of the sun-god, "the feast after the sacrifice", in which, as we have seen, flesh and blood figured prominently.

The passage from Corinthians shows that Paul claimed to have had yet another direct communication from Jesus, describing a Last Supper with his disciples (which was evidently unknown to his immediate followers), and which, Paul decided, must take the place of the Love-Feast. To give Paul his due, he did not institute what afterwards became the purely pagan rite of Transubstantiation, the actual eating of flesh and blood in order to establish communion with the deity.* He intended the bread and wine to be eaten in memory of the Saviour, and partaken as a symbol of his sacrifice, as it still is in the Protestant form of Eucharist, but his innovation was undoubtedly the first step to the pagan idea that has persisted through the ages in the Catholic Church, that communion with Spirit is obtainable through matter.

The Fathers of the Early Church, such as Justin, Tertullian, and, later, Augustine, complained bitterly of the likeness of the sun-god's Eucharist to their own. They attributed it to the precognitive genius of the Devil who, foreseeing what the Christian rites would be, moulded his own upon them in order to discredit them when they appeared. The simple

---

* This idea first came to be promulgated by Justin (1 Apol. 66 ; 2), and *Irenaeus* (Haer. 4, 18, 5; Cf. *Ibid.*, 5, 2, 3).

explanation that the likeness might be due to the eclectic genius of Paul, and those who "improved" on his concept, never seems to have occurred to them; but it must certainly have been an embarrassment to find the pagan congregations of the rival Faith celebrating the Last Supper of the Lord Mithras, and consuming round—as round as the orb of the sky—consecrated wafers of unleavened bread, known as *draona*. These were topped by a piece of sacred flesh, known as *Miẓd*, or *Myaẓd*, a word from which, as J. M. Robertson suggests in *Pagan Christs*, the term *Mass* seems to have been derived. This author also points out that the supper initiated by Paul had no Jesuine authority.

Paul's complicity in this matter has been advanced before. In his *Origin of the Lord's Supper* (1893), Sir Percy Gardner argued that Paul was influenced by the Eleusinian Mysteries, and that if we are to accept 1 Corinthians 11:23, his account of Jesus' directive about the Last Supper came solely from one of his psychic revelations, and not, as has been presumed, from the Gospel records as a recollection of Jesus' immediate disciples.

While the similarity of the two rites may have made an appeal to the Gentiles, which is doubtless why the Christian Eucharist was instituted, it had the tragic effect of strengthening the Jewish theory of atonement, and vicarious salvation through the blood shed for the world, and the martyred flesh, an idea that fatally obscured Jesus' own method of salvation, through self-purification and spiritual-mindedness. It is true that Paul also taught that the Mind of Christ should be put on by the aspirant, but by initiating such a primitive rite he was teaching something completely foreign to this Mind, and focussing attention on the Saviour's martyrdom rather than on his life and victory. This led to the hampering sadism that has always been a feature of Catholicism, with its dreadful penances and mental concentration on misery and violence, especially during the unsuitably named "Good" Friday. Moreover it opened the gate to the still more primitive doctrine of transubstantiation. Nothing further from the thought of Jesus, or indeed of Paul, can possibly be conceived than this pagan rite; and the fallacy of the belief that virtue can be acquired by any such means is shown by the state of Christendom after nearly 2000 years of cannibalistic consumption of deity.

From the evidence found in Romans 5:8–11, Colossians 1:13–14, 19-22, and Philippians 3:10–13, there can be no doubt that the doctrine of vicarious atonement was introduced into the Christian Gospel by Paul, since he was the first New Testament writer. This doctrine was eagerly seized upon by the Jewish scribes that followed him. It was an idea with which their race had always been familiar, and they failed to see that it conflicted with the method taught by their Master. It has proved to be one of the chief stumbling-blocks to making converts among reasonable and honest men. Its appeal is always to the weak, emotional, irresponsible and unethical thought.

While Paul, as a Pharisee, taught the resurrection of the dead, he did not, as the Church was later to do, suggest that the resurrection body would be the same as that which died—an idea which aroused the justifiable scorn of the pagans. As Paul saw it, the body was buried as gross matter but rose in a spiritual form as we find in 1 Corinthians 15:3, 4, 12–54; Romans 6:4–6; 8:9–21. But 1 Thessalonians 4:16, 17 obviously belongs to the concept of the sun-god, and none of these teachings brings out the idea of the soul's pre-existence and co-existence with God which was the teaching of Jesus Christ, as it was of all exponents of the Wisdom religion; and Pauline indecision on this point led to further deterioration until the canonical Christian teachings became indistinguishable from those of the Zoroastrian *Bundahesh*, where we find in Book XXX.

> At the coming of the Saoshyant (Messiah) they prepare the raising of the dead. First the bones of Gayomard (the first man) are raised up, then those of Masha and Mashyoi (the man and woman succeeding him), then those of the rest of mankind. Afterwards, when all material living beings assume again their bodies and forms, then they assign to them a single class. Then is the assembly of the SADVASTARAN, where everyone sees his own good and evil deeds; the righteous are for heaven, and they cast the wicked back to hell.

This is obviously the source of the orthodox Christian teaching as to the resurrection, but it has no relationship to the Wisdom that eternally proclaims: "The Kingdom of God is within you", or to Paul's vision of man as the offspring of God in whom he "lives and moves and has his being". His deviation from this exalted concept, which agreed with that of his Master, gave those who followed him the opportunity to work on the lower conception of the fire-worshippers, which, after the time of Origen, they energetically did.

But probably the greatest and most fatal deviation from the Creed of Christ ever made by Paul was his attitude, described in 1 Corinthians 5:1–5, towards punishment of the sinner and his idea of destroying the flesh that the soul might be saved. This is in keeping with the character of a man who could watch Stephen being stoned to death, but it was utterly alien to the ever-compassionate thought of the Healer of Galilee, and led in the course of time to the fanatical and diabolical persecution of unbelievers and heretics, and to the stake, the rack, and the "holy" wars that have so disgraced and dishonoured the Church supposed to be advocating the way of Jesus Christ.

As we have seen, the pagan concept of a spatial heaven beyond the stars was also perpetuated by Christian theologians on the authority of Paul's reference to the seventh heaven; and this, too, was disastrous to a right comprehension of the Creed of Christ. Jesus being a mystic, God and His Kingdom were, for him, now and forever, the great Realities to be brought into human experience through single-minded attention to the things of the Spirit. Intellectually, Paul could understand this process, as we see from that beautiful passage in 2 Corinthians 3 : 18, which runs: "We all with open face beholding as in a glass the glory of the Lord are changed into the same image from glory to glory, even as by the Spirit of the Lord." But few of the theologians who followed him were mystics, and this was not the sort of instruction they wished to emphasise. Mediation, and not mysticism was the policy of the Church. The great mass of the people must approach God through the priests, then through Jesus, and, later on, when the Mother of the Gods had become the Mother of God, through the Virgin Mary, who would intercede with her Son. It was a long process of mediation, for which the services of a priesthood would be continually needed, instead of the immediate approach of the Son to the Father that Jesus had taught and demonstrated. The theologians, therefore, fastened on to those teachings of Paul that represented Jesus as a Mediator, like Mithras, such as in Philippians 2 :9–11. Where Jesus directed thought to a one-pointed attention to God, Paul, for the most part, directed it to the contemplation of Jesus—to the image rather than to the Original.

But Paul and the theologians were teaching with an eye always on the universal Church they contemplated. Jesus had no thought of a Church. If all men followed him—as if they wished to be saved, they must do— there would be no need for an ecclesiastical organisation. The world would not be perpetuated but transcended, and man would inhabit the Kingdom of God in which there would be no marriage nor giving in marriage, no propagation of fleshly man. In other words, the end of the world which he prophesied, and for which his early followers eagerly looked, would become a fact.

The celibate Exemplar made it perfectly clear in his personal life how this would naturally, painlessly and inevitably come about. The man obsessed with the things of the Spirit would become less and less aware of the flesh and its claims until eventually he lost all consciousness of them, shedding them as the chrysalis is shed by a soaring insect. Paul, as a student of the Mysteries, was well aware of this teaching, but the Jew in him prevented his whole-hearted acceptance and explicit teaching of it. Aware that salvation from the suffering of physical life was impossible without purity, or the outgrowing of the lust of the flesh, he accepted the discipline of celibacy for himself, but, as we see from 1 Corinthians 7:1–17, he rather dishonestly inferred that the same results could be obtained from monogamous marriage, even while affirming that his own state of chastity was the better way. With his usual disinclination to refer to the personal example of the Teacher he had never known, he did not point out that the Perfect Man had been celibate, or that celibacy must inevitably follow from the single-minded attention to the things of the Spirit that was the only means of salvation or evolution.

For Paul, Jesus was less of an Example upon which men should immediately model themselves than a remote ideal that might one day be attained after enormous strivings and wrestlings of spirit, such as the initiates of the Mysteries had to undergo before being offered the Crown. The method of Jesus, of so loving the Highest Good that the one aim of life was to be like the Beloved, an emulation that could begin directly the love was realised, was too "womanish" a concept for Paul, although it was obviously the mainspring of Jesus' life and action.

Therefore the Apostle's teachings on the question of sex were ambiguous. Chastity was right, but it was better to marry than to burn. It was upon this last injunction that the later theologians, avid for congregations, seized, building upon it such a complicated thesis on the subject of matrimony, and so sanctifying it, that it became a sacrament. And the state of matrimony was seen as being quite compatible with following the celibate Jesus, so long as the partners to the contract had received the permission and blessing of the Church.

This policy undoubtedly popularised and filled the Churches that thus became indispensable for those who wished to indulge their animalism without incurring what was, in fact, the inevitable evolutionary penalty for so doing, but did nothing to bring the sufferings of physical life to an end. And the Church, uneasily aware of its departure from the Wisdom of the Goddess, instituted in propitiation a fierce and lasting warfare against the evil of adultery. So far and no further, it commanded with Canute; but inevitably the unheeding ocean flowed in.

CHAPTER XI

The Unfreemasons

Nevertheless, it is obvious from 1 Corinthians 2, and from many other passages in his Epistles that Paul knew a great deal about the Wisdom religion. "We speak the wisdom of God in a mystery", he writes, "even the hidden wisdom, which God ordained before the world unto our glory. . . ." He also advocated love of the Good in what is possibly the finest exposition ever written on that theme, in 1 Corinthians 13, and he eloquently taught the necessity for purification of thought in Philippians 4:8.

Like all the great teachers he recognised that spiritual evolution was the destiny of man, and that the Mark, or evolutionary goal, was to arrive at the stature of the fullness of Christ by putting on the Mind of Christ. Like the Platonists, he despised the flesh, and regarded it as the antithesis of Spirit, as something to be first subdued, and then transcended or put off. He had no illusions whatever about it being eternal or existing in that sphere of Reality that Jesus called the Kingdom of God. His forthright statement that flesh and blood cannot inherit this kingdom has been shamelessly ignored, and seldom studied within the context of Jesus' life and example by the theologians. Indeed, in the present age, it has been so flouted by what claims to be the original Christian Church that the Assumption of the Virgin Mary—the belief that the mother of Jesus was taken up bodily into heaven, like the mother of Bacchus—has of quite recent years been made dogma.

It was not that Paul failed to teach Christianity in so far as he was able to interpret the Mind of Christ, but that he taught so much else, thereby fatally adulterating the original Gospel, and leaving loopholes for further errors to seep in through the efforts of mentalities less enlightened than his own. Among these was that of Justin Martyr (c. 100–167), born in Neapolis in Samaria of Greek parents.

Between the writings of the Epistles of Paul and the conversion of Justin, the Gospel had appeared according to the four Evangelists, two of whom had introduced the theme of the Virgin Mary and the Nativity, a concept unknown to Paul. Nor did it figure in the first Gospel to be written, that of Mark; and if Mark had access to the source known as Q., which is uncertain, it could hardly have been in that or he would certainly have included it. Nor was this idea, so familiar to Greeks and Romans, whose heroes and rulers were frequently believed to have been born of a God and a woman, mentioned by the Hellenistic John.

Matthew who writes as a Jew intent on showing how the prophecies of the Old Testament were fulfilled in the life of Jesus, somewhat illogically traces his genealogy from Abraham to Joseph, following it with an account of the virgin birth! Luke, who was a Gentile, was writing deliberately for a pagan audience that was accustomed to, and would have expected a wonder story to be connected with a great man's birth. There seems to be no means of discovering when or how this idea occurred to the two evangelists, or even how it was expressed in the original version of their gospels, for they have been much written over and what the evangelists actually wrote was probably very different from what is found in the modern New Testament.

We know, for instance, that at least until the second century, as we find from the Protoevangelium of St James, Jesus was believed to have been born in a cave, information that could only have been discovered from Matthew's and Luke's gospels as they were then written. And this is but a single piece of evidence of what appears to have been a continual manipulation of the New Testament records which culminated in Jerome's much criticised translation of the old Latin version in the fourth century. F. G. Gould, in *The New Testament*, quotes Professor Dummelow as saying of this practice:

> A copyist would sometimes put in not what was in the text, but what he thought ought to be in it. He would trust a fickle memory, or he would make the text accord with the views of the school to which he belonged.

Justin writes of the story of the birth of Jesus current in his day, in his *Dialogue with Trypho*:

> With regard to the child having been born at that time, since Joseph had not where to lodge in that village, he lodged in a certain cave nigh the village, and then, while they were there, Mary brought forth the Christ and laid him in a manger, where the wise men of Arabia came and found him.*

He then waxes indignant at the coincidence of the connection of the cult of Mithras with a cave:

> I have already narrated to you . . . what Isaiah proclaimed beforehand concerning this sign also with regard to the cave (Isaiah 33:13-19). . . . On account of these words they who do teach the Mysteries of Mithra were moved by the devil to say that men are initiated by them in a place to which they give the designation of a cave.

* *The Dialogue with Trypho*, translated by A. Lukyn Williams, D.D. (S.P.C.K., 1930).

Justin was one of the worst offenders in pressing the absurd theory that the age-old teachings of Zoroastrianism were plagiarised from the Hebrew Scriptures by men who would have had no knowledge of the Hebrew tongue. To him, also, we owe the ridiculous explanation of the similarity between Pauline Christianity and the pagan religion, which was that the devil, having foreseen what the true Gospel would be centuries before it was preached, made pagan versions of its teachings in order to discredit them when, in due course, they appeared. He writes LXIX: 1,2:

> The very things which the Devil, rightly so called, corrupted, and then made into current tales among the Greeks . . . have confirmed my knowledge of the Scriptures and my faith. For when they say that Dionysos was born son of Zeus by his intercourse with Semele, and relate that he was the discoverer of the vine, and after being torn in pieces and having died rose again, and has ascended into heaven; and when they bring forward an ass in his Mysteries; must not I think that he has imitated the prophecy of the patriarch Jacob which was recorded by Moses.

This *Dialogue with Trypho the Jew* is particularly interesting as evidence of the way the Christian religion had developed by the second century, and also as an illustration of the approach made by Christians to the Jews that they hoped to convert: as, in the following century, Origen, in his *contra Celsum* was to demonstrate the method and arguments employed to convince the pagans; although Celsus who he addressed, was already dead, whereas Trypho was very much alive and full of embarrassing questions. For in this pre-Nicene period the theologians were uncertain as to whether there were two gods or one, as both the Jews and Jesus had always maintained. Having decided, on Pauline evidence, that Jesus was a deity, they had yet to make up their minds as to whether he had existed as a separate God from the Maker of heaven and earth, or merely as a manifestation of His nature. Justin, as a Greek, inclined to the former theory. He pointed out (CXXVII: 1, 2, 3) that the unbegotten God could never come down from heaven or remove Himself from one place to another:

> For the ineffable Father and Lord of all neither comes to any place, nor walks, nor sleeps, nor arises, but abides in His own place . . . nor is He moved, who cannot be contained in any place, even the whole world, who in truth was even before the world came into being. How therefore should he speak unto any, or be seen of any, or appear in a tiny part of the earth. . . ?

Because he could not, he must employ a Messenger to announce to men "whatever the Maker of the Universe, above Whom there is no other God, desires to announce to them". This Messenger is His Son who had recently appeared on earth as Jesus Christ. We now come to a concept so strikingly like the one already quoted on page 228 from Philo's *Confusion of Languages* as to leave no doubt of its pre-Christian, Gnostic origin. Justin writes of the essential nature of the Christ (LXI:1):

> God has begotten as a beginning before all His creatures a kind of Reasoning Power from Himself, which is also called by the Holy Spirit the Glory of the Lord, and sometimes Son, and sometimes Wisdom, and sometimes Angel, and sometimes God, and sometimes Lord and Word.

Had God not become, by common consent, purely masculine, Justin might fairly have added, "and sometimes Minerva, sometimes Cybele, sometimes Sophia", or even, having regard to the Platonic definition, "sometimes *nous*". But no matter by what name it is called, there is certainly a description, recognisable to Gnostics, of the eternal Christ, the divine nature that could be manifested in any form; distinct from the forms that embodied it yet constituting their essence. According to Justin, this Christ had appeared in the Old Testament as one of the three angels who visited Abraham (Genesis 18:2), and also in angelic form to Isaac and Jacob. It was the God who conversed with Moses from the burning bush. It had also appeared as Joshua, the name meaning Jesus. Yet the fact that he appeared in these many forms did not cut the Son off from the Father:

> When we put forth any word we beget a word, not putting it forth by scission, as though the word within us was diminished . . . . (LXI:1).

This divine Word appears in such form as the Father wills. He is called the Logos since he carries the messages from the Father to man, but he can no more be separated from the Father than the light of the sun can be separated from its source.

> When the sun sets the light is borne away with it. So the Father . . . makes when He will His power to spring forward, and when He wills he draws it back again into Himself.

This paraphrase of John 16:28 appeals to reason as well as to our religious sense. That the outcome, or offspring, of an infinite and eternal divine Mind, which is the highest concept that man has ever had of God, must be Wisdom, and that a wise man, as an embodiment of that Wisdom, may be called a son of God, is a logical argument. This premise persisted fitfully in the teachings of the Early Church whenever the mentalities of the theologians were clear enough to sustain it, until, at the

Council of Nicaea, the many conflicting opinions then current as to the nature of Jesus Christ were crystalised into the reasonless doctrine of the Trinity.

This particular concept of the Logos was fundamentally monotheistic, since the light of the sun cannot be said to be something other than its source. But unfortunately, like the theologians who followed him, Justin was not content to abide by this metaphysical simile, but descended to a dialectic dualism that presented God and Jesus as two separate dieties, leading eventually to a third in the form of the Holy Ghost.

All men, according to Justin, were originally made like God:

> Free from suffering and immortal if they kept His precepts, and were deemed worthy of being called by Him His sons. But they became like Adam and Eve and prepared death for themselves. . . They were deemed worthy to become gods, and capable of becoming sons of the Highest. (CXXXIV:4.)

But descending from the Hellenistic view of the eternal Logos, or Christ, to the sacrificial outlook of the Old Testament, he writes:

> The Father of the universe purposed that His own Christ should receive on himself the curse of all, on behalf of men of every race. (XIV: 2.)

So we return to the primitive concept of the scapegoat, and of Jesus as a man, or God, who deliberately took the condemnation upon himself in order to propitiate an angry and bloodthirsty deity. Ignoring Jesus' concept of God as wholly and unchangeably good and compassionate, Justin returns to the diabolical Jehovah found in the Old Testament who could deliberately cause suffering to his faithful son whose lifework had been to heal, or eliminate, suffering. This, of course, makes nonsense of Jesus' words, "the Son can do nothing of himself, but what he seeth the Father do: for what things soever he doeth, these also doeth the Son likewise". (John 5:19.)

Justin seems to think it was rather good of the Father to allow Jesus to grow to manhood:

> The Father had decided that He whom He had begotten should be put to death only after becoming a full-grown man and preaching the Message received from Him.

This is a typical example of the insanity that followed the attempt to reconcile the irreconcilable: the gods of the Old and New Testament. How could anything begotten by the Eternal be put to death? How could death be the will of the Source of life? Abandoning reason, Justin could heartily embrace the doctrine of vicarious atonement: "As the blood of the passover saved them that were in Egypt, so also will the blood of Christ rescue from death them that have believed." (CXI:3.)

Justin believed that the crucifixion was pre-ordained, and that the blood of the passover was sprinkled in the Israelites' doorposts in the form of a cross, as TAW, the last letter in the Hebrew alphabet, foretelling the sacrifice on Calvary. This, he thought, was also pre-figured by the sheep of the passover that was roasted whole, and was "a figure of the suffering of the cross by which Jesus was to suffer . . . for when the sheep is being roasted it is roasted arranged in a fashion like the fashion of the cross, for one spit is pierced straight from the lower parts to the head, and one again at the back, to which also the paws of the sheep are fastened". (XL:111.)

To suggest that this cruel and sadistic idea had already been a thought in the Divine Mind at the time of the exodus from Egypt was to make a mockery of Jesus' constant affirmation of the goodness of God. From such a premise arose the theme of the suffering Lamb of God through whose agonies other men were saved. And from this unhealthy dwelling on suffering and violence, it was but a step to the acceptance of the equally primitive Judaic idea of the eternal punishment of evil-doers in the sight of all men, which we find in CXXX:2, where Justin writes:

> We know even by Isaiah that the limbs of them that have transgressed are to be devoured by worm and never-ceasing fire, abiding immortal so that they may be seen of all flesh.

An idea that Tertullian (A.D. 160–240) was later to seize upon and labour with avidity. Such theories could only come from, or be accepted by, perverted, sadistic minds, mentalities that had not freed themselves from the teachings of primitive Judaism. Yet Justin prides himself on repudiating others far less alien to the Mind of Christ. He reminds Trypho that Christians do not live in accordance with the Jewish law, inasmuch as they do not sacrifice, nor practise circumcision, nor observe the Sabbath. For the supreme and final sacrifice was made on Calvary, and the new circumcision is of the heart, and involves freeing the soul from all anger, hatred and other evils; while the Sabbath must be kept perpetually all day and every day. How about the high priests, he asked Trypho, who sacrificed on the Sabbath? Were they sinning? "Nature does not idle or keep Sabbath." And since before Abraham there was no circumcision, and before Moses no need to keep the Sabbath, these things were obviously unnecessary, but were given as laws to the Jews who needed them as a discipline.

The other Jewish practices that the Christians had rejected were war and polygamy:

> We who were filled full of war and slaughter of one another, and every kind of evil, have from out of the whole earth each changed our weapons of war, our swords into ploughshares and pikes into farming tools . . . each of us dwelling under his own vine, that is, each enjoying only his own wedded wife.

That spiritual healing was still practised among Christians in Justin's day is evident from XXXV : 8, where he writes:

> We pray that you may not blaspheme Jesus Christ who by his works and the miracles that even now take place by his name, and by the words of his teaching . . . is shown to be without blame and without reproach in all respects.

And that the works of Jesus were still cited as secondary evidence of his Messiahship is suggested in LXIX :6, where Justin relates that "by his works he importuned the men of his day to recognise him".

Despite its adulteration by confused and Jewish-influenced mentalities, the Christianity of Justin's day still retained enough of the original spirit of Christ to create in his followers a love and devotion that caused them to die rather than to deny him, a fact which the Fathers of the Early Church were quick to recognise as being one of the best evidences and advertisements of the truth of their Gospel. For which reason, and with a callousness bred of fanaticism, they encouraged and praised to the utmost a willingness to be martyred.

This tendency is seen at its worst in Origen's *Exhortation to Martyrdom*, probably one of the most horrible expositions of sadism ever to have been printed. It is addressed to two of Origen's personal friends who are threatened with martyrdom, and he tells them to hate their life, for so they will keep it unto life eternal. He asks, "How can the soul be slain when it has been given life by the very fact of martyrdom?"

Origen argues that martyrdom is a sort of baptism, and connects it with Jesus' crucifixion, suggesting that it is a perfect way of following the Master. He writes:

> Note also that the baptism of martyrdom, as received by our saviour, atones for the world; so, too, when we receive it, it serves to atone for many. Just as they who assisted at the altar of Moses seemed to procure for the Jews remission of sins by the blood of goats and oxen, so the souls of believers that are beheaded for the testimony of Jesus do not assist in vain at the altar of heaven, but procure for them that pray, the remission of sins.*

* *Origen: Prayer. Exhortation to Martyrdom*, translated and annotated by John J. O'Meara. (Longmans, Green.)

Here, again, we have the dreadful Judaic tradition clouding the thought of a great teacher who, in many ways, and unlike Paul, understood the heart as well as the Mind of Jesus Christ. But his zeal for the prosperity of the Church seemed to eliminate all humaneness. He fairly bullies his friends into not retracting in order to save their lives; for this, he says, will result in the loss of their souls:

> If a man who has a great and glorious hope in God, permits himself in God to be overcome by fear or sufferings with which he is threatened in court, he will hear this: Thy pride, thy great confidence, is brought down to hell. Under thee shall they strew corruption, and worms shall be thy covering.

So the unfortunate victims are left with the choice of a certain immediate acute agony on earth, or eternal suffering in hell. They are offered no alternative. In this *Exhortation* Origen is quite horrifying, not only in his insensitivity to the physical suffering of others—and so the very antithesis of his Exemplar—but in his implication, possibly owed to Paul, that souls may be saved as a result of suffering agony in the flesh. This utterly false reasoning, which was eagerly perpetuated by other churchmen, led eventually to all the horrors of the rack and stake; and the violence which is anti-Christ, the total rejection of Wisdom, became established as a policy in the self-styled Christian Church.

Origen's idea of the value of martyrdom was a fatal materialisation of the truth taught in the Wisdom religion that salvation is gained through naughting and transcending the flesh by spiritual means. But nothing makes the body more real to consciousness than acute sensation, either of pleasure or pain; nothing makes it less real than a concentrated attention on spiritual things which cause it to be forgotten. It can neither be forgotten nor transcended when it is suffering the agonies of hell in the Roman arena or on the rack. Therefore physical martyrdom, whatever it did for the merciless Church by adding to its congregations, provided for the martyrs themselves the very worst conditions for realising the life of the Spirit. The few who were so spiritually disciplined as to be indifferent to the physical torment could not compensate for the many who died in the consciousness that excruciating agony was more real to them than the presence of God. This teaching was as great and deplorable an error as that of vicarious atonement of which it was a form.

The most horrifying part of the *Exhortation* was when Origen, quoting from the *Book of Maccabees*, spoke of seven brothers who were tortured to death. The first was scalped and had his tongue cut out and extremities cut off, and what was left of him, still breathing, was fried in a pan, his mother and brothers looking on, exhorting him to die manfully; "consoling themselves with the thought that God saw all these things".

Being Jews, they may well have thought it of Jehovah, and would not realise that they were worshipping a devil; but Origen professed to worship the God of Jesus Christ, and to identify Him with the monster who could allow or witness such horrors was, in the fullest measure, to betray the Gospel and life-work of Jesus Christ.

This was one of the unhappy consequences of making the Bible of the Jews the Holy Scriptures of the Christians.

From the first, the idea of vicarious atonement was immensely popular with the Church Fathers. Irenaeus, writing in the second century on the correct way of keeping a perpetual Sabbath by the continual purging of sins, says:

> It was not to a bath that Isaiah sent you to wash away murder there and all other sins. . . But, as is probable, this was of old that laver of salvation, which he meant, for those who repent and no longer cleanse themselves with the blood-shedding of goats and sheep, or the ashes of an heifer and offerings of meal, but by faith, through the blood of Christ and his death.

The Teacher whose joy no man could take from him, was now transformed into a figure of sorrow and suffering by the darkness of the primitive idea of blood-sacrifice, so acceptable and familiar to Jew and pagan alike.

The sorrowing figure of the mother of Thammuz and Bacchus had, by Clement of Alexandria's time, been introduced into the new Faith, and her sufferings were soon to be added to those of her son for the many to whom suffering and religion were synonymous. But the new Faith was to lack the orgiastic human compensations to which the pagans were accustomed, and alleviation of suffering was postponed until a far-off geographical heaven was attained. Thus an unhealthy and, in the truest sense, *insane* way of thought gradually replaced what was originally a creed of health, healing and compassion.

Tertullian had a particularly dark and materialistic thought, even imagining that souls were material and so subject to death. The son of a Roman centurion, he was familiar with the idea of great men, like Augustus Caesar, having been born of a God and a woman, and so strove mightily against the heretics who denied the Virgin Birth. In *Adv. Marcion*, IV:7, after using Justin's argument that Joshua, the son of Nun, was but an earlier incarnation of that God which was in Jesus, and that this deity appeared to the patriarchs in many forms, he asks: "How can we be at a loss and not believe that according to the will of the Father of the universe, He can also have been born man by a virgin?"

To a pagan, neither of these ideas would seem impossible, but Tertullian could not foresee that the theory of reincarnation was eventually to be firmly rejected by the Christian theologians, and appears not to have noticed the scorn that they were already pouring on the Greek idea of a woman being filled with the spirit of wisdom by a God. This ancient and universal idea was to be fiercely resisted as having anything in common with the sacred experience of the Virgin Mary, so that the theory of the virgin birth had to be accepted without its pagan and philosophic rationalisation, and regarded as a unique miracle, the sole and inadequate explanation for which was that it had been foretold by a Jewish prophet. That it had been foretold even more explicitly by Zoroaster and Virgil was not taken into account.

The Alexandrians, with their Hellenistic outlook, were more cheerful than Justin or Tertullian, but in the case of Clement (second century) hardly less confused on certain points. His knowledge of the Mysteries in *Protrep*, ii, suggests that before his conversion he had been an initiate. Like Paul, he was an eclectic, and saw Christianity as the point to which both Judaism and Hellenism had been converging. Like Paul, he conceived of the religious life as spiritual evolution—within the Church. In *Church History*, II p. 486, Neander writes of Clement's teachings:

> (The Logos) first conducts the rude heathen to the faith; then progressively reforms their lives by moral precepts; and finally elevates those who have undergone this moral purification to the profounder knowledge of divine things, which he calls Gnosis.

For Clement, the evolved or perfected man is the man of knowledge, the true Gnostic. This follows the pattern of initiation in the Mystery Religions, with which he was familiar, the Gnosis being given only to those of the highest degrees. In *Origen and Patristic Theology*, W. Fairweather writes:

> Clement holds that hidden Mysteries received by the apostles from the Lord had been handed down in direct succession until those who possessed the tradition of the blessed doctrine "came by God's will to us also to deposit those ancestral and apostolic seeds". (Strom. I : 1, VI : 8.) These Christian Mysteries were not disclosed to the general body of pupils attending the Catechetical School. Their proper diet was "milk" or catechetical instruction and not "meat", or mystic contemplation. On this principle the lower grades among the catechumens were not introduced to anything which he reckoned as Gnosis.

As a Gnostic, Clement had a considerable knowledge of what he termed "Divine Science", and was well aware of its unity and universality. In *Strom.* I:13, 57, we find an idea with which students of Eastern religion are very familiar: "Truth is like the body of Pentheus, torn asunder by fanatics; each seizes a limb and thinks he has the whole." In *Strom.* V:10 he gives credence to the idea, based on Genesis 6, that women were originally the imparters of wisdom to the human race since they received it from their angelic husbands. He accepts fully that the one way to salvation is to Love God with all the heart, soul, mind and strength, because "Love makes man like the beloved".

> By love he (the Gnostic) is already in that scene where he will one day dwell. And having anticipated his hope by gnosis he desires nothing, for he holds in closest possession the very object of his desire.

His view on prayer is startlingly modern, but most unlike what his Church was afterwards to teach on the subject. Words, he said, were unnecessary, for God reads the heart. He pictures Him as saying: "Ask, and I will do; think, and I will give." As a mystic he knows that prayer is mental communion with the Parent Mind. In *Strom.* VII:43, he writes most beautifully on the subject of prayer:

> When he who is at once right-minded and thankful makes his request in prayer, he in a way contributes to the granting of his petition. . . . For when the Giver of all good meets with readiness on our part, all good things follow at once on the mere *conception in the mind*. . . . How can God help hearing the soul and the mind by itself, seeing that soul already apprehends soul, and mind apprehends mind? Wherefore God has no need to learn various tongues, as human interpreters have, but understands at once the minds of all men. . . . It is permitted to man therefore to speed his prayer even without a voice, if he only concentrates all his spiritual energy upon the inner voice of the Mind by his undistracted turning to God.

This is an early description of the method of prayer used in modern spiritual healing.

According to Clement, contemplation is the first necessity, for from it comes active benevolence, and the tasks of instruction whereby the Gnostic makes others like himself. He is still pagan enough to ordain that public prayer indulged in by the multitude should be performed with face to the East. In those early days, Christians did not kneel at prayer, but stood with hands and head uplifted looking towards the rising sun.

That to the Gnostics the "blood" of Jesus was purely symbolical. Clement shows in *Adumb. in 1. Ep. Joan*, p. 1,009, where he says: "The blood of His Son cleanseth from all sin. For the doctrine of the Lord, which is very strong, is called the Blood." Had this definition been kept clearly before Christian congregations, the idea of literal vicarious atonement would soon have died a natural death, for the truth that the doctrine and life of Jesus constituted the salvation of mankind would have been recognised.

Like the first Christians, Clement regarded the Eucharistic Bread as merely symbolising the eternal Truth, having no connection with flesh and blood. "Knowledge is our reasonable food." The Christ at the Eucharist is "in the heart not in the hand".

With Paul he believed that the resurrection body is an evolved body, quite different from the one formed of gross matter, which has to be changed as a seed in the ground changes into a flower. In his day, there was no authoritative teaching about the nature and immortality of the soul. Having departed from the age-old and logical premise of one Soul manifesting in many forms in different stages of awareness, the Church's difficulty was to find anything like a reasonable alternative. Most Christians believed that, after death, the individual soul would wait in Hades or Paradise until the resurrection of the body. Tertillian and some others believed that the soul was material and so died with the body to be raised at some future time by an act of God, to suffer or enjoy eternally according to its deserts. Others believed the soul slept until its physical organism was restored to it. But having abandoned the one reasonable theory, nothing else had proved convincing enough to be crystallised into dogma.

On the subject of sex Clement is curiously ambivalent. At one moment he is writing: "Our ideal is not to experience desire at all", which is the teaching of Wisdom and appears to have been his innermost opinion. At the next he is castigating the heretics who forbid marriage and refuse to propagate. Tatian, for instance, at one time a pupil of Justin Martyr, called marriage fornication and incompatible with the practice of Christianity. Marcion refused to believe that the visible, all too imperfect world was ever created by the God and Father of Jesus, and had no intention of helping whoever the creator was to perpetuate his evil work of nature-red-in-tooth-and-claw; and therefore ordained that no member of the Marcionite Church should marry.

This perfectly logical viewpoint that was shared by many others, was hotly denounced by Clement who evidently regarded such a realistic criticism of nature as an affront to God the Creator. And even when the heretics who practised continence argued that they were living in the present life as Jesus told them they would have to live in the world to come, Clement illogically answered that they might as well refuse to eat and drink also. Yet elsewhere he quotes with approval: "Human nature has some wants which are necessary and natural, and others which are only natural. To be clothed is necessary and natural; sexual intercourse is natural but not necessary."

Rejecting both Jesus' celibate example and Marcion's reasonable objection to human propagation, Clement hovers unhappily and unconvincingly between his feeling that the species must be perpetuated and the certainty that a man must be pure in order to be like his Master; in other words, to be really a Christian. "It is absolutely impossible", he admits, "at the same time to be a man of understanding and not to be ashamed to gratify the body."

He is also aware (Ch. 5:43) that "to attain knowledge of God is impossible for those who are still under the control of their passions". Yet after giving the warning that "desire is nourished and invigorated if it is encouraged in indulgence, just as . . . it loses strength if it is kept in check", he suggests that Christians should marry for the purpose of procreation.

He deliberately quotes from the *Gospel According to the Egyptians:* "When Salome asked the Lord: 'How long shall death hold sway?' he answered, 'As long as you women bear children'"; but so dislikes this Marcionite sentiment that he refuses to face its implications, and declares that Jesus did not mean that creation was bad, entirely ignoring the fact that Paul had declared death to be an enemy that must be overcome. Yet he further writes of the same Gospel (Ch. 1:63): "They say that the Saviour himself said, 'I come to destroy the works of the female', meaning by 'female' desire, and by 'works' birth and corruption." But then disputes it on the grounds that this instruction has not been accomplished, for the world continues as before. He is unwilling to face the obvious fact that it could never be accomplished until the would-be followers of the Master were instructed in his doctrine on this point by the Church. He still inclines to marriage, and declares:

> Fornication and marriage are . . . different things, as far apart as God is from the devil. . . . It necessarily follows . . . that it is wrong to forbid marriage, and indeed eating meat or drinking wine.

His rejection of the plain truth led him to this entirely illogical conclusion, and so to the Church's misdirection of its congregations. On Clement's own showing, desire, which prevents the knowledge of God, is encouraged by indulgence, whether in or out of the state of matrimony; eating flesh violates the law of compassion; and drinking wine intoxicates, clouding the mentality that should be a clear mirror for the ideas of God.

So that, contrary to his contention, it would seem to be right that al three indulgences should be avoided. However, reason and desire are apt to war with one another, and the secret reason for his insistence upon wedlock and its fruits seems to be revealed in Ch. 7:103, where he asks:

> Without the body how could the divine plan for us in the church achieve its end?

Accepting Paul's idea of a universal religion to which the whole world must be converted, instead of the perfecting of the individual as taught by Jesus and the Mystery Religions, the continuance of the human race was clearly essential; but this was to accept the Pauline directive instead of the Jesuine example; and this was the policy of those who followed the Apostle to the Gentiles. Desire was permitted in moderation and within the bounds of wedlock. In Ch. 17:102 Clements tells us that "the heretics say man became like the beast when he came to practise sexual intercourse", and comments: "But it is when a man in his passion really wants to go to bed with a strange woman that in truth such a man has become a wild beast."

Desire and the animalistic act proceeding from it are thus represented as not evil *per se*, but only when directed to the wrong or illegal object. With his ecclesiastical eye on congregations he writes:

> True manhood is not shown in the choice of a celibate life. . . . The prize in the contest of life is won by him . . . who in the midst of his solicitude for his family shows himself inseparable from the love of God and rises superior to every temptation which assails him through children and wife and servants and possessions. (Ch. 12:70.)

But having already stated that the desire necessary in order to beget children inevitably separates man from knowledge of God, he goes on to say that begetting children must be an act of the will, not of desire. "A man who marries for the sake of begetting children must practise continence, so that it is not desire he feels for his wife, whom he ought to love, and he may beget children with a chaste and controlled will."

Such revealing ignorance of the simple biological fact that children cannot be begotten merely with a chaste and controlled will, except through the medium of a test tube, would be a source of delight to the modern psychologist, but it was no help to Clement's students on the subject of sexual indulgence.

For him, the most virtuous attitude was deliberately to abstain from sexual intercourse after having known the pleasure of it. Therefore the widow who remained unwed was more virtuous than the virgin. In Ch. 12:76, he writes:

> The great thing is to abstain from pleasure after having had experience of it. For what credit is it to practice self-control where pleasure is unknown?

This distinctly dangerous teaching, though to some extent plausible, entirely shelves the question as to whether the perpetuation of the human species, or the outgrowing and transcending of mortal life, was intended by the celibate Example. It was also a departure from the Pauline outlook, which regarded marriage merely as a concession to weakness. But Clement's view became the popular one with a Church that, in order to thrive, must have congregations.

Eventually the conflict within Clement on this vexed but vital question, which was never reasonably resolved, became too much for him, and in Ch. IX:60, evidently outraged by the more logical standpoint of heretics and pagans, he writes:

> Those who from a hatred of the flesh ungratefully long to have nothing to do with the marriage union and the eating of reasonable food, are both blockheads and atheists, and exercise an irrational chastity like the other heathen. For example, the Brahmins neither eat animal flesh nor drink wine.

Such smug assumption of his own, and the orthodox Christian's, superiority in these respects would be laughable if it were not for the suffering and unhappiness that has been endured throughout the ages by such misdirectives from those in authority; and Clement's personal opinions on these all-important matters were later to become the popular policy of the Church.

On the question of flesh-eating, however, Clement was as painfully divided as he was on the question of sex. He permitted it but did not inwardly approve of it. In fact he believed that the practice of animal sacrifice, of which, as a Christian, he naturally disapproved, was originally "an invention of mankind to excuse the eating of flesh". Ch. 4:22. He traces the sacrificial habit back to those primitive times when, under the direction of Prometheus, men were recorded to have set before the gods "the rump, the gall, and dry bones" of the beast, "while they consumed the rest themselves". He then goes on to say:

> If any of the righteous refuses to weigh down his soul by the eating of flesh, he does this on some reasonable ground, not as Pythagoras and his school from some dream as to the transmigration of souls. (Book VII, Ch. 4:32.)

It may be that fear lest a non-carnivorous diet might be adopted from pagan motives prevented his advocating something of which he obviously approved more whole-heartedly; but, blindly or intentionally, he misrepresented Pythagoras's chief motive which, as we have seen, was compassion for helpless, sentient creatures, a motive entirely consistent with the Mind of Christ but completely lacking in Clement. He does not even consider it. Instead, he approaches the subject from the purely "scientific" angle of those times, and writes:

> Xenocrates in a special treatise on animal food, and Polemon (successive heads of the Platonic Academy) in his book on Life According to Nature, seem to lay it down clearly that a flesh diet is inexpedient, as it has already passed through a process of digestion and been thus assimilated to the souls of irrational creatures. . . . Further they tell us that . . . owing to the sluggishness produced by eating flesh, it is of no use to those who try to encourage the growth of the soul. A Gnostic might therefore abstain from flesh, both for the sake of discipline and to weaken the sexual appetite. For, as Androcydes says, "wine and flesh gorging make the body strong, but the soul more sluggish. . . . The Egyptians in their purifications forbid their priests to eat flesh . . ."

All very admirable, commonsensible and true, but not a hint in it anywhere of the compassion for suffering, sentient creatures that was the keynote of the life and character of Jesus Christ. But this was generally the failing of the Alexandrians who, like Paul, knew so much about the Mind of Christ, since they had access to the same sources of wisdom as he had had, but so little about his heart.

Clement regarded the spiritual life as a science, devoid of emotion. For him, Gnosis was the highest peak of spiritual attainment. He referred to it as, "the knowledge of insight . . . the science of divine things"; and for him, as for James (2:22), it was by this insight, or science, that faith was made perfect. Single-minded attention to the things of the Spirit he spoke of as "Scientific contemplation". And in Ch. 12:70, he refers to the poise that this one-pointedness produces when he writes:

> The Gnostic never departs from his own set habit in any emergency. For the scientific possession of good is fixed and unchangeable, being the science of things divine and human.

Despite his mistakes, caused by double-minedness and too little sensitivity, Clements was undoubtedly a fine exponent of this Divine Science on many points, and it is commonly agreed that his notable successor, Origen, said to have been "the greatest Teacher of the Church after the Apostles", owed him a great deal.

Origen (c. 185–253) is quite the most extraordinary figure among all the theologians of the Early Church. His father, Leonidas, suffered martyrdom for the Christian Faith when Origen was seventeen. It is supposed that he was a convert from the pagan faith to which he evidently belonged at the time of Origen's birth, for the name, "Origen" may be rendered "generated of Horus", or son of the sun-god. And indeed he proved to be a link between the old Faith and the new.

Although his worst enemies never attempted to deny his sincerity as a Christian, he was, in many particulars, also a priest of the goddess, even, in his youth, going so far as to castrate himself, after taking too literally the instruction found in Matthew 19:12. He was afterwards said to have regretted this, not, apparently, because he ever wished to marry, but because it brought such denunciation upon him from the Judaistic-influenced men of his Church who had evidently accepted Moses' injunction not to allow any mutilated person into the priesthood. Instead of applauding him for his sincerity in determining to follow the example of his celibate Master, they made it a reason for not giving him the bishopric he so richly deserved. Demetrious, an uncultured peasant, who, as a result of a vision experienced by Bishop Julian, had been seated in the throne of St Mark, hearing that the Church of Caesarea was about to raise Origen to the episcopate, "spread the information about his act of self-mutilation when a young man for the purpose of not only stopping Origen's consecration, but also of censuring even those who had raised him to the presbyterate".*

It was, perhaps, only natural that Origen should have aroused the jealousy of an unlettered man so much his intellectual and spiritual inferior. For Origen, possibly because he could not use his energy on the physical level, had immense mental power, and was a literary genius. He is supposed to have written six hundred books, of which only a few remain. But these are sufficient to show how great a devotee of the Wisdom-Goddess he was in fact, however little he realised it in theory. Like Solomon and other wise men, he referred to Wisdom in the feminine gender. In his *First Principles* (Book III:2) he writes:

> Wisdom is the Word of God. For Wisdom opens to all other beings . . . the meaning of the mysteries and secrets which are contained within the wisdom of God, and so she is called the Word, because she is, as it were, the interpreter of the mind's secrets.†

* *Alexandrian Christianity*, J. E. L. Oulton, D.D. and Henry Chadwick, B.A. Library of Christian Classics. (SCM Press Ltd.)
† *First Principles*, by Origen. (Koetchau's Text of De Principiis). Translated by G. W. Butterworth, Litt.D. (S.P.C.K., 1936.)

This statement, coming somewhat oddly from a member of a Church whose perfect *man* was known as the Logos, or Word, of Wisdom, is probably explained by the prevalent idea at that time of the third Person of the Trinity, the Holy Spirit, the feminine Dove. In Ch. 3 : 5, Origen also quotes from Solomon's *Book of Wisdom*, a passage referring to the goddess, which says:

> She is the breath of the power of God, and a pure effluence (that is emanation) of the glory of the Almighty. . . . Nothing that is defiled can enter into her. For she is the brightness of the eternal Light and an unspotted mirror of the workings of God and an image of his goodness.

What is this but a description of the Mind that was in Jesus Christ, the holy "Mother"? Writing further on this theme, Origen explains:

> When Wisdom is called the "unspotted mirror" of the Father's power and working, she would have us understand her nature to be like the image reflected in a mirror, which moves and acts in correspondence with the movements and actions of him who looks into the mirror, not deviating from them in any way whatever. So, too, the Lord Jesus Christ, who is the wisdom of God speaks of himself when he says . . . "The son can do nothing of himself but what he seeth the Father doing".

This is surely a recognition of the Goddess as well as of the God that was in Jesus Christ, and is perhaps one of the most illuminating illustrations ever given of the relation of the Perfect Man to the divine Parent Mind that is God.

Origen undoubtedly preached the Gospel of the goddess on many points, especially on the basic subject of man's pre-existence and co-existence with God. No one in the Early Church ever taught this more explicitly; and it was this logical and age-old doctrine that was so fiercely resented by the Emperor Justinian, and declared anathema at the Second Council of Constantinople in 553.

For Origen, the Father and origin of all being was pure Spirit, as Jesus had taught, of which the mind is an intellectual image; so that, as mind, man is able to perceive to some extent the divine nature, and therefore to be that nature. It is as Mind that he lives eternally. The "Son" is not born in time; he is eternally begotten of the Father in the same way that the light of the sun is eternally begotten by its source. Such generation is not division, as in human birth, but expansion. Origen does not conceive of God as a Lord God who created the world in six days, but as a perpetual generator of His own likeness from all eternity, as the sun is a perpetual generator of his rays that exist not as creations but as emanations. Therefore "all genera and species have forever existed, and some would say individual things; but either way it is clear that God did not begin to create after spending a period in idleness". (Ch. 4:10).

The Creator never begins to create. What seems to be creation is perpetual emanation, as eternal as the source is eternal.

For Origen as for Paul, spiritual evolution was the aim of life, and was made possible by man's embodiment of Wisdom, goodness and Love. For him, Jesus was not born Christ, but *became* Christ. He writes:

> The man became Christ for he obtained this lot by reason of his goodness. This soul which belongs to Christ so chose to love righteousness as to cling to it unchangeably and inseparably in accordance with the immensity of its love; the result being that by firmness of purpose, immensity of affection and an inextinguishable warmth of love all susceptibility to change or alteration was destroyed, and what formerly depended upon the will was by the influence of long custom changed into nature.

Here we have a very valuable and practical illustration of the method of spiritual evolution. First comes the will to good which, when persisted in, leads to habitual righteousness; but with the increase of the immensity of love for the Good, that which at first required an act of will becomes the very nature, the embodiment of the love that was loved. It is the susceptibility to change that must be overcome, for any change from single-minded attention to the Good must result in a descent of the soul—the fall of man, as described by the Mystery Religions. "So long as a soul continues to abide in the good it has no experience of unity with a body."

But of the descent that results from inattention to the Highest, he writes (Ch. 4:1):

> All rational creatures who are incorporal and invisible, if they become negligent, gradually sink to a lower level and take to themselves bodies suitable to the regions into which they descend; that is to say, first etherial bodies, and then aerial. And when they reach the neighbourhood of earth they are enclosed in grosser bodies, and last of all are tied to human flesh. . . . It is a mark of extreme negligence and sloth for any soul to descend and to lose its own nature so completely as to be bound, in consequence of its vices, to the gross body of one of the irrational animals.

Unlike the modern Catholic Church, however, Origen did not deny that animals have souls. On the contrary, since there was one Creator, all livings things possessed something of the deific Spirit. In Ch. 8:1, he writes:

> No one will doubt that all living creatures whatever, even those who live in water, have souls . . . for soul is defined thus, as an existence possessing imagination and desire . . . capable of feeling and movement. This may

be said of all living creatures, including those who live in water, and the same definition of soul may be shown to apply to birds also.

When a totalitarian Church discredited Origen's teachings, it rejected this humane and rational point of view, so vital a part of the Wisdom of the Goddess. Nevertheless, like Clement, Origen was far from consistent on this subject, and both must be accounted as in part responsible for the appallingly inhuman policy of the Church on the subject of the lesser creatures. Neither of them ever approached the matter from the point of view of compassion, and, what is worse, they refused to credit Pythagoras with this pure motive. Instead, they both indicated that his attitude was based entirely on the teaching of metempsychosis. Origen writes with the same ludicrous self-righteousness as Clement (*contra Celsum*, Book V :49):

> Notice the difference in the reason from the abstention from living things between the Pythagoreans and the ascetics amongst us. For they abstain from living things on account of the myth about the soul's reincarnation.... But if we are abstemious we do this because we bruise the body and bring it into subjection, and "want to mortify our members that are on earth, fornication, impurity, licentiousness, passion, evil desire"; and we do everything in our power to mortify the deeds of the body.*

It is interesting to discover that a fleshless diet was adopted by Christian ascetics in Origen's day, but owing to the wrong motive upon which it was based, it was never recognised as an essential part of the spiritual life. The habit therefore did not spread and persist, and has practically vanished from religious circles, surviving only in the curious and inadequate custom of slaughtering fish instead of animals on Friday.

Another point to be noted in the above citation is Origen's dismissal of the idea of reincarnation or transmigration as a myth, when it not only figured in his own philosophy but was the very teaching for which he and his works were to be anathematised in the sixth century. Why he should have assumed this attitude, as he does in several other passages of the *contra Celsum*, is difficult to understand. It is true that this book was written long after *First Principles*, and his opinion may have changed in the meantime; or the Church may have shown a disinclination for the theory. But in this case, why did he not have the references to this subject in the earlier book eliminated? For this age-old conception was no mere personal theory; it was a basic premise from which totally different conclusions as to life, humanity, God and the after-life must be drawn from those based on the idea of a creation in time. It may be that he was just toeing the

---

* *contra Celsum*, by Origen. Translated by Henry Chadwick. (Cambridge University Press.)

official party line of the moment, but this is unlikely as eschatological teaching had not at that time been finally crystallised into dogma, and great latitude was allowed for personal opinions of the theologians.

It may just possibly be that, as is often the case with people who have written extensively on metaphysical subjects, in writing so many books, he had said almost everything that there was to be said on the subject of religion, and had expressed a variety of ideas, some of which were incompatible with one another. In which case his worth as a philosopher must be diminished. But whatever the reason for his retraction on this vital point, the fact remains that, at their highest level, his works contained much of the Wisdom teaching.

The *contra Celsum* is supposed to be his literary masterpiece. It is certainly most valuable as an exposition of the Christian beliefs and practices of its time. It is Origen's reply to the objections made to Christianity by Celsus, a pagan who had died some years previously. In Book 1 : 14, 16, 24, he quotes Celsus as saying that "there is an ancient doctrine which has existed from the beginning, which has always been maintained by the wisest nations and cities, and wise men . . . that the Galactophagi of Homer, the Druids of the Gauls, and the Getae are very wise and ancient nations, who believe doctrines akin to those of the Jews. . . . He says that Linus, Musaeus, Orpheus, Pherecydes, Zoroaster the Persian, and Pythagoras understood these doctrines and their opinions are put down in books and are preserved to this day."

Later he speaks of a "certain mysterious Science that is related to the Creator of the universe". Both these allusions obviously refer to the universal Wisdom-religion.

In the *contra Celsum*, we are given positive evidence that, at least until Origen's time, the Christian Church remained firmly based on Jesus Christ's policy of non-violence and reverence for life. It was not only pacifist, but taught that it was wrong to take human life for any cause whatever. In answer to the charge made by Celsus that Christianity was merely the result of a revolt from the orthodox Jewish community, Origen writes:

> If a revolt had been the cause of Christians existing as a separate group (and they originated from the Jews for whom it was lawful to take up arms in defence of their families and to serve in the wars), the lawgiver of the Christians would not have forbidden entirely the taking of human life. He taught that it was never right for his disciples to go so far against a man even if he should be very wicked; for he did not consider it compatible with his inspired legislation to allow the taking of human life in any form at all. (Book III: 7, 8.)

On the subject of pacifism Origen is forthright:

> No longer do we take the sword against any nation, nor do we learn war any more, since we have become sons of peace through Jesus. (Book V:37.)

He then points out that when the laws of men conflict with the law of God, a man must live according to the latter even though the penalty is shame and death.

That the Christians were absolutely immoveable on this basic policy, which was one of the chief causes of the Romans' disapproval of them, is proved by the earnest plea made by Celsus at the end of the book to them to help the Emperor and to fight for him. To which Origen replies that they will help him in the only way open to them if they are to keep faith with their Legislator—by prayer, which seeks to eliminate the causes of wars, and by leading exemplary lives, and educating men to be devoted to God who guards the city.

It is equally certain from statements in the *contra Celsum* that spiritual healing among the Christians was still a common occurrence, known to, and admitted by the pagans. Not only does Origen say that Christians "charm demons away and perform many cures" (Book I:46), and that he has "seen many delivered from serious ailments and from mental distractions and madness, and countless other diseases which men had failed to cure" (Book III:24), but Celsus frequently refers to this power, ascribing it to magic (Book I:26).

To this charge Origen reasonably replies that "no sorcerer does his tricks to call the spectators to moral reformation . . . nor does he attempt to persuade the onlookers to live as men who will be judged by God. Sorcerers do none of these things, since they have neither the ability nor even the will to do so" (Book I:68); whereas "the name of Jesus still takes away mental distractions from men, and daemons and diseases as well, and implants a wonderful meekness and tranquility of character, and a kindness and gentleness. . . ". (Book I:67.) He uses the same convincing argument when Celsus suggests that Jesus was a magician:

> I do not know why a magician should have taken the trouble to teach a doctrine which persuades every man to do his every action as before God who judges each man for all his works, and to instil this conviction into his disciples whom he intended to use as the ministers of his teaching.

Origen clearly perceives that spiritual healing is inextricably interwoven with the preaching of the Gospel; and by his description of the method used to bring it about, it is obvious that it is the long-advocated healing by the Word, as well as by faith in Jesus. He writes of the Christians:

> Upon those who need healing they use no other invocation than that of the supreme God and of the name of Jesus together with the history about him.

Origen certainly realises that Jesus meant his miracles to be proofs of his Messiahship, for he writes (Book II:9): "Jesus showed himself among the Jews to be 'the power of God' by the miracles that he did." And in Book II:39, he says that the multitude believed on account of the works even when they could not understand his arguments. Admitting that the pagans also produced healings by means of oracles and divination, Origen explains that the superiority of the Christian method is that it reforms the morals of the people who are healed, which was not the case when healings were performed by oracles. This is substantial evidence that the Christians of his time were practising the true spiritual healing which always included the moral reformation of the patient, and was not merely a cure for the physical complaint.

Nevertheless, Origen seems to have felt, with the Essenes, that spiritual healing should only be practised by the initiate, the dedicated Christian, who is truly following the Master. In Book VIII:60 he writes:

> A man ought to use medical means to heal his body if he aims to live in the simple and ordinary way. If he wishes to live in a way superior to that of the multitude, he should do this by devotion to the supreme God and by praying to Him.

That chastity was still the ideal among Christians, though marriage was permitted, may be gathered from Book I:26, where Origen says of Christians that, "from the time that they accepted the word . . . some of them through a desire for a higher chastity and for purer worship of God do not even indulge in the sexual pleasures that are allowed by the law".

As we know, he was of this number; and that he was convinced that Jesus intended this ruling, and did not expect the present world with all its sufferings to be perpetuated, is implied by:

> Jesus . . . taught . . . that life in what is called "the present world" is a calamity, or the first and greatest struggle of the soul.

He believed that the practice of self-control proved, beyond all other things, man's superiority to the brute beasts and his relationship to God, the controlling Mind. In reply to Celsus' suggestion that men are mere worms in comparison with God, Origen asks (Book IV:26):

> Do we think that these people are the brothers of worms . . . who master the most violent desire for sexual pleasure, which has made the minds of

many soft and pliable as wax, and who master it for the reason that they have been persuaded that in no other way can they become intimate with God unless they ascend to Him by self-control?

A very illuminating passage on the meaning of the ascent and descent of the soul, as well as of the literal teaching that Jesus "came down" from, and ascended into heaven, is found in Book IV:12:

> Just as people commonly say that teachers come down to the level of children ... without meaning that they make a physical descent; so if anywhere in the divine Scriptures God is said to "come down", it is to be understood in a similar sense to that of the common usage. The same is also true of "going up".

Origen always makes it quite clear that God can only do what is compatible with His nature. He will not allow, as so many other Christian and Jewish theologians have done, that *anything* is possible to God. He can, as Plato believed and Jesus taught, only "act in character": "We say that God cannot do what is shameful, since then God could not possibly be God. For if God does anything shameful he is not God." (Book V:23.)

Like Clement, Origen realises that Truth is One and universal, and writes (Book VIII:12):

> None of us is so stupid as to suppose that before the date of Christ's manifestation the truth did not exist. Therefore we worship the Father of the Truth and the Son who is the Truth: they are two distinct existences, but one in mental unity, in agreement, and in identity of will.

How badly this definition was to be needed—although it was never quoted—in the arguments later brought forth at the Council of Nicaea as to the relationship of Father and Son, when, for lack of Greek lucidity, the theologians plunged Christendom into a welter of obscurities and a maze of tangled trinities.

From Book VIII:17 we must infer that, in the days of Origen, the Alexandrian Christians had no church edifices and were still worshipping either privately or in gatherings assembled in private houses, for there we find:

> Celsus says that we avoid setting up altars and of images and temples. . . . He does not notice that our altars are the mind of each righteous man.

It was evidently only from the time of the Church-building Constantine that the pagan habit of worshipping in temples built with hands started among the Christians, bringing with it all the perils and evils of material organisation; while the true worship of the Mystic at the altar of Mind, such as Jesus and his disciples practised, was abandoned.

Origen's teachings on prayer are particularly beautiful. For him as for Jesus and all mystics, prayer meant individual communion with God. He who prays aright "pays no attention to, nor does he desire, anything outside, but closes all doors of sensation so that he may not be drawn away by the senses, nor any sensory image come into his mind".*

He considered that prayer should be offered at least three times a day, facing East, in the direction of the rising sun, "an act which symbolises the soul looking towards where the true light shines". This is obviously a heritage from the solar religion, and is not at all the same concept as that which lay behind the injunction to "pray without ceasing", which signifies a constant mental communion with the Parent Mind. Nevertheless, parts of his spiritual interpretation of the Lord's Prayer are very illuminating.

Commenting on its first clause, "Our Father . . . " he reminds us that only the practising Christian, one who is indeed like the Son, can really offer up such a prayer, for God is only our Father inasmuch as we are like His image, or Son; those who are "reformed in the newness of their mind". He points out that the heaven referred to is by no means geographical, but is reached by the ascent of the mind, and he speaks of the "degrading notion" of believing God to be in heaven in a local sense. Citing "Thy kingdom come", he reminds us that the kingdom of God is within us, and that this prayer is for that kingdom to be established and perfected in our consciousness; so that he who prays "dwells within himself as in a well-ordered city", ruled over by the Mind of Christ. He adds:

> By the kingdom of God I believe is meant the happy enthronement of reason and the rule of wise counsels; and by the "kingdom of Christ" the saving words that reach those that hear, and the accomplished works of justice and the other virtues. (84.)

Yet the Catholic Church has continued for centuries to allow its humbler and more credulous congregations to believe that heaven is "above" in the spatial sense, in the sky where it was naturally located by the primitive worshippers of the hosts of heaven. And now that this pagan belief has been found by the disclosures of materialistic science to be without foundation, the faith of untold numbers of people has been undermined, and disillusioned mankind pathetically strives to reach heaven wherein its

* Origen; *Prayer; Exhortation to Martyrdom.* Translation and Introduction by John J. O'Meare. (Longmans, Green & Co.)

hopes were so long placed—via space-ship to the moon! Such mis-teaching has therefore betrayed not only the Creed of Christ but humanity itself. It stemmed, of course, from the dangerous and dishonest practice of Reserve, of which both Clement and Origen were guilty, that kept the Truth for the initiate and gave fables to the multitude.

Of "Thy will be done", Origen says that since Christ perfectly accomplished the will of God, we, by becoming one in spirit with him will also fulfil the will of God, since "he who is joined to the Lord, according to Paul, is one Spirit". (89, 90, 91.)

Man's citizenship in heaven is a matter of his dispositions, not of locality. As the will of God is done on earth, so earth will remain earth no longer, but be seen as heaven, for heaven is the inevitable result of the will of God being done.

"Give us this day our daily bread" was evidently, in Origen's day, rendered: "Give us this day our supersubstantial bread", which certainly better describes the meaning that must have been in the Mind of Christ, for he had warned his disciples not to pray for small, material things of this earth, but for great and heavenly things. They must "seek first the kingdom of God", and then all the lesser, necessary things would be added. "The bread that is given to our flesh is neither heavenly nor is the request for it a great request." (92) The true bread for which we must pray is the wisdom of God through which he who is nourished by it becomes the image of God:

> Just as material bread which is used for the body of him who is being nourished enters into his substance, so the living bread ... offered to the mind and the soul, gives a share of its own proper power to him who presents himself to be nourished by it. And so this will be the supersubstantial bread which we ask for. (98.)

This definition not only elucidates the meaning of the word bread as used in the Lord's Prayer, but shows clearly what was originally intended by the Bread of the Eucharist, which, as we know from the *Didache*, was regarded in just this sense when broken at the Christian Love-Feast, before Paul's confusion of it with martyred flesh and blood.

Unlike what afterwards came to be the policy of his Church, Origen taught, with his Master, that prayer must be addressed to the Father alone. It must be the pure communion of mind with Mind: "We may never pray to anything generated—not even to Christ but only to God and the Father of all." This idea was rejected by the other theologians, and prayers and hymns were, from quite early times, sung to Jesus, the last thing that he, as a monotheist, would have wished.

The discrediting of Origen and his teachings, containing, as they did, so much of the truth of the Wisdom religion and therefore of the original Gospel of Jesus Christ, did irreparable damage to the theology of the Church, since a departure from Truth obviously involves a descent to error. Owing to this lack of love of the Truth *per se*, and a complete absence of humility which led the theologians to reject everything in the pagan faith with which they were striving, even when it was patently true, Christendom was deprived of the eternal truth that alone could make it free.

The fact was that Origen, like his Master, was too spiritually-minded for the churchmen that came after him. His insistence that only the soul, Mind, or spiritual entity was immortal, and that there could be no re-surrection of the gross, material body after its disintegration, was what in particular enraged the carnal mentalities of Christian laymen and Church-men alike. They clung to the life they knew best—life lived in and for the body. Origen and the Neo-Platonists who lived so very much in and through the mind, understood its substantial nature, and realised, in consequence, the inferiority and transience of physical life.

Anathema XI of the Second Council of Constantinople ran:

(If anyone shall say) that the judgment to come signifies the complete destruction of bodies and that the end of the story is an immaterial exis-tence, and that nothing material will thereafter exist but only mind (let him be Anathema).

Anathema II reads:

(If anyone shall say that) the creation of all rational creatures consisted of minds bodiless and immaterial, without any number or name, so that they all formed a unity by reason of the identity of their essence and power and energy and by their union with and knowledge of God, the Word; but that they were seized by weariness of the divine law and contemplation, and changed for the worse . . . and that they took bodies either fine in substance or grosser . . . (let him be Anathema.)

Both of these doctrines were, of course, what Origen and, before him, Pythagoras and Plato had taught, and what the Neo-Platonists after him were to teach, since they were the basis of the Wisdom Religion that had existed from the beginning of recorded time, and seems to have come to the human race as a recollection from some previous and higher mode of life. Indeed, there appears to be no more convincing explanation than this to account for its existence in the primitive times to which it is traceable. We owe it to Origen that it was explicitly taught in the early days of the Christian Church, which abandoned it at the cost of its soul.

The last teaching of Origen to have been printed to date is such a beautiful statement as to the true nature of man that it must be quoted as his final benediction. Found in a cave in Tura, near Cairo, in August 1941, that the British Army was using as an ammunition store, it was among a small library of books. It was written on papyrus apparently in the sixth century, probably after Justinian's decree promulgated by the Church Council at Constantinople had proscribed Origen's works, making it necessary to conceal them. It is contained in the *Dialogue with Heraclides*, and reads:

> At the creation of man . . . there was first created the man that is "after the image", in whom there was nothing material. He who is in the image is not made out of matter (Genesis 1:26,27). . . . That that which is in the image of God is understood as immaterial and superior to all corporeal existence not only by Moses but also by the Apostle is shown by his words (Colossians 3:9).*

It is to this concept of Being, according to the Wisdom of the Goddess, that it is the destiny of man to return.

---

* *Dialogue of Origen with Heraclides and the Bishops with Him.* Alexandrian Christianity. J. E. L. Oulton and Henry Chadwick. (SCM Press Ltd.)

CHAPTER XII

The Wise Woman and the Pagan Messiah

While the Christian theologians, with an eye to a Universal Church, were busily hammering out a colossal doctrinal edifice containing elements of primitive Judaism, Pauline Christianity, paganism, and the original Gospel of Jesus Christ, which could be synchronised only when, and as, they reached the heights of the Wisdom Religion, but, on lower levels, as Celsus said of Philo's allegorisations, could not "by any means be made to fit", their rivals, the pagans, stirred by such industry, were working just as busily, and far more logically, on what they hoped would provide the spiritual basis for a universal religion, transcending, yet including, all lesser Faiths at their summit.

One of the most enthusiastic of these learned eclectics was that highly intellectual woman, the Empress Julia Domna. Wife of the Roman Emperor, Lucius Septimus Severus, and mother of Geta and Caracalla, Gibbon writes of her that "she possessed, even in advanced age, the attractions of beauty, and united to a lively imagination, a firmness of mind and strength of judgement seldom bestowed on her sex. . . . Julia applied herself to letters and philosophy . . . she was patroness of every art, and the friend of every man of genius". And it was in this capacity that she was able to commission Philostratus of Lemnos, a famous sophist and Pythagorean, to write an account of the life of Apollonius Thyanaeus, of whom Eunapius, writing in the fourth and fifth centuries, says:

> Apollonius of Tyana was a philosopher indeed, but more than a philosopher being somewhat between the gods and man; for following the philosophy of Pythagoras, he raised the reputation of it as truly divine and excellent. Philostratus of Lemnos has written his history in several books, calling his work *The Life of Apollonius* which might have been more properly entitled *The Peregrination of God Among Men.*

It is quite obvious that the much debated Eclogue IV of Virgil, written 40 B.C., which Constantine the Great, among many other overzealous Christians, insisted was a prophecy of the advent of Jesus Christ, referred instead to this great Teacher of the first century. The reference to the Golden Age which was a specifically Pythagorean teaching, should have been sufficient proof of that, but, in addition, there is actually the name of Apollo, and its derivative "Pollio", so that there was no excuse at all for the obtuseness of Constantine whose sole concern seems to have been to relate everything appertaining to the old religion to the new God in order to strengthen the State by the power of the Church, with utter disregard for Truth.

The passage relating to the divine child's advent runs:

> Only do thou
> Smile, chaste Lucina, on the infant boy,
> With whom the iron age will pass away,
> The Golden Age in all the earth be born;
> For thine Apollo reigns. Under thy rule,
> Thine Pollio, shall this glorious era spring . . .
> Under thy rule all footprints of our guilt
> Shall perish, and the peaceful earth be freed
> From everlasting fear. Thou, Child, shall know
> The life of Gods . . . and be seen by them,
> And rule a world by righteous father tamed.*

And this prophecy might well have come about if the Pythagorean-Essenic philosophy of Apollonius, which was also the basic philosophy of the original Gospel of Jesus Christ, had not been finally defeated and abandoned in the fourth century.

This great teacher of the first century who lived at the time when the Emperor Domitian was persecuting the philosophers, fearing that their other-world theories would distract the Romans from the all-important physical culture and militarism so necessary for empire-building, might have been entirely overlooked by posterity had not his companion and disciple, Damis, a native of Nineveh, who had attended Apollonius in his extensive travels in Europe, Asia and Africa, written down his deeds, sayings and prophecies. These, in manuscript form, nearly 200 years later came into the possession of Julia Domna, who, quickly perceiving their propaganda value in the current ideological struggle with the new Faith, decided that they must at once be given to the world, and so employed Philostratus to compile them into a history.

Julia Domna was no bigot, and did not let her own preference for the pagan religion prejudice her against Christianity. Pagans and Christians worked together in her household, and she was well acquainted with the beliefs embodied in the new Faith, as well as with the history of Jesus. It seems highly probable that a woman of her intelligence, comparing the latter with the theological teachings of the Church that was so dangerously rivalling her own more ancient Faith, would have realised that something had gone badly wrong with Christianity since the days when its Founder had walked the earth.

* *The Eclogues and Georgics of Virgil*, translated into English verse by T. F. Royds, M.A. (J. M. Dent & Sons Ltd.).

Her knowledge of the Mysteries would have led her to the conclusion that Jesus had been "brought to perfection"; that he was, in fact, a perfected man. This would have been evident to her from the healings that had resulted from his Word, as they had done from the teachings of Apollonius. But clearly there was much that, to a devotee of Wisdom, was not perfect in the current teachings of the new Faith that was challenging her own. It was, therefore, imperative that a way of life that both she and the Goddess would consider perfect, should be brought to the attention of mankind, when perhaps the imperfections of the Christian ideal—as it was represented in her time, owing to the tampering of the theologians—would be exposed.

We know that in her day, the rivalry between the old Faith and the new was at its keenest, and the challenge of the new had led the champions of the old to rise to the highest possible conception of the worship of the hosts of heaven. *The Life of Apollonius*, by Philostratus, depicting the Perfect Man of the Pythagoreans, was soon to be followed by the *Enneads* of Plotinus, containing the most exalted spiritual teachings that the world had ever been given.

However, it was not as a rival of Jesus that Apollonius was represented, but as a disciple of Pythagoras who had exceeded his Master in the demonstration of their mutual principles; and, being a Pythagorean himself, Philostratus was well equipped for interpreting the mind of his subject. In the Bampton Lectures 1886, Dr Biggs writes of Julia Domna that she,

> Was deeply interested in the Syrian worship of the Sun, to which her family owed its consequence, and she presided over a coterie of lawyers and men of letters, which was ardent in the defence of Paganism. To a lady so learned . . . the settlement of ecclesiastical disputes . . . seemed an easy task. Let Paganism be set forth at its best . . . and then the reformed Judaism would be compelled to renounce its exclusive pretensions, and fall at once into its proper place in the imperial pantheon. The necessary ideas were already current in the imperial saloons. What was wanting was a Messiah, some personage, not too ancient, not too modern, who would inspire the system with the needful human interest and vitality. Such a figure was to be found in Apollonius, a sage. . . . *

It was therefore of this figure that Philostratus was asked to write. In his *Life of Apollonius*, he says:

> They who admire Pythagoras of Samos say of him that he wore no clothing taken from animals, and that he forbore the use of animals in food

---

* *Christian Platonists of Alexandria*, being the Bampton Lectures of the year 1886 by the late Charles Biggs, D.D. (Oxford, 1913.)

and sacrifice, offering up only cakes with honey, and frankincense and hymns. And they say that he conversed with the gods, and from themselves knew what things were most acceptable to them and what were displeasing. And many other things are said of him by those who philosophize after the institution of Pythagoras which I must forbear to relate. . . . For Apollonius, who lived not very long ago nor yet very lately, attempted the like things in a more perfect manner than Pythagoras.

Philostratus tells us that the birth of Apollonius was announced to his mother by Proteus, the holy ghost of Platonism. And when she asked, "What is it that I shall bring forth?" she was told by God, "Myself".

At sixteen, having been made acquainted with the Pythagorean way of life, he was led by higher powers to adopt it. In obedience to the compassionate Wisdom of the Goddess, he wore linen garments, practised the strictest abstinence from animal food, and observed the five years' silence imposed on his followers by Pythagoras. He allowed his hair to grow long, and wore nothing on his feet (sandals being made of leather). He was said to be radiantly beautiful. Biggs writes, quoting the *Life:* "He dwelt in temples, especially those of Aesculapius, the Healer, like a child in his Father's house."

Although apparently a natural healer, he seems to have gained many of his psychic powers from the Brahmins under whom he studied in India before returning "to be the saviour of the Hellenic world", where he healed the sick and raised the dead.

Eusebius tells us that Hierocles, in his work *Philalethes*, or *Lover of Truth*, wrote:

> They are continually crying up Jesus for opening the eyes of the blind, and other like works. . . . In the reign of Nero flourished Apollonius of Tyana, who having when very young sacrificed at Aegis in Cilicia to that good God Aesculapius, wrought many wonderful works.

From the Arabians, among whom the ability was common, Apollonius learnt to understand the language of birds and beasts. And when Damis, who was going with him on his travels, suggested that, knowing foreign tongues, he might be useful to his Master as an interpreter of the speech of the barbarians, Apollonius told him: "I understand them all though I have learnt none of them. . . . Do not wonder in that I know all the languages of men: for I know their secret thoughts."

His goodness and his power aroused the wrath of the heathen priests. As a Pythagorean, he naturally refused to be present at their bloody sacrificial rites, and, instead, sprinkled incense on the altar of the Sun. As in the cases of the Buddha and Jesus Christ, compassion was the keynote of his life, and he preached against the cruelties of the amphitheatre; always and everywhere evincing loving kindness both to man and beast.

Hearing that the Emperor Domitian, was persecuting the philosophers, he decided to offer himself as a voluntary sacrifice to appease his rage, in spite of all his disciples could do to dissuade him. In Rome, he was imprisoned and chained, his captors mocking him and telling him to work a miracle and save himself. Brought to the tribunal of the Emperor, he vanished from sight, appearing later in the day to Damis and another disciple at Puleoli, where they were sorrowing for his loss. Only the grasp of his hand could convince Damis that this was his beloved Master.

Like Jesus, he demonstrated his at-one-ment with all-knowing Mind. At the moment when Domitian was being stabbed in Rome, Apollonius was preaching at Ephesus, but broke off suddenly to describe the incident being enacted in the capital of the empire. He was accredited with many magical works, and was courted by kings and princes. He had his circle of disciples, and he drew the common people to him by his constant beneficence and healing works.

Of his death nothing is known. Philostratus suggests that he was translated after being imprisoned in the temple of Dictynna by the priests. At midnight, he tells us, Apollonius arose in full view of his gaoler, the chains having fallen from him, and, as the gate swung open, angels were heard to sing, "Away from earth to heaven, away." After which he was lost to human sight, although he reappeared once to a disciple who was mourning for him, to reassure him as to man's immortality.

Apollonius was, in fact, the Perfected Man of the pagans. He had evolved to "somewhere between the gods and man", and was regarded by the heathen as they regarded Pythagoras and Socrates, as a Son of God. And although his history falls considerably short of the magnificent and convincing exposition of the life of the Perfect Man, and his Gospel of the kingdom of God that we find in the New Testament, it was of great significance and value in that it stressed what was being largely ignored at that date by the Church Fathers—the practical compassion so essential to the nature of a Perfect Man. It also recalled attention to the importance of spiritual healing which had almost departed from among the Christians by the time of Severus.

If the theologians of the Early Church had had the humility to appreciate the significance of the humane way of life advocated by Apollonius, they would have placed greater emphasis on the need for compassion in diet and apparel as well as in politics among their own ranks. As it was, they refused to learn anything from the revived Wisdom-teachings, and, instead, did their utmost to discredit Apollonius, and all those who had anything to do with the writings of his *Life*.

Unable to deny that he had lived, they called him a charlatan, and attributed his obvious psychic gifts, so like those of their own Master, to magic. In fact, they used the same arguments against his works and life as the pagans, such as Celsus, had used against the works and life of Jesus. It was all part of the deadly struggle for power between the two religious systems. Instead of focusing on the undoubted likeness that existed between the teachings of the two Masters and their ways of life, they concentrated on the superficial differences.

Nevertheless, *The Life of Apollonius* seems to have been written not only as a reply to the challenge of the Christian's Perfected Man, but also as an attempt to clean up the ancient Faith which still indulged in the blood-sacrifices forbidden by the Goddess and her prophet, insensitivity to the suffering of sentient creatures, and flesh-eating. Over a hundred years after the death of Philostratus, the Emperor Julianus was gleefully sacrificing hecatombs of oxen to the warrior-god, Mithras.

The exoteric religion of the pagans needed as much purification as exoteric Christianity, and *The Life of Apollonius* might have effected this cleansing had the priesthood and theologians been prepared to receive the higher ethic. Julia Domna was obviously well aware of what was lacking in both religions, and evidently hoped that Philostratus' portrait of yet another Perfected Man would awaken mankind to the overwhelming need for non-violence and compassion in religion and in the nature of man.

But the habit of animal sacrifice was too firmly entrenched in the pagan religion to be dislodged. It was a vested interest bringing in enormous revenues to the temples, and had ever been a privilege of the priests to which they tenaciously clung. Also, the belief in the efficacy of divination by means of studying the entrails and liver of the sacrificed beasts was one of the oldest and most universal in the ancient world.

In Porphyry's *Abstinence from Animals*, an opponent of Pythagoreanism argues that "if animals are not killed, we shall be deprived of the benefits of divination, which depends upon searching their entrails"; to which Porphyry reasonably replies that a philosopher—and, according to the Pythagoreans, *all* men should be philosophers—"abstracted from the world, seldom has occasion to go to daemons or priests, and diviners, and the entrails of animals. He rarely wants advice about marriage, a lost servant, commerce; and as for things of religion, he consults his own breast, and goes to God dwelling in him. Concerning such things as he is most desirous to know, no certain information can be had from diviners and the entrails of animals".

But despite all the truth of his argument Porphyry was not able to move the orthodox religionists of his day; and the Christian congregations were equally unteachable. Although they had condemned the practice of animal sacrifice, and the Jews had been forced to abandon it after the final razing of their Temple, both clung obstinately to the flesh diet insisted upon by the Jewish priests.

Their complete inability to understand the compassionate Pythagorean viewpoint, and their utter insensitivity to the suffering involved by carnivorous habits, is illustrated in the story told by Eusebius, of Alcibiades, one of the Christian martyrs, who led a very abstemious life on bread and water, "and still observing the same course of life in prison, it was revealed to Attalus, after his first combat in the amphitheatre, that Alcibiades did not do well in not using the creatures of God, and was an occasion of scandal to others (1 Timothy 4:4); and Alcibiades submitted, and after that partook of all sorts of food promiscuously, and gave God thanks".

This is an example of how ecclesiastical teaching has kept humanity from evolving to a more harmless species. By entirely ignoring the necessity for compassion, and quoting certain discreditable utterances ascribed to Jehovah in the Old Testament, it has been possible to argue that flesh-eating is morally right and according to the will of God.

In Julia Domna's day, there were four religious concepts competing for acceptance by the civilised world: the ancient pagan Faith of Greeks and Romans; church-Christianity; Judaism, and the Wisdom Religion as enshrined in the philosophy of Pythagoras, Plato and the Neo-Platonists. Of the four, the last was nearest to the spirit of the, by then, largely lost creed of compassion that was the original Gospel of Jesus Christ. In its humaneness, loving-kindness, pure spirituality, and kinship with the philosophy of the Essenes, Neo-Platonism was far closer to the teaching of Jesus than the confused and complicated theology of the so-called Christian Church, a fact that must have become apparent to the clear-sighted when only a few years after the publication of *The Life of Apollonius*, Plotinus produced his *Enneads*.

Of their author, the late W. R. Inge, probably the most enlightened and perceptive churchman of the twentieth century, wrote in his book, *The Philosophy of Plotinus*:

> It is to Plotinus more than to any other thinker that we owe a definite doctrine of spiritual experience.

After the age-old revolt against the Queen of Heaven and her wisdom, an eminent modern scholar and priest comes to the conclusion that the teachings of Plotinus, or the philosophy of the Wisdom-Religion, constitutes the one definite doctrine of spiritual existence, the living of which should be the chief preoccupation of every true religionist.

It was, then, by means of Plotinus whose teachings have survived, rather than by Philostratus whose history of Apollonius has been neglected or forgotten, that the ambition of the wise woman, Julia Domna, was eventually fulfilled. Nevertheless, the part she played in the writing and publication of a book which was to remind the world of the high ethics of the age-old Wisdom teachings, was probably her greatest achievement. For her personal history was tragic, despite her marriage which had raised her to royal rank. As Gibbon writes of her last days:

> The Empress Julia had experienced all the vicissitudes of fortune. She had been raised to greatness only to taste the superior bitterness of an exalted rank. She was doomed to weep over the death of one of her sons, and over the life of the other.

But her name endures since it must be forever linked with the publication of *The Life of Apollonius*—the pagan Messiah.

CHAPTER XIII

The Summit

The teachings of Plotinus were the philosophy of the Wisdom Religion more fully and perfectly expressed than it had ever been before, even by Plato who was a philosopher but not a mystic, whereas Plotinus was both.

In his book *Origen and Greek Patristic Theology*, W. Fairweather writes of Neo-Platonism, of which Plotinus was the most famous exponent, that "at the commencement of the fourth century it became the prevailing philosophy in Christian as well as in pagan circles".* As well it might, for in fact it provided a meeting-ground for both Faiths "at the summit". As Fairweather says, "It took for its religious ideal the direct apprehension of the divine essence." In other words, it was the religion, or spiritual life, of the true mystic, and as such could appeal to men of all Faiths. "The Neo-Platonist", he continues, "contemplated nothing less than the introduction of a universal religion, constructed on principles so broad that the wise of all the earth could adhere to it." Combined with the teachings of the New Testament and their practical application, it could, in fact, have provided a firm basis for the spiritual unification of mankind. During his period of enthusiasm for Neo-Platonism, Augustine wrote:

> The message of Plato, the purest and most luminous in all philosophy, has at last scattered the darkness of error, and now shines forth mainly in Plotinus, a Platonist so like his Master that one would think they had lived together, or rather since so long a period of time separates them— that Plato was born again in Plotinus.

Plotinus made no secret of the source of his inspiration. Of his metaphysical system he wrote:

> These teachings are . . . no novelties, no inventions of today, but long since stated, if not stressed; our doctrine here is an explanation of an earlier, and can show the antiquity of these opinions on the testimony of Plato himself.

Born at Lycopolis in Egypt, and for many years a pupil of Ammonius, Plotinus (A.D. 205–270), is, without doubt, the clearest exponent of what is usually referred to in the present age as the Perennial Philosophy, that

---

* *Origen and Greek Patristic Theology*, by the Rev. W. Fairweather, M.A. (T. & T. Clark Edinburgh, 1901.)

the Western world has ever known. The Founders of the major world-faiths have all given their individual interpretations of the same universal truth, but Plotinus rescued the essence of their teachings from the accretions of myth, superstition and dogma which, in the case of every exoteric religion, have succeeded in perverting, materialising, and, in some cases, completely reversing the original Gospel, thus preventing it from performing its work of saving mankind from spiritual ignorance. His comprehensive knowledge of the age-old Wisdom religions of East and West enabled him to separate the metaphysical wheat from the tares of debased theology, and to arrive at the central truth of all the great religious systems. It seems, therefore advisable to consider his philosophy in some detail since it is at once a climax to, and recapitulation of all that has gone before in this book.

His viewpoint, based squarely on the spiritual hypothesis, is the direct antithesis of the prevailing spirit of the present age, the spirit of materialistic science that has brought humanity to the verge of self-destruction.

In the sixth Ennead (*On the Good or the One*), he writes:

> Those to whom existence comes about by chance and automatic action and is held together by material forces have drifted far from God and from the concept of unity; we are not here addressing them but only such as accept another nature than body and have some conception of soul.*

Indeed, his view and experience of life completely contradict the view of life upon which the modern world is built; and for those of us who deplore the present world-pattern, they not only offer the reverse hypothesis but the reverse effect. Therefore Plotinus shows us the way of salvation from the almost total materialism in which mankind is immersed. But although this perennial philosophy is opposed to all materialism, it is by no means opposed to pure science; for pure science is pure knowledge which is The Good of all true philosophers, which explains the fact that many of our best physicists have already begun to come into line with the central truth embodied in the *Philosophia Perennis*.

Plotinus, for instance, describes "the summit of our being as Divine Mind, which he calls Authentic Existence, outside of which nothing has any permanence, or, finally, reality. This universal, metaphysical hypothesis—the Ahura Mazda, or Good Mind, of Zoroastrianism, the Pure Consciousness of Vedanta, the Divine Mind of the Sufis of Islam—is now being advanced by such notable scientists as Sir James Jeans who wrote in *The Mysterious Universe:* "The universe can best be pictured as consisting of pure thought . . . its creation must have been an act of

---

* *Plotinus: The Enneads*, translation by Stephen MacKenna. (Faber & Faber.)

thought"; and Professor Eddington who observed in *The Nature of the Physical World*, "the stuff of the world is mind-stuff"; curiously using a phrase long known in the East. Patanjali, the father of Indian Yoga philosophy, and one of the earliest teachers of the theory of evolution, according to Swami Prabhavananda in *Vedanta for the West*, defined Yoga as the means of "restraining the mind-stuff (Chitta) from taking forms". And Sir J. Arthur Thompson once remarked that "after a long circuit there is a return to the old truth; in the beginning was Mind".

It is with the nature of this mind, and its relation to man, that the greatest religionists and philosophers of all times have been concerned, and the result of their separate researches has seldom been put more clearly and concisely than in the *First Ennead* (1st Tractate), where we find:

> This (Divine Mind) we possess as the summit of our being. And we have it either as common to all or as our own immediate possession: or again we may possess It in both degrees, that is in common, since it is individiable—one, everywhere and always its entire self—and severally in that each personality possesses It entire in the First-Soul (i.e. in the Intellectual as distinct from the lower phase of the Soul).

For Plotinus, the Intellectual Principle, or Divine Mind, is the summit of being, that to which all existing things are bound, and to which, in its fulness, they aspire. But beyond even this is The Good, which is so far above what is commonly meant by that term, so far beyond finite description, that it cannot be defined in words, and can only be experienced by those who, reaching the summit, the highest phase of the Intellectual Principle, are fit to be at-one with the Ultimate Good.

In the symbology of the Persian religion and the Jewish Kabbalah, Plotinus pictures all things as emanations from the Highest; most real in their primal and ultimate connection with The Good, less and less real as they draw further away from Authentic Existence, even as sun-rays gradually lose their heat in their earthward descent.

The First Soul, the enduring reality in a man, gains its immortality and retains its hold on The Good by the connection of its highest nature with the lower reach of the Intellectual Principle, which, in turn, on its higher level, continually contemplates The Good. Hence the existence of what we call "conscience", which, unless it has been corrupted, has always before it the perfect pattern. The lower reach of the soul, enchanted by a sort of hypnotic spell, or dream state, is apt to become involved with the things of matter and nature, which Plotinus describes as the antithesis of Authentic Being, and therefore as Non-Being. When this happens, the Soul must turn upon itself, away from this unreality, and retrace its footsteps, putting off all that is alien to the nature of Soul, that which has accrued to it in the course of its descent earthward.

The Soul, being infinite, its "fall" is explained as being the result of its reaching the outer periphery of the emanations of The Good, and being deluded as by a sort of bewitchment or spell into believing that the dark Non-Being of matter beyond this periphery is real, when, in fact, it is her own illumination of it that makes it appear to be real. The Soul's return to the Source of its being is, as we know, a feature of every religion, while the re-ascent to the Highest is the process of evolution advocated as the way of salvation by the greatest Teachers of all the creeds.

Plotinus teaches that the method of salvation, or ascent, is by the persistent contemplation of The Good, allowing no distraction to turn the gaze downward and so back to the illusion from which the Soul must escape. Possibly the story of Lot's wife was a crude allegory of the same idea. For the Soul cannot be aware of anything better than that which it persistently contemplates. Therefore if a man wishes to be free from the evils that beset human life, he must fix his gaze on that which is higher than this life. "We must ascend", says Plotinus, "again towards the Good, the desired of every Soul . . . to attain it is for those who will take the upward path, who will set all their faces towards it, who will divest themselves of all that we have put on in our descent."*

The earthly blemishes, mortal failings and passions are not, according to Plotinus, a part of the Soul, which, owing to her inner hold on the Good, remains perfect despite appearances; but they besmirch her like mud clinging to a man which, while it is no part of him, must be removed before he can be seen for what he really is. The true ascent of the Soul is this inward purification, the putting off of all unlike the Good, until it is seen in its original state—the emanation and likeness of the Good. To achieve this, the persistent contemplation of the Good is all-essential, since, as Plotinus tells us of the nature of the Soul, "in all its memory, the thing it has in mind, it is and grows to".

It was after contemplating and communing with the Father unceasingly that Jesus declared (John 16:28): "I came forth from the Father, and come into the world: again, I leave the world, and go to the Father." He spoke with the certainty of one who had maintained his conscious hold on the Good, despite the pressing illusions of physical life; and with betrayal and crucifixion threatening his human and temporal entity, he could say of his essential, untouchable being: "I and my Father are one."

---

* This is the explanation of the emergence from the Cave, entirely naked, of the Mithraic initiate, so adversely commented upon by Christian critics.

The Good, the Source, the Father of all, was most certainly to Jesus, as later it was to Plotinus, the one enduring Reality.

Writing of the Soul's present attainment in its process of re-ascent, Plotinus observes in the *Third Ennead:*

> Humanity is poised mid-way between gods and beasts and inclines now to the one order, now to the other; some men grow like to the divine, others to the brute, the greatest number stand neutral. . . When the life-principle leaves the body it is what it is, what it most intensely lived. . . . Those that have maintained the human level are men once more. Those that have lived wholly to sense become animals. . . . Those who in their pleasures . . . have gone their way in torpid grossness become mere growing things, for only or mainly, the vegetative principle was active in them, and such men have been busy be-treeing themselves.

The Soul of man determines its fate by that to which it gives its attention. "Everything that looks to another is under spell to that: what we look to draws us magically." As there is a sorcery, or magnetism, that draws the lower soul to matter as soon as its attention is given to the world of nature, the realm of process, so there is an eternal and far stronger spiritual magnetism of the Good which draws, as a Christian mystic has said, with cords of affinity, drawing that in the Soul which is like to It.

As all things turn to the sun, their physical source, so "where there is life the longing for Good sets up in pursuit".

The longing for the Good is, in fact, the longing for the real life, Authentic Existence, as distinct from the delusive, transient life of sense-perception: "All that exists desires and aspires towards the supreme by a compulsion of nature, as if all had received the oracle that without it they cannot be."

The eternal oneness of being is maintained consistently by Plotinus. All real life—Authentic Existence—being included in the Good, even the apparent multiplicity of souls is found, in the last analysis, to be merely different though individual aspects of one undivided Soul, or Mind, even as a sunbeam shining upon the sea is apparently, but not actually, broken into a thousand sparkling sequins.

> The souls are apart without partition, present each to all as never having been set in opposition; they are no more hedged off by boundaries than are the multiple items of knowledge in one mind; the one Soul so exists as to include all souls.

It is this concept of oneness, the unity of being, that constitutes the unbridgeable gulf between the Wisdom teachings and the exoteric religions that teach of divisable and separated souls created in time. The former concept produces a sense of kinship with all life, the latter a sense of separateness resulting in sectarianism and such evils as "holy wars". The former postulates an unchangingly good God, and an eternal life to which all forms of consciousness are, in essence, united; the latter involves the belief in an external God, the maker of a diversity of souls that may be saved or damned, elect or cast out; while sub-human creatures are believed either to have no souls, or souls of a totally different sort. According to this view, there is no fundamental and inseverable link between the Source of life and its manifestations. It is not, therefore, true religion since it neither binds man irrevocably to God, nor man to man. Nor can it give any assurance of immortality since eternal life can obviously only be achieved through oneness with the Eternal. In orthodox religion, the relationship with the Father is not like that of a ray to the sun, an unbreakable union as taught by the Wisdom religion, but an uncertain, capricious connection, since the soul consigned to hell cannot still retain its hold on the Father Mind. Nor is the idea of brotherhood sufficient to establish unity among men, for we know the disunity that can exist between sons of the same family. Only the realisation of essential spiritual oneness can induce the integrated love of God called for by Jesus and the pagan Plotinus alike, and which alone can preserve a conscious and unalterable sense of unity with one's fellow men.

For Plotinus, as for Jesus, Authentic Being is eternal perfection. Everything that is real has its source or roots in this perfection. But how do we know what is real? Everything is real inasmuch as it seeks the Good, since "nothing absolutely void of the Good would ever go seeking the Good". Like calls to like, and the good is inevitably drawn to the Good as steel to a magnet. And that which is good is eternal, for "nothing from the realm of real being shall pass away".

All that ever dies is false accretion, illusion, that which is unlike the Good. Yet it cannot be said to die since, in truth, it never had any being. Plotinus describes matter, which, like the Eastern seers, he considers to be the root of all evil, as complete non-being. "What appears in matter is not Reality." Matter is what seems to be and is not. Having described Authentic Existence as the Good, he deals with its antithesis in the following words:

> Matter is not Soul; it is not Intellect, is not Life, is no Ideal Principle, no Reason-Principle; it is no limit or bound, for it is mere indetermination; it is not a power, for what does it produce? It lives on the farther side of all these categories and so has no title to the name of Being. It will more plausibly be called a non-being, and this not in the sense that movement

and station are Not-Being (i.e. as merely different from Being) but in the sense of veritable Non-Being, so that it is no more than the image and phantasm of Mass, a bare aspiration towards substantial existence ... a phantasm unabiding and yet unable to withdraw—not even strong enough to withdraw, so utterly has it failed to accept strength from the Intellectual-Principle, so absolute its lack of all Being.

In complete contradiction to the modern hypothesis, Mind and Spirit are, for Plotinus, Reality, and matter finally nothingness. He defines Soul as the infinite emanation of the Good reaching out in its infinity even to Non-Being which acts as a "check to the forthwelling of Authentic Existence", and as a repellent to emanation, sending it back, as it were, on an upward course, or the re-ascent that, to the senses, appears as spiritual evolution.

All that impinges upon this Non-Being is flung back as from a repelling substance; we may think of an echo returned from a repercussive plane surface; it is precisely because of the lack of retention that the phenomenon is supposed to belong to that particular place and even to arise there.

Thus we have the illusion of everything arising and evolving from matter; whereas the truth is that what appears so to rise and evolve is that which has been repelled—the Soul-substance, or Reality. And the return of that intact Substance to its source is what we describe as the evolution of consciousness, which Plotinus sees as a casting off of the illusory accretions collected during the descent, and a gradual realisation of that which already IS.

Spirit and goodness, he teaches, are native and real to the Soul; matter is alien to Authentic Being, "its actuality is that of being a phantasm, the actuality of being a falsity; and the false in actualisation is the veritably false, which again is Authentic Non-existence". Therefore, physical life is an evil, a state of falsity or illusion, which may only be overcome by ceasing to have mental and emotional commerce with it. Only so can man escape from the Realm of Process to the Realm of Authentic Being.

Spiritual man, made in the image and likeness of the Good, remains essentially himself: "Man exists from eternity and must therefore be complete." Any other belief about man is an illusion or falsity that must be dispelled by higher knowledge. Man as co-existent with God is the basic teaching of the Wisdom religion, and contradicts all theories concerning a creation in time.

The body, Plotinus teaches, is not wholly material. It is matter illumined by Soul. Only by this contact with Soul can Non-Being appear to have life. But such illumination involves the lower soul's concern with the

unreal, and its sufferings result from identifying itself with what it sees—
the antithesis of the Authentic Being that it loves, and which alone can
give it peace and bliss. It is then that "you must turn appearances about
or you will be left void of God".

Turning appearances about involves reversing the evidence of the
senses, turning the attention in the opposite direction, and beginning the
re-ascent in which everything immediately above constitutes the good
until, having become at-one with it, the Soul perceives still a higher good,
and, attaining that, yet a higher. But always it is the Good that is the Soul's
inmost desire, and nothing less will satisfy. Even the love of Life and Mind
is called forth by something higher than both.

> The intense love called forth by Life and the Intellectual-Principle, is due
> not to what they are but to their receiving from above something quite
> apart from their nature.

Yet though we talk of aspiration and re-ascent, we are attempting thereby to describe spiritual facts in material terms, which is always misleading.
In truth the God we seek is already within, and must be not reached but
realised within consciousness. As we separate ourselves from the Alien,
from all that is material, and concern ourselves wholly with what is
native to us, the spiritual, we achieve the harmony which is the goal of
life, "the least alloyed and nearest to the Good are most at peace within
themselves".

In one of his best-known passages (*On the Good or the One*), Plotinus
likens the situation to a choir singing about a conductor. So long as they
keep their faces turned to the director of their singing, there will be harmony. Looking away produces discord.

Spiritual living, when the Soul is filled with God, is the only true life.
The life lived with, and for, the things of the earth, in the service of the
perishable, Plotinus describes beautifully as a sinking, a defeat, "a
failing of the wing".

The Good is the Soul's veritable love. Nothing less than complete
unity with the Beloved will satisfy her. All earthly loves produce a sense
of shame because they are the result of a fall from the Highest. They
bring no enduring happiness since they are perishable, and so productive
of sorrow. From them the disillusioned turn to their real love, and do not
cease in their quest until they have found what they seek.

> We must put aside all else and rest in This alone . . . all the earthly environ-
> ment done away, in haste to be free, impatient of any bond holding us to
> the baser, so that with our being entire we may cling about This, no part
> in us remaining but through it we have touch with God.

While all this sounds transcendental and unrelated to life as it is lived by human beings in the present age, it is, in fact, the most practical means of producing the sort of man that is necessary if the world is ever to be a happier and better place than it is today. When the late Professor Einstein, who may be presumed to have known the potentialities of materialistic science for ensuring an improved way of life, was asked: "What can we do to get a better world?" he made the classic reply, "You have to have better people." And this is precisely what Plotinus' system aims to produce.

Self-perfectioning by the contemplation of the Good is not the unrealistic, time-wasting method that the materialists would have us believe it is, for the effect of integrated contemplation is assimilation. As the Soul gazes, so she becomes one with that which she perceives and adores.

Such contemplation of the Good is no easy task. It involves a steadfast rejection of distractions, and an intelligent apprehension and assimilation of all the attributes and qualities that we conceive of as appertaining to the Good. As an instance, by his continual contemplation of the Good as the Spirit of compassionate Love and spiritual power, Jesus became the embodiment of these attributes. So identified was he with That which he worshipped that he could truthfully say: "He that hath seen me hath seen the Father", in the sense that a clear lake mirroring the moon and stars, if it could speak, might say, "He that hath seen me hath seen the heavens."

Gautama the Buddha, who worshipped Wisdom as the Highest Good, became known as the Enlightened, and could say, even as he walked the earth, "I have attained Nirvana", which he described as a state of all-knowingness. Nearer to our times, Mohandas Gandhi, whose God was Truth, was not only one of the most truthful men the world has ever known—the stark candour of his *Autobiography* is, at times, almost embarrassing—but Truth was the very positive power by which he performed his political miracles. And this self-identification with what inwardly is most worshipped, or desired, may be traced in the lives of all successful men and women, whether the beloved objective is sacred or profane, an intensive desire to be perfect as the Father is perfect, or to be wealthy, powerful or famous.

Therefore, far from being unrealistic, Plotinus' system is the most practical measure so far conceived for ensuring the evolution of man to a higher, better and more harmless species, which is the fundamental need of the world today. Unless this policy is adopted, and this step taken, there is a very real danger of humanity finding itself on the cosmic scrap-heap as a failure of evolution, not by the decree of a punishing God but by reason of mankind's inability or unwillingness to outgrow its animalism and the self-destroying violence of the jungle, which today can be expressed in terms of nuclear deterrents with their potentiality for deterring the continuance of the human race.

Man can never be better, never be himself, unless he understands his relationship to God and the universe; unless he realises the unity and oneness of being, and therefore understands what his conduct should be towards all other forms of sentient life. In the eyes of tame and harmless beasts, we cannot fail to recognise the brightness of the life-simulating Soul such as we find in those we love, shining from these lesser manifestations of Mind. The scientific man exploits this likeness; the understanding man has compassion on it.

Had the Christian theologians been more intelligent or more honest, they would have recognised that Plotinus had resolved all their philosophical difficulties by raising thought to an altitude where they no longer existed. For by denying validity to matter or evil, he was able to maintain the immaculate conception of the one perfect God, which is what the theologians, those un-freemasons fettered to the Judaic belief in the reality of matter and all its ills for which a single Creator must in some measure have been responsible, were continually but unsuccessfully trying to do.

Moreover, Plotinus relegated the theory of metempsychosis, which was so violently opposed by the Church Fathers, to the realm of process, or Non-Being, the antithesis of Authentic Being, which at once justified their objection and explained how the illusion seemed to be. For in his system, metempsychosis, like evolution, is seen to be a part of the sorcery and betwitchment to which the hypnotised lower soul becomes a prey when she focusses her attention in the wrong direction. It is a phantom of *Maya*, no more real than a night-dream. Yet is is this phantasmagoria that materialistic science investigates in the hope of arriving at the truth about life. Small wonder that the hypotheses of such a science are in a state of continual flux and change.

Plotinus provides for the Christian, and others, a vision of the eternally perfect God and perfect man demanded by Jesus, the goal of the *Teteles-menoi*, while conceding to the materialists the appearance of an ascent from the lowest forms of consciousness, mineral, vegetable and animal, up to the highest philosophical thought. He demonstrates how, from the premise of an Ultimate Perfection, the universal concept of the fall of man can be rationalised, by postulating the downward look of a dreaming mind; the reverse process of evolution being seen as the external effect of an inwardly ascending consciousness.

Yet neither explanation is the final one. In absolute truth, the Higher Soul has never fallen, has never ceased to contemplate the Good. It is this fact which makes the appearance of evolution possible, since if the evolutionary goal were not already known by something far deeper than surface consciousness, there would be nothing to which the Soul could aspire or progress. We can only arrive at our destination when we know what that destination is.

On the other hand, the Higher Soul that has never looked downwards to the enchantment of matter, the fully conscious Soul, being already perfect in its relationship with the Good, does not evolve. The realm of process, and all that is therein, are of the nature of a dream. What may be said more truly to happen is that the hypnotised lower soul awakes to the facts of Being.

The world of becoming is, according to Plotinus, actually Authentic Being viewed in the deceptive light of sense-perception. Yonder is already Here to the clarified vision. The fully awakened consciousness, no longer deluded by the senses, is aware only of the Reality of Being.

Since man in his essence is not a material being but an emanation of Soul, and therefore of the nature of Mind, or consciousness, he is always identified with that which he contemplates. The truth of this is apparent even in the outer world. Husbands and wives frequently grow amazingly like one another. Startling resemblances may often be traced between domestic pets and their owners. A continual focus of attention on pornography and the things of the flesh produces over-sexed behaviour. Persistent contemplation, or "imaging" of crime and violence, as in the case of American television, increases these tendencies in the viewers. On the other hand, the true religious contemplative is marked with a serenity and quiet beauty, evidencing inward peace.

With such examples before us, how can we doubt what the effect would be of perpetual and consistent contemplation and assimilation of the Highest Good? Indeed, humanity has already been shown the result in the lives of such perfectionists as Gautama and Jesus Christ. But if characters such as these are produced by contemplation of the Highest, it is obvious that contemplation of the lowest will tend to produce the reverse—sub-human—effects. And if consciousness that has fallen to the human level looks downward rather than upward, and thinks and lives as an animal, despite his human form, he becomes inwardly an animal. May not Plotinus, therefore, be right in assuming, as Pythagoras and Plato did before him, that "when the Life-Principle leaves the body, it is what it is, what it most intensely lived". Thus the fate of man is not decided by some arbitrary, external, punishing and rewarding God, but by the judgment of his own soul. Therefore, Plotinus warns us, we must break away from the sorcery induced by wrongfully applied attention:

> We dare not keep ourselves set towards the sensuous principle, following the images of sense, or towards the merely vegetative, intent upon the gratification of eating and procreation; our life must be pointed towards the Intellective, towards the Intellectual Principle (Divine Mind), towards God.

He has already shown that those who live like human beings, balanced between the soul and the flesh, return as human beings. But more often in the modern world we find people "tilted towards the animal", putting their bodily needs, lusts and urges before all else. In fact, psychologists of the Freudian and similar schools of thought deliberately encourage this obsession with animalism, teaching that this is the true nature of man, and that to repress it will result in mental unbalance; whereas the unbalance really lies in the reversion to the animal.

We have most of us encountered, too, the kind of people that Plotinus describes in a former citation as being busy "be-treeing" themselves in vegetative apathy; people who have found thought too difficult or too disillusioning, and so have given up the attempt, allowing themselves, like unresisting sponges, to absorb the propaganda levelled at them by radio, television and press, or some totalitarian State or Church, quoting what they take in as their own opinion. They excuse this apathy by saying that they have no time to think; that they must get on with the job of earning a living in order to eat, in order to work . . . a monotonous cycle of externalism, concerned only with things that can be seen, touched and heard, "The service of the perishable." Their inward life may be said to be dead, especially when what remains of their mentality is being perpetually drugged by narcotics and intoxicants, no matter how active their bodies may be. And if this is how death finds them, as far from the reasoning Principle as a vegetable or shrub, they have indeed be-treed themselves; or, rather, have effected the great betrayal of their inmost nature, which is potentially the manifestation of the Intellectual Principle, or ever-active Divine Mind.

From this judgment of the Soul, this inevitable relationship of manifestation to consciousness, naturally followed the doctrine of retribution: Nemesis for the Greek, Karma for the Hindu, and, for the Jew and Christian, the law of "Whatsoever a man soweth that also shall he reap." When this perfectly logical and just law is recognised and accepted, the result must be an attitude of compassion, benevolence and mercy to all living beings; the feeling of "there go I but for the grace of God", realised within.

The Golden Rule is a natural consequence of the recognition of the unity of being. The sufferings of other living creatures then evoke the tenderness and care that we should wish for ourselves in like circumstances, and a determination to do nothing that will add to the general misery of sentient life, but instead to live harmlessly and lovingly as expressions of the Good towards which all things are so painfully striving.

And that, indeed, has been the attitude and way of life of all the great Teachers—Pythagoras, Socrates, Gautama, Mahavira, Jesus and Plotinus himself. Porphyry, the author of the Pythagorean treatise entitled *Of Abstinence from the Flesh of Living Animals*, and the devoted disciple and editor of Plotinus, himself an ardent advocate of a harmless diet, wrote of the Master that "he refused such medicaments as contain any substance taken from wild beasts and reptiles: all the more, he remarked, since he could not approve of eating the flesh of animals reared for the table".

Porphyry also informs us that Plotinus seemed ashamed of being in the body, and refused to talk of his human ancestry—a perfectly consistent attitude in one who was teaching that to live in a physical body is itself a proof of fallen consciousness, and that one should rightly be ashamed, having fallen to the level of matter and having any commerce with it, when he has it in him to be at one with the spiritual and the Good. Equally logical was his refusal ever to have his portrait painted, saying to those who suggested it:

> Is it not enough to carry about this image in which nature has enclosed us? Do you think I must also consent to leave, as a desirable spectacle to posterity, an image of the image?

Obviously no portrait could be painted of the real man who, like the Good, is purely spiritual; and it showed an obtuseness in those who had listened to, and apparently accepted, his theories, that they should have been surprised at his firm refusal.

Like all true philosophers, and most unlike our modern pseudo-philosophers, Plotinus lived as consistently as possible with all that he taught. Both he and Porphyry seem to have lived purified lives, having as little commerce as possible with the flesh, and living most intensely as manifestations of the Intellectual Principle.

In rejecting Plotinus and his *Enneads* the policy makers of the Catholic Church were rejecting the perfect philosophy, or rationalisation of the Creed of Christ. It evidently did not occur to them that if they rejected the corner-stone, the true hypothesis, they must necessarily build on the sands of error. What they were determined to do was to keep what they had made of this Creed free from what they thought of as pagan influences, and Plotinus was a pagan even though he taught the highest truth known to the Essenes, and, through them, to Jesus. Therefore what might have blessed mankind, healing all divisions and resolving all theological difficulties, became the greatest stumbling-block to the salvation of the world by the pure Christian Faith; for in rejecting the Truth, Christianity ceased to be Christian.

Plotinus rejected the current Catholic theology because it had ceased to be the truth that liberates. The Church Fathers rejected that Truth because it came from Plotinus instead of from Palestine. And, on account of this rejection, humanity has suffered the acute agonies of mortal life, war, sickness and domination by Church and State—all things from which Jesus sought to save his fellow-men—for 1,700 years.

CHAPTER XIV

The Great Betrayal

The Catholic Church was admittedly in a very difficult position after the publication of *The Enneads*. The only way to avoid the charge of having capitulated to the teachings of the pagan Plotinus was to teach something other than the truth he taught, and that must mean a departure from the truth.

The "something other" turned out to be the exoteric and false teachings of Judaism and the pagan religion. In particular, as I have shown in *Mithras: The Fellow in the Cap*, the militancy was stressed that was the keynote of the cult of Mithras, and greatly appealed to the temporal powers of the period while not being entirely incompatible with certain aspects of Pauline Christianity and the general tone of the Apocalypse. It was only necessary to lay stress on these in order to evolve a theology quite unlike the philosophy of Plotinus, and therefore unlike the Wisdom Religion and the Gospel of Jesus Christ. It was undoubtedly this decision that made Origen's works so disliked and opposed by those who recognised in the Alexandrian thought so many facets of the Neo-Platonism that, in his day, had been in the making. Yet only by means of Hellenistic philosophy could the many pagan teachings that had by then crept into the Church be made to make sense.

This was particularly true in the case of the idea of the Trinity, which, as we have seen, was a purely pagan concept dating from the days of Semiramis. Its metaphysical meaning was most clearly stated in the works of Plato and Plotinus. For some reason hard to understand, it was considered necessary by the theologians of the Early Church to include this popular age-old "Mystery" in Christian theology, however difficult it might be to assimilate. The hair-splitting arguments as to the exact meaning of this doctrine, which had no connection whatever with the essentially monotheistic teachings of Jesus, led, in what had originally been a determinedly pacifist sect, first to blows among the clergy themselves, and eventually, as the opposing factions of Arius and Athanasius grew more numerous and heated, to the loss of thousands of human lives in bloody massacres.

In more modern times, the theologians attempted to associate this still unresolved doctrine with the passage in 1 John 5:7, thus claiming that it had Scriptural authority; but in the eighteenth century, this was proved by Richard Porson to have been an interpolation that first appeared in

Latin manuscripts of the New Testament about A.D. 400, that is, almost 150 years after it had been presented in the rational and intellectual form of the *Three Hypostases*, by Plotinus. Porson proved that, although it was found in the *Vulgate* prepared by Jerome in the fourth century, and pronounced authentic by the Council of Trent, there was no sign of it in the oldest Greek manuscripts, nor was it ever quoted by any of the Christian Fathers in their references to the Trinity, which it certainly would have been had it been available.

Bentley had been the first to point out this forgery in his *Praelection* as Professor of Divinity in 1717; while Gibbon, in his *Decline and Fall of the Roman Empire*, suggested that the passage had been added to provide an answer to the Arians in the great controversy.

During the fourth century the theologians mainly responsible for the existence of the doctrine in its present mystifying and confusing form, were, in the East, Gregory of Nazianus, Basil the Great, and his younger brother, Gregory of Nyssa; and in the next century, in the West, the Trinity-obsessed Augustine, Bishop of Hippo, who staunchly defended without attempting to prove the doctrine. It was something about which one might argue, fight, and "have faith", but it was not be to understood, although he confessed that the best explanation of it that he had found was in the *Three Hypostases* of Plotinus. But even Augustine could not make this explanation acceptable to a Church that had committed itself to the policy agreed upon at the Council of Nicaea, where the bishops had made themselves ridiculous in the eyes of the cultured Roman world with their reasonless discussions. Such discussions convinced Julian the Apostate that the Eastern bishops "neither understood nor believed the religion for which they so fiercely contended", while he himself maintained truly that "the Christian Trinity was not derived from the doctrine of Paul, or Jesus or of Moses".* It was indeed an anachronistic protuberance on the Christian Faith.

Of the Arian controversy so fiercely waged in the reign of Constantine, Gregory of Nyssa wrote:

> Every corner of Constantinople was full of their discussions, the streets, the market-place, the shops of the money-changers and the victuallers. Ask a tradesman how many obols he wants for some article in his shop, and he replies with a disquisition on generated and ungenerated being. Ask the price of bread to-day, and the baker tells you," the Son is subordinate to the Father". Ask your servant if the bath is ready and he makes answer, "the Son arose out of nothing".

* *The Decline and Fall of the Roman Empire*, by Edward Gibbon. (John Murray.)

Yet Plotinus had provided a rationalisation of the idea in his *Three Hypostases:* the Good, the Mind, and the world-regarding Soul; or, echoing Philo, the Divine Mind, Wisdom, and the embodiment of Wisdom, which could be quite easily equated with Jesus Christ, and which, from the Gospel of John, was obviously how he regarded his divine nature. Yet, nearly 300 years after the crucifixion the learned bishops were endangering the Church which was supposed to be perpetuating his teachings, and confusing the mentality of their congregations, by futile arguments as to whether the Founder of the Christian Faith was begotten of God (which he had affirmed), or was indeed very God, which he had emphatically and explicitly denied, and was a concept utterly alien to his monotheistic thought.

Constantine, in his shimmering sidereal robes of Pontifex Maximus of the pagan Faith, convened and presided over the Council of Nicaea. He and the bishops of the Church were united in a single aim: to establish one religion in place of the many that resulted in so much bad feeling and bitter feuds; he, in order to unify his empire under a single ethic; they, in order to convert the whole world to what they regarded as Christianity. Both had a totalitarian régime in mind. Since the new religion was better organised for such a régime than the pagan Faith, it seemed to the Emperor the more likely of the two for his purpose. Constantine needed help in holding together his far-flung empire; he evidently foresaw what Archbishop Maury was centuries later to declare, that with a good police force and a good clergy the Emperor could always be sure of public order.* Yet when a controversy arose among the bishops so violent as to split the Church regarding the nature of the God that was to be worshipped, and led to street fighting and insults being hurled at the Emperor's statues, Constantine must have entertained serious doubts as to the wisdom of his choice. For he was used to the worship of many gods, and had no fanatical preference for the new Faith, remaining an adherent of both religions until his death-bed baptism. His triumphal arch in Rome has reliefs of Mithras, not of Jesus Christ. The famous Labarum that accompanied him into battle, and was afterwards said to represent the Christian cross and crown, was quite obviously the Sword and Crown that figured in the rites of the Soldiers of Mithras, laced with the initials of Jesus Christ, thus symbolising the design of Constantine even at that early date to unite the militaristic Cult of Mithras with the pacific Gospel of Jesus Christ, a syncretism that seems, to their shame, to have met with no opposition from the bishops of the all too Catholic Church. Furthermore, after the Emperor's death, coins were struck

* *Montalembert I.* G. P. Gooch, D.Litt., F.B.A.

depicting him sitting in Mithras' four-horse chariot, and being drawn up into the heavens by a divine hand extended from the clouds—a most obvious portrait of the ascent of the sun-god, or of his representative on earth.

Therefore, to his eclectic mind, which saw all gods as but different forms of the one supreme divinity, the violent battle between the Christian theologians must have seemed a great and unnecessary fuss about a trivial cause; as indeed we know it did from a letter of his addressed to Alexander and Arius wherein he reprimanded them for wrangling about "these small and insignificant questions".*

The bishops, aware of the delicacy of the situation, and being unable to define the Trinity in the terms in which it had originally been conceived, concocted a statement, or Creed, that would obviously be acceptable to the pagan Constantine, used to the symbology of the descending and ascending sun-god, but which has continued to confuse the mentality of Christendom and blind it to the real nature of Christianity until this day; for it is neither true Christianity nor true paganism, but an unintelligible hybrid. The first clause of the creed agreed upon at the Council of Nicaea ran:

> We believe in one God, the Father Almighty, Maker of things both visible and invisible.

Neither Jesus nor the Neo-Platonists taught that Spirit, the Highest Good made the material, visible world of nature-red-in-tooth-and-claw, with its hideous pattern of one form of life forever preying painfully and violently upon another, or, as it is sometimes more discreetly described, of "life being sacrificed on the altar of life". This jungle of predatory animals, lesser or human, of tse-tse flies, death-dealing germs and mosquitos, this animalistic kingdom with its inexorable law of the survival of the fittest cannot possibly be conceived of as having proceeded from, or being the creation of, the God of unchanging Love and goodness that Jesus proclaimed to all men. Nor did he teach anything of the sort. Throughout his ministry he maintained the sharpest possible distinction between this world and the Love-begotten kingdom of God.

Although he had himself realised this heavenly inward kingdom, and so was able to use its all-beneficent laws in works of healing, he told his followers to pray for it to *come*, which would involve the departure of the present world. We do not pray for what we already consciously possess. *This* world the disciples already had. Why should they pray for anything else if it were God-created or God-ordained? But that it was not

---

* *Vita Constantini*, by Eusebius, Bishop of Caesarea.

"of God" was made clear by the next clause in the Lord's Prayer: "Thy will be done on earth as it is in heaven." The invisible world within was the Realm of God where His will was forever done. The disciples were told to pray for a recognition of this kingdom and its laws that would ensure the will of God being done even while they inhabited the earth. Jesus explicitly stated: "My kingdom is not of this world", and the writer of 1 John 2:17 assures us that the world passeth away, which nothing begotten of the Eternal could ever do. For the true Christian, the world was finite. God was Eternal and infinite. That which was eternal in man existed apart from the world: "And now, Father, glorify me . . . with the glory which I had with thee before the world was." (John 17:5.)

The world was something which, unlike the Eternal and its emanations, had a beginning, and so was transient and temporal, and was therefore not something to cultivate and perpetuate, but to transcend and overcome. "Be of good cheer, I have overcome the world." (John 16:33.) Would the Son "overcome" the creation of the Father? Throughout, Jesus manifested an indifference to the world—though not to its temporal beauties which were a transient reflection of a divine Reality—"What shall it profit a man if he shall gain the whole world and lose his own soul?" (Mark 8:36.) But if the world were the work of God, how could it be despised, discarded and transcended by the Son? The creation must be of the same nature as the Creator.

The Gospel of Jesus Christ was the Gospel of the Kingdom of God which he represented as being the antithesis of the visible world:

> The children of *this* world marry . . . but they which shall be accounted worthy to obtain *that* world . . . neither marry nor are given in marriage.

The end of the world was, as we have seen, eagerly looked forward to both by Jesus and his early followers. Such an attitude would have been impossible had they believed that the world was of God. As Jews they knew that "Whatsoever God doeth it shall be forever. Nothing can be added to it nor anything taken from it." It was obvious that, to Jesus, as to the Brahmins, Buddhists and Neo-Platonists, the physical world was of the nature of *Maya*, the effect not of truth but of ignorance; an illusory, transient state resting on the evidence of the fallible, external senses, that must be replaced by the reality of the kingdom of the eternal and invisible God which was the abiding place of the Perfected Man. "Ye are of this world; I am not of this world" (John 8:23). The Son was a citizen of the perfect, invisible realm of the invisible God who could never be responsible for the imperfections of the visible world.

But perhaps the most vigorous refutation of the Nicene Creed occurs in John 2:15, 17, where we find:

> Love not the world, neither the things that are in the world. If any man love the world, the love of the Father is not in him. For all that is in the world, the lust of the flesh, and the lust of the eyes, and the pride of life, is not of the Father, but is of the world. And the world passeth away, and the lust thereof; but he that doeth the will of God abideth forever.

Therefore the Creed that was to be universally subscribed to by Christians as representing the doctrine of their religion, opened with a statement that completely contradicted the teachings of Jesus Christ. The second clause made an even greater departure from these teachings alluding as it did to Jesus, first as "the Son of God begotten that is from the substance of the Father"—which was what Jesus himself taught— and then as "God of god . . . very God of very God", a definition that would have been considered blasphemous by the monotheistic "Son".

Having postulated two gods instead of one, thus losing the essential unity upon which both Judaism and Christianity were founded, the Creed stated of the second God:

> Who for us men and for our salvation came down and was made flesh, and was made man, suffered and rose on the third day, ascended into the heavens and will come again to judge the quick and the dead.

Small wonder that Constantine, the devotee of the sun-god, accepted such a statement, which was but another version of the rising of Thammuz or Dionysos from the dead, the ascent of Attis from the cave, and Mithras departing skyward in the chariot of Helios. Such an ascent was perfectly possible to the gods with which he was familiar, whose realm was in the sky above, and who also judged the underworld; but it had no place in the teachings of Jesus whose heaven was within, and who firmly denied that he was a judge of his fellow men. "I judge no man" (John 8:15), "Who made me a judge or a divider over you?" (Luke 12: 14), "Judge not that ye be not judged" (Matthew 7:1).

Finally, the Christians were expected to declare, "We believe in the Holy Ghost", which instead of being what it had originally been in the Wisdom Religion—the divine Spirit of Wisdom emanating from the Divine Mind—was now presented as a spectral Third God, the third person of the Trinity, and Christendom was ordered to accept the idea of three gods in one God that has strained the credulity of mankind to the utmost throughout the centuries, and has had to be "believed in" since it couldn't be rationalised, owing to the theologians' rejection of the one reasonable explanation.

The Council of Nicaea was the first public exposure of the appalling theological muddle that had been made of the original simple and comprehensible Creed of Christ, by Paul and the Fathers of the Church. This great betrayal of the sacred charge of perpetuating the teachings of Jesus had begun with the substitution of the primitive and immoral idea of vicarious atonement as the means of salvation in place of the essential spiritual rebirth and total purification demanded by the Teacher of Wisdom; and with the acceptance of Paul's easier way of escaping the wages of sin by a simple faith or belief in the crucified Messiah, instead of following him in thought and in life. To Jesus' explicit teaching, "not everyone that saith unto me, Lord, Lord shall enter into the kingdom of heaven", Paul had replied :"Whosoever shall call upon the name of the Lord shall be saved" (Romans 10:13). Few, given the choice, were likely to choose the more difficult procedure.

To Jesus' firm stipulation that "if you forgive men their trespasses, your heavenly Father will also forgive you. But if ye forgive not men their trespasses, neither will your Father forgive your trespasses" (Matthew 6:14, 15), Paul answered that "we have redemption through his blood, even the forgiveness of sins", a means that appealed to all that is weak, apathetic and unreasoning in human nature.

It is not surprising, therefore, that faith and vicarious atonement, Paul's means of salvation, had usurped the place of understanding and striving for perfection and at-one-ment with the Source of Being that was the way of the Mysteries and of Jesus Christ.

This serious deviation not only led men astray but undid Jesus' fundamental and greatest work of purifying man's concept of God by revealing Him as the Spirit of unchanging goodness and love. Paul's teaching ensured that the Deity reverted to type, and became once more a primitive, vengeful, bloodthirsty Jehovah: "Being now justified by his blood, we shall be saved from the *wrath of God* through him" (Romans 5:9).

Paul's concept of God made it impossible to obey the greatest of all commandments, an obedience which Jesus had said was essential to entry into the kingdom of Heaven: to love God with all the heart, soul, mind and strength, the only true basis of morality. In this instance, Paul behaved like the Pharisee he originally was, who would not enter the kingdom himself, and refused to let others enter. By such manipulation of the pure Creed of Christ, whether intentional or unintentional, Judaism survived, but at the price of the loss of the healing and redemption that could only result from knowing the unadulterated Truth taught in the hills of Galilee.

The substitution of faith in the redemptive efficacy of spilled blood for obedience to the law of God made it possible to ignore what was well known to have been Jesus' explicit refusal to "allow the taking of human life in any form at all"; and Christians, who had previously been forbidden to bear arms, were, after the treacherous accommodation made with Constantine, not only allowed to fight for their champion, but, as John B. Firth tells us in his *Constantine The Great*, "at the council of Arles the Gallican bishops passed a canon anathematizing any Christian who flung down his arms in times of peace". And, later, Augustine was to say, when asked whether a Christian could serve God as a soldier, that a man could do his duty to his God and his Emperor as well in a camp as elsewhere!

In becoming the State religion, and conniving at the policy of militaristic imperialism, the Catholic Church very factually gained much of the world but lost its own soul—the one justification for its existence. And the blind leading the blind, both have fallen into a very uncomfortable ditch.

Sixty-two years after the Council of Nicaea, an African who was to become a Bishop of Hippo and the greatest theologian of the established Church, was baptised into the Christian Faith after an apprenticeship with the Manichees and the Neo-Platonists. Augustine professed to love Plato, and was aware of the lucidity of his reasoning, but it is quite obvious that his own blurred mentality was incapable of really understanding and following the logic of the Greeks, wherefore the involved theology of the Church eventually appealed to him more than the philosophy of Plotinus.

Abnormally sin-conscious, not very ethical, and having long and ineffectually struggled against sexuality which was an obsession with him, he was perhaps naturally drawn to the idea of vicarious atonement. Self-discipline was obviously not his strong point. As a Manichee, he remained in the lower class of auditor instead of rising to the Elect who were strict vegetarians and abstained both from wine and sexual indulgence. He had more success with Plotinus whose philosophy induced in him a brief mystic experience which he describes in *Confessions*, VII:17, when, he says, the power within him withdrew from the sensible world and "in the flash of a trembling glance, it arrived at That Which Is. Then indeed I came to have a sight of Thy invisible things, which are understood by the things that are made; but I could not fix my gaze upon them."

Once again he was hindered by his incapacity for self-discipline, but even more by the fact that he was fundamentally at variance with both Platonists and Neo-Platonists. For, to Augustine, the flesh, far from being an encumbrance or a delusion, was good. Jesus' declaration that it profited nothing meant little to his Bishop. In *Confessions*, Ch. 5, he writes: "We should not wrong our creator in imputing our vices to our flesh; the flesh is good."

His thought is hopelessly confused. Of creation he writes (Book XII, Ch. 6), "God made man of dust, yet he made dust of nothing, which he joined with the body making full man." In Book IX:31, he asks why Christians believe that man is not co-eternal with God as the Platonists aver, but created by God; and quotes the Platonists' reasonable argument that that which has not been forever cannot be forever. But instead of giving any plausible answer to his own question, he simply states that "the blessedness of the soul has a beginning, but it shall never have an end". Unable to argue against the truth, he merely evades it. He adheres stubbornly to the theory of the resurrection of the body, while being unable to reply to the scoffing questions of the pagans who, he says, ask:

> Whether the abortive births shall have any part in the resurrection. . . . They pass to deformities . . . misshapen members, scars, and such-like; enquiring with scoffs what forms these shall have in the resurrection. If we say they shall all be taken away, then they come upon us with our doctrine that Christ arose with his wounds upon him still. But their most difficult question of all is, whose flesh shall that man's be in the resurrection which is eaten by another man through compulsion of hunger? For it is turned into his flesh that eats it, and fills the parts that famine has made hollow and lean. Whether therefore shall he have it again that owned it at first, or he that eats it and so owned it afterwards? These doubts are put into our resolutions by the scorners of our faith in the Resurrection.

That a professed follower of Jesus Christ, and a feeder of his sheep, should be engaged in such ridiculous speculations which could never have arisen had the Gospel been properly taught, shows into what depths of ignorance and credulity the Churchmen had fallen by the Fourth Century, as a result of the great betrayal.

For Augustine, hell is no allegory; it is a physical reality. In Book VII, Ch. 10, he writes:

> But that hell, that lake of fire and brimstone, shall be real and the fire corporeal, burning both men and devils, the one in the flesh and the other in the air; the one in the body adherent to the spirit, and the other in spirit only adherent to the fire, and yet both infusing life, but feeling torment, for one fire shall torment both men and devils. Christ has spoken it.

It is quite evident to any reasonable student of the Gospels that nothing of the sort could ever have proceeded from the Mind of Christ. The passage in Matthew 25:41–46, which conflicts with the whole spirit of Jesus' teachings, as well as with the explicit statement found in Luke

9:54–56, was obviously a later interpolation, when the doctrine of a literal hell-fire had been agreed upon by the theologians evidently as a means of ensuring conformity by terrorisation, instead of, as Jesus had taught, by an integrated love of God. We find the same primitive teaching in 11 Peter 2:4, and Jude 6, and later in Justin's *Dialogue With Trypho;* but the gleeful embroideries provided by Augustine show how agreeable it was to the greatest theologian of the Church. To the objection that it was impossible for flesh to burn without being consumed, he replied that all things are possible to God. Has He not made the salamander? Entirely ignoring the dictum of the more rational Alexandrians, that God cannot do what is unworthy of Him, Augustine goes on seriously to debate "whether the fire of hell if it be corporeal can take less effect upon the incorporeal devils?" and decides that, owing to the omnipotence of God, it cannot. Furthermore, if anyone shall oppose such teachings and the Church that supports them, he will share the fate of the devils:

> If any man shall die her (the Church's) impenitent foes, and not return unto her bosom, does she pray for them? No, because they that before death are not engrafted into Christ, are afterwards reputed as associates of the devils. (Ch. 34.)

In other words, if men did not consent to hold the sadistic views of the Church, they were to be eternally damned.

The curious thing about the hell-fire teaching is that it was no part even of ancient Judaism. The concept of the fiery lake is purely Zoroastrian, and is found in the *Zend Avesta*. At least 500 years B.C. Zoroaster was teaching allegorically that an evil mentality with its thoughts was mercifully to be consigned to destruction in a fiery lake prepared for the purpose, and not human beings. But when the Jews, at some time in their history, absorbed the Persian Angelology, and, with it, the concept of the fiery lake, they materialised the latter so that it became the torture chamber of their vengeful and merciless Jehovah, an idea utterly incompatible with the compassionate Creed of Christ. It had, however, a marked affinity with the pagan concept of a subterranean hell, described by the poets from Virgil to Dante—the land of shades to which all go hereafter, some to continue a shadowy form of the life previously lived on earth, others to be confined to hell's prison, known as the Abode of the Accursed, where the wicked suffer the inevitable consequences of their sins. Here Tantalus forever thirsts, Sisyphus pursues and pushes his wayward stone; the vultures continually gnaw at the liver of Tityus, who was guilty of introducing to mankind the unnecessary habit of flesh-eating, and reaped a karma of eternal indigestion.

The origins of hell, therefore, were all pre-Christian, and could have no place in the thought and teaching of one who believed God to be unchangeably perfect and merciful. But the Fathers of the Church were more concerned with the expansion and prosperity of their offspring than with the Truth it was supposed to be propagating. What it must have as its necessary food was—congregations; and while sweet persuasion, such as that practised by Jesus, might gain one convert in sixty, the ambitious Fathers wanted the other fifty-nine. Arguing from the premise that men could only be saved by becoming members of the Catholic Church, it was obviously a kindness and duty to them to terrorise them into it if they could not be persuaded. But to do this was to induce in them an idea of God totally unlike the merciful Father of the Christian Gospel, but extremely like the Jehovah He was intended to replace.

Augustine went further than the pagans in his sadistic view of the after-life, for his concept of heaven prepared for the saints included an awareness of the fate and agonies of sinners. Gloatingly he writes:

> The saints shall want all evils, so that they shall be abolished utterly from their senses. Nevertheless, that power of knowledge which shall be great in them, shall not only know their own evils past, but also *the everlasting misery of the damned*. (This is the sabbath of rest!) (Book XVIII:18).

This idea did not originate with Augustine; it was also one of Tertullian's favourite themes: but any mentality that could believe such things must be considered to some extent insane. And as Augustine is said to have greatly influenced such men as St. Thomas, Wyclif and Luther, we need not wonder at the Western world being in the condition that it is today.

The peculiar thing about Augustine is that in his personal life he experienced what reads like a human version of the myth of Cybele and Attis. His *Confessions* while they contain passages of real beauty for the mystic, must seem to the ordinary modern reader a rather tedious exposition of the trouble the writer endured from the sexual urge, a trouble that was largely of his own making, and sprang from an habitual double-mindedness all too often apparent in his theology. As he puts it, for many years he was praying: "Give me Chastity and Continence, but do not give it yet." A very common sentiment in those who wish to be delivered from the bondage of their own passions but not from the pleasure of them. Augustine admits that he wished them to be glutted rather than quenched.

The idea of self-purification was early fostered in his mind by his adored Christian mother whom he regarded as the handmaid of the Lord. Of her he writes:

> My mother in whose heart Thou hadst already begun to build a temple and a holy habitation for thyself* . . . advised me that I should keep myself pure from all women . . . which seemed to me to be but old wives counsels, the which I should be ashamed to follow.

Nevertheless, by the time he wrote his *Confessions* he had realised that it was the voice of God speaking to him through his mother. What brings his story into a still closer parallel with that of Cybele and Attis was that one of the reasons why his mother did not want him to marry was because both she and his father had great ambitions for him as a scholar, and she feared "lest the clog of a wife might have hindered her hopes of me, not those hopes of another world, but the hope of fame through learning" —a modern version of Cybele imploring her son only to beget in the intellectual realms!

Monica's one prayer was that her beloved son should be converted to Christianity, and walk closely in the Master's footsteps. When she heard that he had become a Manichee, "she did weep for me in thy presence more bitterly than mothers are used to bewail the corporeal death of their children", believing that his soul was in jeopardy. At this time she received a vision of a glorious young man who assured her that where she was, there was Augustine also. He at once interpreted it as meaning that his mother would become a Manichee, but Monica quickly corrected him, saying: "No, I was not told, 'where he is thou shalt be', but 'where thou art he will be'," which even then Augustine recognised as the voice of God.

But nine years passed before the prayers and tears of his mother had the desired effect. Meanwhile Augustine was finding a good deal of help in Neo-Platonism. Indeed, it has been suggested that his purification actually took place some time before the date he gives for it, through his study of the works of Plotinus. In an interesting footnote found in his book, *The Varieties of Religious Experience*, William James tells us that Louis Gourdon (*Essai Sur la Conversion de St. Augustine*), has shown by an analysis of Augustine's writings immediately after the date of his conversion (A.D. 386) that the account he gives in the *Confessions* is premature. The crisis in the garden marked a definite conversion from his former life, but it was to *Neo-Platonic spiritualism*, and only a half-way stage towards Christianity. The latter he appears not fully and radically to have embraced until four more years had passed. Augustine's own

* It is noteworthy that the Queen of Heaven was often described by the pagans as "the habitation of God".

version, in the *Confessions*, written many years after the event, says that after studying the Platonists, he turned to the writings of the Apostle, Paul, "and found all the truth I had read in the older books to be re-affirmed by him with the commendation of thy grace".

His actual conversion, he tells us, took place in a garden where he had gone with his dearest friend Alipius while having one of his customary wrestlings of spirit with the all too demanding flesh. Opening the works of Paul at random, he found the message that was to change his life:

> Not in rioting and drunkenness, not in chambering and wantonness, not in strife and envying; but put ye on the Lord Christ, and make no provision for the flesh and its concupiscence.

This seeming to him and also to Alipius to be the very voice of God speaking to them, they both dedicated themselves from that time to the life of the Spirit. They went immediately to Augustine's mother to tell her of the change of heart; whereupon he writes:

> She did exult and triumph and bless thee, O Lord, who art able to do above that which we can either ask or think. . . . For thou didst so convert me to thyself, as that I did no more desire a wife nor any other ambition of this world; setting my feet upon that Rule of Faith, whereon thou hadst revealed unto her (his mother) so many years before that I should stand. Thus didst thou turn her mourning into joy, more plentiful than she had dared to wish for, and far more clear and purer than she could have found in the offspring of my flesh.

Monica's prayers and tears had, in a word, at last effected her son's spiritual castration, and, as in the case of Cybele, the Hilaria, or rejoicing followed.

Augustine writes most movingly of their communion together, and their mutual realisation of eternal life, a few days before Monica's death at Ostia, and says:

> When our discourse was drawn to such a point, as that the greatest delights of flesh and blood . . . did seem not only unworthy to be compared, but even so much as to be remembered in respect of the sweetness of that life eternal . . . we struck inward upon the consideration of our souls, and did even transcend and pass beyond them also, that we might touch upon the confines of that region of plenty that never faileth . . . and where life is that very Wisdom of thine . . . And this Wisdom is not made, but it is, so as it was and shall ever be. Or, rather, to have been in times past, and to be hereafter, is not in it, but only to be now, because it is eternal; for to have been, and to be hereafter, is not eternal. . . . We said therefore. . . . "We made not ourselves, but he made us who remains forever."

The necessity for purity in the leading of the spiritual life seems always to have been intuitively felt by religionists of ancient times, and it is certainly one of the few right ideas that has been fostered, however imperfectly, by Catholicism through the ages, in the face of intense opposition from human nature in general and Protestants in particular. Even in this post-Freudian period it lingers in the Catholic Church in the form of a celibate priesthood.

It would almost seem as though an instinctive realisation of the need for evolution had persisted, unrationalised and inarticulate, in the race-consciousness since man's transition from a purely animal state, and that what can now be understood intellectually was, in the past, intuitively sensed, namely, that the only means of sloughing our animalism is by ceasing to act like the brute beasts, and by outgrowing violence and lust—which is a form of violence—thus becoming capable of experiencing a higher life than that lived at present by the great majority of men on this earth.

The nearest the old-time religionists could come to a rationalisation of this urge to self-purification was to say that it was the will of God, or of the Goddess of their Faith, which was certainly not far from the truth. Other explanations of this instinct were apt to leave a loophole for departure from the ideal. Paul's plea for purity on the grounds that we must not pollute the temple of the living God, was afterwards nullified by the teaching that monogamous marriage was honourable, and did not pollute it. Both Monica and Augustine had arrived at the absolutist position that was, in their day, more common among the followers of the Mystery Religions than among the Christians; and it undoubtedly contributed to their spiritual attainment, which, on the whole, was considerable, despite the many grave errors in Augustine's theology.

Owing to some extent to pagan rivalry in this matter, the need for purity, the demand of the Goddess, continued to be a pronounced feature of the Church until the disruption of the Roman Empire, and it is obvious that many thinkers recognised its connection with the attainment of the evolutionary Mark described by Paul as "the stature of the fulness of Christ". Of Virginity, Methodius, Bishop of Tyre declared:

> Viriginity is exceeding great and wonderful and glorious, and to speak plainly, following Holy Scriptures, this most noble and fair practice is alone the ripe fruit, the flower and first-fruits of incorruption. And therefore the Lord promises to admit those who have preserved their virginity into the kingdom of heaven. For we must consider that virginity walks on earth, but reaches heaven.

While Ambrose, writing in the Fourth Century, clearly discerned it as a break-away and distinction from the animal kingdom, saying:

> This virtue is our exclusive possession. It is not found among any of the animals. We breathe the same air, we share in all the conditions of an earthly life, we are not distinguished from them in birth; we escape from the miseries of a nature similar to theirs only by our virgin chastity.

This is probably the clearest statement of the viewpoint of the Goddess that a Christian theologian ever made. Unfortunately this rationalisation of a necessary feature of the spiritual life was not generally understood, and in time chastity came to be practised as traditionally "correct" without understanding why it was necessary. The flesh became an evil to subdue, and gradually the absurd idea arose among the *Flagellantes*, and other fanatical ascetics, that they could "deny" it by making it acutely real to themselves; and instead of evolving to a higher state than the animals, they became more obsessed with the body and its lusts than any healthy animal has ever been. We give power to that to which we give our attention, and the attention ascetics of the Church gave to their bodies, with their hair shirts and continual scourgings, kept their mentalities firmly bound to the flesh instead of raising thought to that which is above it. Asceticism in its many forms became a war against the unfortunate body instead of a transcendence of it by means of replacing thought *about* the flesh—which induces sensation in it—with the Spirit-obsessed Mind of Christ. Nevertheless, the association of chastity with the spiritual life remained until the time of the Dark Ages when sexuality became rife among laity and clergy alike.

Curiously enough, it was the stressing of abstinence from sexual indulgence and flesh-eating by the heretics that, for many centuries, made both these disciplines unpopular in the Church, and, in the latter case, absolutely forbidden. This is brought out clearly in a story told by Coulton, who wrote:

> About 1233 a suspect, brought before the Tribunal, protested as follows in order to clear himself from all suspicion of heresy: "Hear me, my Lords! I am no heretic. I have a wife and cohabit with her, and have children; and I eat flesh and lie and swear and am a faithful Christian."

The reformation failed to revive an enthusiasm for celibacy, except among the Catholic clergy, for Protestantism has always aimed at restraining animalism but not at transcending it. As Inge tells us, Luther "denied the possibility of continence . . . his remedy is universal marriage; he wished to stone adulterers".

To hold animalism on a leash, to restrict lust and legalise it in matrimony, but not to eliminate it, was ever the unrealistic policy of Jews, Protestants and all those whose nearest approach to spirituality was respectability and social conformity. The further descent—a logical one if lust *per se* is not wrong—was brought about by the teachings of Freud, who insisted that the healthy and normal procedure was a return to the jungle; all else was prudery and dangerous repression. This sounded a delightful and most acceptable theory to those who did not understand the purpose of life, but has had the most disastrous consequences, as the sexual immorality of the West at the present time bears eloquent witness; and has successfully impeded and postponed the further evolution of the human race.

The Manichees with whom Augustine had been associated, were the successors of the Marcionites and inherited their outlook on the necessity for celibacy and on the diabolical character of the natural world. Like their predecessors, they repudiated the God of the Old Testament, and therefore the Scriptures that were written about him. This argument, which was also that of the Gnostics, so difficult to deny in the face of visual evidence, was a constant thorn in the flesh of the Church. The Old Testament, which ascribed the physical creation to Jehovah, having been pronounced canonical, such a criticism of the visible world, however rational, threatened the very foundation of what was thought of as Christian theology, and this accounted for the Church's violent persecution of the Manichees. They managed to survive however, well into the Middle Ages when they handed on the torch to the Albigenses. This unfortunate sect was the last articulate manifestation of the ethics of the Wisdom Religion within the Catholic fold. In *The Return of the Magi*, translated from the French of Maurice Magré, by Reginald Merton, the author writes of them:

> Life to them was a kind of penitence, and if a man did not desire eternally to enter new bodies, to reincarnate endlessly, it was necessary for him to attain to detachment from everything, for that alone would allow him to become united with God. It was necessary also, but only when a man had reached a certain degree of perfection, to abstain from marriage and from the act by which life is perpetuated.

Further on he says:

> Their souls were like the souls of the Early Christians. . . . There was to be found in their words the pure doctrine of the Master Jesus. That which the Church called "the abominable leprosy of the South" manifested itself as an epidemic of unselfishness, a handing on of goodness, a chain of sacrifice. . . . They worshipped the inner God, Whose light grew brighter the more they lived pure lives filled with love for their fellow-men.

But the last thing that the Church could afford at that period of its history was a restatement of "the pure doctrine of the Master Jesus", for its bright light could not fail to show up the abysmal darkness into which the Church that officiated in his name had fallen. Accordingly, the Albigenses were ruthlessly exterminated by the "Christian" soldiers of Pope Innocent III, who, as we read, seized babies from their mothers, threw them up and caught them on the points of their swords, thus fully confirming the Albigenses' conviction that the unfortunate little creature should never have been born. Writing of this persecution, W. R. Inge says:

> The worst criminal was Pope Innocent III (1198–1216), who ordered a crusade to exterminate the harmless Albigenses in the South of France. In 1209, the Abbot Arnold Amaury, Papal Legate, wrote jubilantly that at the capture of Beziers 20,000 persons were massacred, men, women and children together. . . . The Archbishop of Toulouse was said to have destroyed half a million lives.*

And these homicides professed to be followers of one who had forbidden the taking of human life in any form at all!

In the Church's eyes, however, the sins of the Albigenses were many. They believed that the natural world was the work of a devil, not of God; and that matter was evil, therefore not to be perpetuated by sexual intercourse. They refused to believe in Transubstantiation, and so did not go to Mass. They scoffed at the doctrine of the Trinity, refused to worship images and denied the Virgin Birth. In other words, they separated the pagan tares from the Christian wheat. On the credit side, they refused to take the life of any living thing, and their aim was to become perfect, like their priests, who were both vegetarian and celibate. They evinced tender care for the sick and impoverished, and punished no man but prayed for the criminal's redemption.

The Church so hated these good people whose Christ-like compassion was such a judgment on its own pagan and anti-Christian violence, that their vegetarian habits were not only resented as signs of a diabolical heresy, but were also used as a means to detect and convict them. For when prisoners were taken, sheep were led to them and knives provided for their butchery. Those who refused to kill the animals were burnt at the stake, and the majority did refuse since to take sentient life violated the very basis of their Faith. W. R. Inge writes:

> History seems to show that the powers of evil have won their greatest triumphs by capturing the organisations which were formed to defeat

* *Christian Ethics and Modern Problems*, by W. R. Inge, K.C.V.O., D.D. (Hodder & Stoughton, 1930.)

them, and that when the devil has thus changed the contents of the bottles, he never alters the labels.

This was never more true than in the case of the Catholic Church that has nurtured the authoritarianism, violence and other evils of imperial Rome, which, as Inge remarks, "perpetuated itself in a marvellous fashion in the institution which it first tried vainly to destroy and then tried only too successfully to capture". He points out that the development of what was meant to be the Church of Christ into a political corporation run by power addicts has been excused by the argument that it had to make this transformation or perish; and as it was the will of its Founder that it should not perish, it obviously had to be so transformed. But as E. W. Barnes points out in *The Rise of Christianity*, Paul and not Jesus, was the founder of the Catholic Church. Jesus, who was expecting an immediate end of the world, had no reason to found a Church. Of Matthew 16:17, 18, Barnes writes:

> This saying attributed to Jesus is one of the passages in Matthew which come neither from Mark nor from Q. Like most of such passages, it is probably a late addition of no historical value. . . . It is a clumsy anticipation of later developments to make Jesus speak of "my church". The theme of his preaching was the kingdom of God. His mission was to call men to join this Kingdom: he did not set out to found a Church. . . . He either expected that the kingdom would come with visible splendour, or else that its manifestation would be inward and spiritual.

W. R. Inge writes:

> It is absolutely clear that the idea of a politically ordered Church was totally foreign to the Mind of Christ Himself. While He was on earth He never contemplated a new Church or a new religion. His earthly mission was that of a prophet and reformer within the Jewish State. . . . Nothing could be further removed from ecclesiastical Theocratism than the original Gospel.

Yet it was always in the name of Christ that the most terrible and vile of acts, such as the Massacre of the Albigenses, the revocation of the Edict of Nantes, the Massacre of St Bartholomew, torture on the rack, burning at the stake, and persecution of heretics, were performed. In the early seventeenth century appeared a great work, entitled *Criminal Theory and Practice*, by Farinocci, who was procurator-general of Paul V in which it was stated that the children of heretics ought "so to sink in misery and want, that life will be a punishment to them and death a comfort".

The hypocrisy of papal policy is shown in the fact that, although the use of torture was ordered by Papal Bulls of 1252 and 1259, the actual killing of heretics was carried out by the secular rulers who, by order of the Oecumenical Council in the Lateran convened in 1216, were threatened with excommunication if they did not exterminate the enemies of the Church. Others must perform the evil work so that the Church could technically keep its hands clean from actual murder.

Few people realise today that the Spanish Inquisition which, between 1498 and 1809 is recorded to have burnt over 23,000 persons, was still functioning in the days of Napoleon who abolished it in 1808, and that it was restored when he fell from power.

When in August 1572, 70,000 Protestants were slain in the great massacres, Gregory XIV was so delighted that he ordered a High Mass of thanksgiving to be celebrated. When the Bavarian Constitution granted liberty to Protestants in the early nineteenth century, Gregory XVI issued an encyclical containing the words:

> From this most foul fountain of indifferentism flows that absurd and erroneous opinion, or rather *deliramentum*, that liberty of conscience is to be assented to and vindicated for everybody.

As Inge so comparatively recently warned us:

> In the Catholic Encyclopaedia (1908–1912) the statement is several times repeated that the Church has never relinquished the right to resort to the old methods of extinguishing heresy.

And this is obvious from the fact that, as late as 1927, a female Protestant of Segovia was imprisoned for two years for quoting from the Gospel that Mary had children by Joseph after the birth of Jesus.

Those today, and there are many, who regard the Roman Catholic Church as the one ideological rallying ground against Communism, should therefore remember that it has never repented of its conduct and tyranny in the days when it had almost unlimited power, and that its policy has served as a blueprint for all the forms of political totalitarianism with which the modern age has been plagued. Inge wrote in the 1930s:

> Even the Bolsheviks have not quite equalled the reign of terror which lay heavily over Western Europe for centuries, cowing all except the most heroic, and effectually preventing intellectual progress, which cannot exist without freedom of thought and speech.

He then issued the serious warning that "there is the gravest reason to expect that the Church of Rome would revive its persecuting edicts, which have never been disavowed, if ever circumstances made such a thing possible".

This evidence of the great betrayal of the Creed of Christ coming from a once eminent Orthodox Churchman cannot be lightly dismissed, although his own Judaistic-controlled Church had also had a share in that betrayal. But this does not alter the truth of his verdict on the Catholic Church which we find at the end of the chapter on Theocratic Imperialism:

> The Roman Church is a most formidable corporation, and we can understand the arrogance of those who belong to it. But as an institution it represents a complete apostasy from the Gospel of Christ. In almost every particular it has restored that kind of religion to destroy which He suffered Himself to be nailed to the cross. . . . As soon as we recognise that the history of the great Church is the history of a monstrous abuse, which has made the word of God of no effect by its traditions, we shall be more ready to go back to the fountain-head and to judge of modern problems by the broad principles of the New Testament in entire detachment from ecclesiastical tradition, which has completely upset the moral standard of the Gospels, counting disobedience to the hierarchy a graver offence than sins against love, truthfulness, humility, or purity.

CHAPTER XV

Broken Lights

Just as religion reached its highest point in the original Gospel of Jesus Christ, and all the theologians who attempted to explain or to improve on it only succeeded in falling short of it, so the Philosophy of Religion reached its summit in the *Enneads* of Plotinus, and all the idealistic philosophers who came after him and tried to be "different" detracted both from his idealism and his logic, becoming at best but broken lights of that clear illumination afforded by the Master of philosophic idealism. Only the mystics, such as Boehme, John of the Cross, Meister Eckhart, and so on, succeeded in approaching similar heights of spiritual apprehension, which, in fact, were, and are, only really comprehensible to the Mystic, or to one who seeks direct communion with the Divine Mind; that is, the true religionist; for, as W. R. Inge writes:

> Mysticism is pure religion. For this reason the great Churches have never been able to do without it, and yet have never been able to control it or subordinate it to their aims.

It has been through the vision, consecration and teachings of the mystic, whether of the great Mystic who declared, "I and my Father are one", or the simple Jacob Boehme who knew that "God is in heaven and God is everywhere", that the spring of spiritual truth has been kept flowing and unsullied amid the polluted, stagnant waters of exoteric religion. Many thoughtful people today are coming to the conclusion that the way of the mystic, relieved from all intermediaries between man and God, and from church organisation, constitutes the true life of the Spirit, and may well prove to be the means by which the spiritual hypothesis is preserved in a civilisation based on a materialism that may eventually turn all its churches into Science museums.

"Religion is too pure for corporations", wrote Landor. "It is best meditated on in our privacy and best acted on in our ordinary intercourse with mankind." Such a religion, however, would have to include a study of idealistic philosophy since that is one of the best means of the all-essential concentration on the Good.

Unfortunately, when Western philosophers departed from the lucidity of the Platonic and Neo-Platonic premiss of the essential Reality of the unseen Perfection, and the transience and final unreality of the imperfect *seen*; when, in fact, they looked downwards into Non-Being, as materialists always do, they inevitably became lost in dialectical confusion, leaving their systems incomplete, and their students unsatisfied. In varying degrees this is what happened to the European philosophers from Descartes to Schopenhauer, the former obviously attempting to modernise the Neo-Platonism that, after a period of almost total neglect in the Dark Ages, was revived and gained immense popularity during the Renaissance among the intelligentsia of Europe, especially at the courts of François I and Henri II of France.

Descartes, in the early seventeenth century, attempted the first restatement of Neoplatonic idealism, doubtless with the idea of rationalising it in the light of current "scientific" ideas. His *Discourse on Method* bears unmistakable traces of Neoplatonism with which he probably came into contact through his life-long friend, Marsenne.

In Descartes' time (1596–1650) all education was in the hands of the Church, and he had an extremely good one according to the standards of the period. At the age of eight he became a pupil at the Jesuit college of La Fleche in Maine, meeting there Marsenne who, first a monk, was afterwards appointed head of a Parisian convent where his "cell" became a "salon" for the intelligentsia of his times, scientific as well as philosophical. Through him, Descartes came in contact with the most enlightened thought of his day, which doubtless included the philosophy of Plotinus.

Descartes is often spoken of as the father of modern science, but while he certainly fell into the error of wishing to use mind for utilitarian rather than for idealistic purposes, his premiss of the allness and superiority of mind, and his Pauline-like distinction between the body and mind, are as unlike the dialectical materialism of the present day as they could possibly be. He was a man of his times and spoke in their idiom, which was the opposite of that of modern philosophy.

Realising the importance of reason as opposed to blind belief, he considered that philosophy was absolutely essential to religion as an explanation of it, which should not be left to the vagaries of theology, especially in defining such questions as the nature of God and the soul:

> For although to us, the faithful, it be sufficient to hold as matters of Faith that the human soul does not perish with the body, and that God exists, it yet assuredly seems impossible ever to persuade infidels of the reality of any religion, or almost even any moral virtue, unless, first of all, these two things be proved to them by natural reason. (*Meditations* 65.)*

* *Discourse on Method*, etc., by René Descartes. Translated by John Veitch, LL.D. Introduction by A. D. Lindsay. (J. M. Dent & Sons Ltd.)

He could, perhaps, foresee, even in his day, a time when a higher standard of popular education would bring a revolt from the demand for credulity, and an insistence on a reasonable explanation of things previously accepted in blind faith. He had himself thought his way to such a rationalisation.

> I was led to enquire whence I had learned to think of something more perfect than myself; and I clearly recognised that I must hold this notion from some nature which in reality was more perfect.

The very existence of what we now think of as the evolutionary goal proved the possibility of its attainment. Descartes' much disputed, "I think, therefore I am", may have its philosophical flaws; but, "I can perceive an evolutionary goal, therefore it exists" must surely be indisputable. And by thinking of what he inwardly was, he came to the realisation of what the Perfect Being was, and also what it could not be. It could not fall short of perfection, and therefore sadness, doubt, change and similar human failings could not be of God, since even men admitted their imperfections by wishing to be free of them.

> Because I had very clearly recognised in myself that the intelligent nature is distinct from the corporeal, and as I observed that all composition is an evidence of dependency, and that a state of dependency is manifestly a state of imperfection, I therefore determined that it could not be a perfection in God to be compounded of these two natures and that consequently he was not so compounded.

Of the two, the intelligent nature was obviously so greatly the superior that, through philosophy, Descartes came to the same conclusion that Jesus had, through religion: that God is Spirit, or Divine Mind, and that, as a thinking being, man is produced by this Mind, which is finally the only real substance.

> By substance we can conceive nothing else than a thing which exists in such a way as to stand in need of nothing beyond itself in order to its existence. And, in truth, there can be conceived but one substance which is absolutely independent, and that is God. (Part 1, 184-5.)

That Spirit or Mind is substance reverses the evidence of the senses which tell us that what is visible and tangible is substance. But it is this belief in, and dependence on, the evidence of the senses that must be renounced if metaphysical truths are to be understood, as the scientist has long since discovered to be the case with scientific truths.

> I request my readers to consider how feeble are the reasons that have hitherto led them to repose faith in their senses, and how uncertain are all the judgments which they afterwards founded on them; and that they will

resolve this consideration in their mind so long and so frequently that . . . they may acquire the habit of no longer trusting so confidently in their senses: for I hold that this is necessary to render one capable of apprehending metaphysical truths.

He points out that not only do the senses constantly deceive us with regard to things external to ourselves, but also to that which is internal. He cites cases of men feeling pain in the place where an amputated limb has been, which suggests to him that the reverse might also be true, and that when pain seemed to be in any of his members, it might not, in fact, be there at all. In both cases the pain might be in the mind.

In a passage which clearly discloses his devotion to the Wisdom-teachings, he points out that all men have at some time longed to turn from the evidence of the senses and aspire to some higher good, and this, he feels, is the chief distinction between man and the brute creation which is only concerned with physical nourishment and procreation.

But men of whom the chief part is mind, ought to make the search after wisdom their principal care, for wisdom is the true nourishment of the mind. . . . The supreme good, considered by natural reason without the light of faith, is nothing more than the knowledge of truth through its first causes, in other words, the wisdom of which philosophy is the study.

This wisdom convinced him that what is created by God can never cease to be. The body is corruptible, divisible, made up of accidents, but Mind is pure substance and indivisible, "from which it follows that the body may, indeed, without difficulty perish, but that the mind is in its own nature immortal".

His proof of the existence of God is logical and must be quoted at length. "The existence of God is demonstrated, *a posteriori*", he maintains, "from this alone, that His idea is in us." Those who argue that there is no God must explain how the thought of Perfect Being, something higher than is in the visible world, ever came to be in human consciousness.

Because we discover in our minds the idea of God, or of an all-perfect Being, we have a right to enquire into the source whence we derive it; and we will discover that the perfections it represents are so immense as to render it quite certain that we could only derive it from an all-perfect being; that is, from a God really existing. For it is not only manifest by the natural light that nothing cannot be the cause of anything whatever, and that the more perfect cannot arise from the less perfect, so as to be thereby produced as by its efficient and total cause, but also that it is impossible we can have the idea or representation of anything whatever, unless there be somewhere, either in us or out of us, an original which comprises in reality, all the perfections that are thus represented to us; but as we do not in any way find in ourselves those absolute perfections of which we have the idea, we must conclude that they exist in some nature different from ours, that is, in God. . . .

The fact that we can conceive of this idea, however, proves our relation to it. If we had nothing in us akin to it, we could not hold or cherish it. As a finite being, he asks, how could anyone have the idea of an infinite substance if it were not derived from that which is infinite?

I clearly perceive that there is more reality in the infinite substance than in the finite, and therefore that in some way I possess the perception (notion) of the infinite before that of the finite, that is, the perception of God before that of myself, for how could I know that I doubt, desire, or that something is wanting in me, and that I am not wholly perfect, if I possessed no idea of a being more perfect than myself by comparison of which I knew the deficiencies of my nature?

Had he lived in this century, he would doubtless have asked: "How can we account for the existence of an evolutionary goal if man is, as the materialists tell us, already all that he inwardly can be?"

But for Descartes, it is primarily the existence of will and freedom of choice which convinces him that he bears a likeness to deity, and that it is the lack of restraint of this will which results in the experience of evil rather than of good. The evil is not in or of God, but results from our deliberately turning from the Good.

He comes so near to the thought of Plotinus at the beginning of the following passage as almost to seem to be quoting from the *Enneads*:

It is true that when I think only of God (when I look upon myself as coming from God [Fr.]), and turn wholly to Him, I discover (in myself) no cause of error or falsity: but immediately thereafter, recurring to myself, experience assures me that I am neverthelss subject to innumerable errors. When I come to enquire into the cause of these, I observe that there is not only present to my consciousness a real and positive idea of God, or of a being supremely perfect, but also, so to speak, a certain negative idea of nothing—in other words, of that which is at an infinite distance from every sort of perfection, and that I am, as it were, a mean between God and nothing, or placed in such a way between absolute existence and non-existence, and that there is in truth nothing in me to lead me into error, in so far as an absolute being is my creator; but that on the other hand, I likewise participate in some degree of nothing or Non-Being.

But, at this point, when he reaches Plotinus' vision of the non-being of matter, he fails to arrive at the older philosopher's explanation that this is a dream experience, or enchantment, due to turning from the contemplation of the Good, and seeks instead to explain it by the suggestion that it is a defect in his nature. Not that God made him capable of such a fall, but that the power he gave him to discriminate between truth and error was not infinite.

He is not, however, satisfied by this explanation, because, as he logically asks, how can the supreme Creator of the universe produce anything less than perfection? Because he will not follow Plotinus to the explicit statement of : "He cannot", he is left with the unsatisfactory alternative that the fall into error is a result of a defect of will, which, true as far as it goes, leaves us with the question: Whence a defective will since the will of the sole Creator is wholly good?

Having departed so far from the Neoplatonic answer, he falls further. After admitting that while thought is focused firmly on the Good, one remains unaware of evil, he now proposes that the great power of Mind which Plotinus taught should be wholly concentrated on the things of the Spirit, should be diverted to the external world, and used for utilitarian purposes. Instead of ascending to the Real, it should descend to the natural world of Non-Being, and *conquer* it, making a reality of the unreal, and seeking satisfaction in the reverse direction to where alone it can be found. In his *Discourse on Method*, Part IV, he writes:

> I perceived it to be possible to arrive at knowledge highly useful in life; and in room of the speculative philosophy usually taught in the schools, to discover a practical, by means of which, knowing the force and action of fire, water, air, stars, the heavens, and all other bodies that surround us, as distinctly as we know the various crafts of the artisans, we might also apply them in the same way to all the uses to which they are adapted, and thus render ourselves the lords and possessors of nature. And this is a result to be desired ... especially for the preservation of health, which is without doubt of all the blessings of this life, the first and fundamental one.

The "fall" of Cartesian consciousness certainly opened the door to the flood of scientific materialism which has now immersed the world. Such plans diverted the mind from the all-important task of self-perfectioning, or spiritual evolution, to the perfectioning of externals, with the result that today humanity loudly and truly complains that man's knowledge far exceeds his spiritual capacity to deal with the fruits of that knowledge. He has, in fact, chosen knowledge which now threatens his destruction, rather than wisdom which alone can protect and preserve him.

But dazzled by the prospect of turning the desert of Non-Being into an earthly paradise by mental means, Descartes apparently forgot that we cannot arrive at a destination by walking in the reverse direction. With his natural concern for health, he could not foresee the present scientific civilisation in which a mighty army of medical men strive to conquer sickness in man by torturing and killing annually millions of other sentient beings, and by injecting into the pure blood-stream of children concoctions made from diseased matter induced in a calf or the kidneys of monkeys. Nor could he know that after nearly a century of ever-increasing "scientific" experimentation on animals, such ailments as cancer would be steadily on the increase, and that, as a direct result of trying to be "lords and possessors of nature", the whole atmosphere of the earth would be in danger of becoming poisoned with death-and-disease-bringing substances, in order that man could achieve the ultimate triumph of being able to blast all sentient beings from the face of the globe.

Living nearer to a time when men still strove for moral perfection, Descartes could not foresee that when this striving gave place to the philosophy of utilitarianiam, perfection would recede ever farther from humanity's horizon, and the Lords of nature, having ceased to exercise their spiritual energies owing to the demands made on the physical variety, would become unregenerate, irresponsible power-addicts.

Locke and Hume were greatly influenced by Descartes, the latter completing his education at La Fleche, where he wrote his *Treatise on Human Nature*. These "natural" philosophers seized eagerly upon Descartes' utilitarianism, ignoring the great illumination of his metaphysical teachings, so that today few seem to know that they ever existed. Both Locke and Berkeley, however, seriously doubted the reality of matter *per se*, and resolved it into ideas, which was not far off the latest findings of modern science that conceives it as being essentially energy.

Leibnitz quotes Spinoza as saying: "The popular philosophy starts from the creatures: Descartes starts from Mind: I start from God."

For Plotinus, as we have seen, Perfect Being was the Intellectual Principle when totally identified with The Good, which is probably the nearest the human mind has ever came to a correct definition of That Which IS. But Spinosa (1632–1677) thought like a Jew and not like a Greek, so reverted to the more ambiguous term of God. Nevertheless, he, like other exponents of the Wisdom-philosophy, taught that a man's salvation depended upon his becoming exactly like God, and that all his suffering was the result of his unlikeness to Him. Only by an integrated, rational, or spiritual love of God that leaves us with the sole desire to become like the Beloved, can we generate the will and power to break away from the bonds of our animalism, and be free. Reason is pure activity. The rational man is no longer the slave of his emotions and passions, and therefore his actions and motives become pure.

Unfortunately Spinosa's idea of God was defective. Excommunicated at twenty-four for having expressed sympathy with Descartes, he seems to have reverted to the God not, perhaps, of the Old Testament, but of Philo, without Philo's element of compassion, a quality markedly lacking in Spinosa himself. As he earned his living by grinding optical lenses, and seems to have had an idea that this occupation was killing him, as indeed it did, at the age of forty-five, it is perhaps not surprising that this, added to his treatment by the Church, resulted in a certain hardness of character towards other sentient creatures. But as regards his idea of God, his love was well-nigh perfect, and he rose to great heights of God-realisation in such declarations as: "Whatever is, is in God, and nothing can exist or be conceived without God."

Released from the burden of the Trinitarian view of Deity, he reverted to the essential unity of the Godhead and of all living things. In an article on him in the *Harmsworth Encyclopaedia*, we read:

> The leading idea of the ethical part of Spinosa's great work is that in becoming conscious of the unity of all things in God we rise above the bondage of the passions and desires which belong to our finitude.

For him, as for Plotinus and Descartes, God, or the great incorporeal spirit, was the one substance and absolutely the First Cause:

> God and all the attributes of God are eternal. God is a substance which necessarily exists. . . . By the attributes of God must be understood that which expresses the essence of divine substance. Eternity appertains to the nature of substance. Therefore each of the attributes must involve eternity, and therefore they are all eternal.*

Man's eternality consists of his embodiment of the attributes of God and his manifestation of the knowing Mind, for "the Mind in as far as it truly perceives is part of the infinite intellect of God".

Man learns to perceive truly only through the Tertium Organum, or the third kind of knowledge, which is reason perceiving things "under a certain species of eternity". Spinosa writes:

> The greatest virtue of the mind is to know God, or to understand according to the third class of knowledge. . . . He who knows things according to this third class of knowledge passes to the greatest state of perfection (215). . . . The more perfect anything is, the more reality it has (222).

---

* *Ethics: Spinosa.* Introduction by T. S. Gregory, M.A. Oxon. (Everyman's.)

Knowledge of God alone ensures man's immortality, for:

> The human mind in so far as it knows itself under the species of eternity, thus far it necessarily has knowledge of God, and knows that it exists in God, and is conceived through God.

Man becomes one with God through love of God, for:

> Mental intellectual love towards God is part of the infinite love with which God loves Himself. . . . Hence it follows that God, in so far as he loves himself, loves men, and consequently that the love of God for men and the mind's intellectual love towards God is one and the same thing.

True though this is, Spinosa's concept of love, like his concept of God, lacked compassion, and he was aware of this but regarded it as a virtue. Like Kant after him he considered the emotions of compassion and pity bad in themselves, and believed that all good acts to others should be motivated by reason. "Pity is sadness", he writes, "and therefore is bad in itself. The good which follows from it, namely, that we endeavour to free the man whom we pity from his misery, we desire to do from the mere command of reason, nor can we do anything which we know to be good save under the guidance of reason. And therefore pity in a man who lives under the guidance of reason is bad and useless in itself." (175.)

The obvious objection to this reasoning—that, without compassion there would be no desire to help the fellow man—never seems to have occurred to Spinosa; and this very dangerous theory, that compassion must never be indulged, evidently accounts for his Jehovahistic attitude to the lesser creatures. On this subject he writes:

> Men have far more rights over beasts than beasts over men. I do not deny that beasts feel; but I deny that on that account we should not consult our necessity and use them as much as we wish and treat them as we will, since they do not agree with us in nature, and their emotions are in nature different from human emotions.

This is, of course, the modern scientific point of view. But, apart from the fallacy of the argument as to the emotions of animals and men being wholly dissimilar, a fallacy obvious to anyone who has had personal experience of the lesser creatures, the idea that one may kill and ill-treat helpless sentient creatures because their emotions are different from our own, is not only utterly inhumane but verges on the ridiculous. Remembering the treachery, violence, lust and cruelty of many human beings, the "difference" in the comparatively mild emotions of most animals points to their superiority. Living in times so much nearer to the Dark and Middle Ages than our own, when men behaved far worse than any brute beast, Spinosa's view of man's superiority at that stage of evolution sounds quite fantastic.

"Save man", he writes, "we do not know any individual thing in nature in whose mind we may rejoice or which we may join to us in bonds of friendship or any other kind of habit."

It is unfortunate that he never experienced the devotion of a dog, and lived too early to read Alan Boone's testimony to the love and friendship of animals in his *Kinship With All Life.* As it is, no compassion can be detected anywhere in Spinosa's attitude to other sentient creatures. He continues:

> Therefore whatever exists in nature besides man, reason does not postulate that we should preserve for our advantage, but teaches us that we should preserve or destroy it according to our various need, or adapt it in any manner we please to suit ourselves.

This reads so strangely like the official directive found in the *Catholic Dictionary* as to what the attitude of the Faithful should be to animals that it seems as though the insensitivity to the suffering of animals evinced by orthodox Christianity may have stemmed originally, and mainly, from Jewish sources. Once again, we find in the Jew that peculiar lack of the "woman" noticeable in Paul and others of his Faith, which is such a fundamental deviation from the Wisdom of the Goddess. This deficiency is particularly dangerous in anyone who understands as clearly as Spinosa did the importance and potency of thought. "The more a thinking being can think, the more reality or perfection we conceive it to have." Yet if that potent thinking is not governed by compassion, how far from perfection it falls, and how dangerous it becomes! The modern scientific mind is an illustration of this.

Nevertheless, it is true that thought is our link with Deity, and this Spinosa well understood. "Thought is an attribute of God, or God is a thinking thing. Therefore man as a thinking thing is the image of God."

Evil he considers to be a form of ignorance:

> The knowledge of evil is inadequate knowledge. . . . Hence it follows that if the human mind had only adequate ideas it would form no notion of evil.

Therefore man's salvation depends on his gaining the third sort of knowledge, which, through reason, brings a man to perfection:

> Under the guidance of reason we desire what is good, and thus far only we avoid what is evil.

We trace in this line of thought the first step to Kant's absolutist position of instating reason in the place of God, a position which Spinosa, as a pious Jew, would fiercely have resisted, but to which, as a philosopher, he almost comes. Yet, as a mystic, he knew the freedom and joy of pure love and contemplation of the Good:

> The love towards a thing eternal and infinite alone feeds the mind with pleasure, and it is free from all pain; so it is much to be desired and to be sought out with all our might.

The love of God itself arises from the third kind of knowledge, which must therefore be gained at all costs. Spinosa believed that Reality and perfection were one and the same, therefore all is as real as it approaches perfection, which brought him logically to the aim and essence of the Mysteries—the self-perfectioning which is salvation.

In his *Basis of Morality*, Schopenhauer says of Kant that "by separating the *a priori* from the *a posteriori* in human knowledge he made the most brilliant and pregnant discovery that metaphysics can boast of ". But Plato and Plotinus had long since done this with their distinction between the ideal and the empirical, the intelligible and the sensible worlds.

Kant (1724–1804) had the extraordinary and not very intelligent idea of restating these concepts in his system but dismissing the foundation on which they were based as "mysticism". The task he set himself was to rationalise a rationalisation, i.e. to rationalise the Philosophy of Religion. What he succeeded in doing was to show how, dialectically, philosophy could be divorced from religion, and in this very real and tragic sense, he was, as he has been so frequently described, "the founder of modern philosophy". As we look about us at the chaos, materialism and violence of the present age, which are the direct results of the prevailing philosophy this hardly seems to be a recommendation.

It was evidently his own personal lack of any psychic or spiritual experience that induced in him the idea that there was no need to postulate anything higher in existence than the rational human mind. This lack was as much a defect in him as a philosopher as the loss of a limb would be in an athlete. On the subject of psychic experience he showed such ignorance that the rest of his teaching might well have been discredited if he had not been preaching chiefly to a similarly defective audience in an age which had never had the benefit of systematic psychical research. It is owing to this defect that he presents us with an entirely fallacious concept of "intuition", which plays a large part in his system. He says:

> All intuition possible to us is sensuous; consequently our thought of an object by means of a pure conception of the understanding, can become

cognition for us, only in so far as this conception is applied to objects of the senses.*

But as any intuitive person knows from experience, this is precisely what intuition is not. It is reason that at least commences its activities from the evidence of the senses; intuition is the antithesis of reason. How often does the intuitive person find that when a certain action is obviously demanded on visual evidence, and, according to every reasonable argument, is shown as being the right thing to do, intuition, an inner instinct based on nothing but a quite inexplicable "feeling", and impossible to rationalise, warns him or her that it must not be done! Intuition in such cases almost invariably proves to be right. But Kant was literally suffering from mental deficiency in this connection, for he categorically denies pre-cognitive experiences and telepathy which, since his time, have been proved to exist by scientific experimentation, as well as having been experienced throughout the ages by those who possess such capacities. He writes:

> A peculiar fundamental power of the mind of intuiting the future by anticipation (instead of merely inferring from past and present events), or . . . a power of the mind to place itself in community of thought with other men, however distant they may be . . . these are conceptions the possibility of which has no grounds to rest. For they are not based upon experience and its known laws; and without experience they are merely arbitrary conjunction of thoughts.†

In point of fact they are, as we know, based very positively on the experience of a great number of people, both primitive and modern, and Kant appears, in this instance, like a blind man who is stubbornly convinced of the complete untruth that the rest of mankind cannot see. He denies what he is incapable of understanding, and his *Critique of Pure Reason* is a valiant, if turgid and obscure, attempt to separate philosophy from the spiritual hypothesis upon which both Plato and Plotinus built their superb systems. Eventually, by the use of pure reason alone, he arrived at a rather feeble and inadequate approximation to that very hypothesis.

He believed of Reason, as the materialists of our day believe of Science, that it could eventually prove a sufficient explanation of life without postulating anything higher. He also imagined that it could constitute

---

* *Critique of Pure Reason*, by Immanuel Kant. Translated by J. M. D. Meiklejohn. (Bohn's Philosophical Library.)

† Before he died, Kant had irrefutable proof of the reality of both these "conceptions" through the well-substantiated experiences of Swedenborg, about which Kant wrote a long, convinced and convincing account.

the ultimate form of government through man's acceptance of the Categorical Imperative of the moral law. But of how the common man was to be brought to the voluntary acceptance of this aid to self-government when it conflicted with his desires and passions, the philosopher gave no hint, beyond assuming that the means would be the same as the ends, and that reason *per se* would lead to the acceptance of reason as an omnipresent guide and counsellor. But this conflicts with what Kant so highly rated—empirical experience, which teaches us that the majority of mankind are far from rational, and are continually swayed by far stronger and more compelling forces than pure reason.

It is true that the noble morality enshrined in the concept of the Categorical Imperative appeals to what is finest in man, and might be accepted—at least in theory—by other philosophers and the élite of the human race. But in practice desire plays havoc with the best of moral resolutions, and the trouble with the exalted and austere moral law is that it lacks the short-term attraction of the temptations of the flesh. Noble and necessary as it may seem when Mind, or Reason, is enthroned, it assumes the most shadowy and intangible proportions when weighed against some vitally urgent human desire. In fact, it becomes the metaphysical "what ought to be" as distinct from the all too demanding "what is". From the conflict with desire, as Schopenhauer was afterwards to point out, reason seldom emerges victorious.

However noble a Categorical Imperative may be, it is not something one can love with all the heart, soul, mind and strength, to the exclusion of all other desires; and nothing less than this can produce a true and reliable morality.

Unlike the modern materialists, Kant recognised the necessity for the evolution of mankind, at least up to the point where he would be prepared to accept and apply the Categorical Imperative, which thus becomes the Kantian evolutionary goal. He points out that people, so far, have evolved by pretending to be better than they are; by setting a high standard and affecting to live up to it. Therefore, "the seemingly good examples which we see around us, form an excellent school for moral improvement, so long as our belief in their genuineness remains unshaken". But this method can only be a temporary means of leading men from an uncivilised state to at least an attempt to emulate the appearance of the good we see, for:

> When true principles have been developed, and have obtained a sure foundation in our habit of thought, this conventionalism must be attacked with earnest vigour, otherwise it corrupts the heart and checks the growth of good disposition with the mischievous weed of fair appearances.

In a word, the evolution must be genuine as far as it goes. But Kant evidently does not aim at anything so exalted as the Perfect Man. He believes that Plato's concept of man as an Idea of the Divine Mind was only an unattainable ideal, "a human being existing only in thought, and in complete conformity with the idea of wisdom". He understands the use and value of such an evolutionary model as a guide to conduct, but does not believe that men can ever become like the pattern, which must remain an ideal:

> The conduct of this wise and divine man serves us as a standard of action, with which we may compare and judge ourselves, which may help us to reform ourselves, although the perfection it demands can never be attained by us.

Illogically, he denies the possibility of the perfection demanded by Jesus and the Wisdom-Religions, in spite of the fact that without that moral perfection no man could live by his Categorical Imperative. He does admit, however, that the Platonic view of life can be maintained by reason, though it can neither be proved nor disproved by that means.

> We may adduce the transcendental hypothesis, that all life is properly intelligible, and not subject to changes of time, and that it neither began in birth, nor will end in death. We may assume that this life is nothing more than a sensuous representation of pure, spiritual life; that the whole world of sense is but an image, hovering before the faculty of cognition which we exercise in this sphere, and with no more objective reality than a dream; and that if we could intuite ourselves and other things as they really are, we should see ourselves in a world of spiritual natures, our connection with which did not begin at our birth, and will not cease with the destruction of the body.

While this is an admirable statement of Neo-Platonic philosophy, he cautiously adds:

> We cannot be said to know what has been above asserted, nor do we seriously maintain the truth of these assertions; and the notions therein indicated are not even ideas of reason, they are purely fictitious conceptions. But this hypothetical procedure is in perfect conformity with the laws of reason.

His own arguments for the possible immortality of man's essential being are far more tentative, keeping rigidly within the limits of what he holds to be reason, which he says convinces us that nothing in nature is useless, superfluous or unsuited to its end, everything appearing to be "perfectly conformed to its destination in life", except man "who alone is the final end and aim of this order"; for his gifts, and especially the moral law that exists in him

> stretch so far beyond all merely earthly utility and advantage, that he feels himself bound to prize the mere consciousness of probity, apart from all advantageous consequences—even the shadowy gift of posthumous fame—above everything; and he is conscious of an inward call to constitute himself, by his conduct in this world—without regard to mere sublunary interests—the citizen of a better. This mighty irresistible proof—accompanied by an ever-increasing knowledge of the conformability to a purpose in everything we see around us, by the conviction of the boundless immensity of creation, by the consciousness of a certain illimitableness in the possible extension of our knowledge, and by a desire commensurate therewith—remains to humanity, even after the theoretical cognition of ourselves has failed to establish the necessity of an existence after death.

The application of the Categorical Imperative seemed to Kant to be a simple matter. All a man need ask himself before performing an action was: "Would I wish this to become a universal practice?" and behave in accordance with the answer. But who, supported only by the very faint hope of immortality offered by Kant, would be willing to apply this rule in every eventuality? Possibly some rare, selfless, and dedicated saint-philosopher might accept such a discipline, but the ordinary man well knows that when reason comes into conflict with desire, the latter only too often insists that the former shall do some special pleading in order to justify the indulgence of its irrational urges; or else "old barren reason" is divorced from the bed, and the daughter of the vine taken to spouse. It was not only Socrates' reason, but his integrated love of the Good that enabled him to resist the advances of the beautiful Alcibiades. For only when the love of the Good is greater than any lesser desire will man be able to resist all that the world, the flesh and its glamorous evil can offer him.

Reason alone can never hope to arouse in man that integrated and overwhelming love, for Love itself is the power which inspires such feeling, the magnet that irresistibly draws. Yet, according to Kant, reason demands that compassionate Love shall be subservient to its own dictates. Therefore the acceptance of the rule of reason—which, however, as a ladder, or aid to understanding should never be despised—cannot ensure at-one-ment with that compassionate Love which the Western world has for nearly two thousand years nominally accepted as God; and without it there can be no full satisfaction for, beyond all else, the highest Good is Love.

It is precisely the lack of this divine attribute that is so much in evidence in the world today, where the emphasis is all on power, violence, materialistic reasoning, and scientific intellect with its insatiable and devastating curiosity that overrides all considerations of mercy and compassion. So that although the influences of Freud and Marx are even more obvious, it is not difficult to trace the influence of Kant's essentially masculine and cerebral philosophy in the present world situation. In fairness it should be admitted, however, that he would probably be appalled at the manner in which his deity is sometimes used by the materialists. He could not have foreseen, for instance, that Reason might one day be employed by those with a genius for perversion, who could prove on perfectly *reasonable* grounds that all moral law must be subservient to class warfare. Kant's God was a patently inadequate one, but he never had any intention of advocating the devil. His *schema* was intellectually admirable but emotionally deficient. Going even further than Spinosa in his distrust of compassion, he insisted that the man who acted from a sense of duty was infinitely superior to one moved by the impulse of compassionate love. Quoting Kant, Schopenhauer wrote:

> An action, he says, has no genuine moral worth, unless it be done simply as a matter of duty, and for duty's sake, without any liking for it being felt; and the character only begins to have value, if a man, who has no sympathy in his heart, and is cold and indifferent to others' sufferings, and who is not by nature a lover of his kind, is nevertheless a doer of good actions, solely out of a pitiful sense of duty.

Schopenhauer then condemns this assertion as being revolting to true moral sentiment, an "apotheosis of lovelessness, the exact opposite . . . of the Christian doctrine of morals, which places love before everything else, and teaches that without it nothing profiteth".

In a word, Kant, believing himself to be wiser than the Greeks, or, indeed, than God, planned a system without a heart. But without a heart there is, finally, no life, and Kant's *schema*, which has so effectually permeated modern philosophy, may well account for the death wish that is so much a feature of this age.

CHAPTER XVI

Recovery

Kant and his successors having denuded philosophy of the spiritual hypothesis, Hegel (1770–1831) perceived the urgent necessity for rescuing it, not only from the arguments of the materialistic philosophers but also from the absurdities of theology, and enshrining it once more in a philosophy of religion. This he succeeded in doing more perfectly than any idealistic philosopher since Plotinus, to whom he obviously owed a great deal.

In Hegel's age, as in ours, this hypothesis seemed to be in danger of vanishing from the face of the earth. On the one hand, the materialists had banished it from philosophy, on the other, the religionists had abandoned any attempt to rationalise the confused jumble of myth and superstition that the theologians had made of a once clear, simple and and practical Faith. The churchmen were at least intelligent enough to see that if the searching light of logic were turned on the current beliefs of the Church, they would be revealed as the fantastic, archaic fallacies they were, and the whole creaking edifice of Orthodoxy might well collapse like a building of cards. Therefore they assiduously indoctrinated their congregations with the idea that their salvation lay, not in understanding, or Gnosis, but in blind belief: "Do not attempt to discover the Truth. Believe everything the Church tells you", had become the directive to those endeavouring to follow a Master who had said: "Ye shall know the truth and the truth will make you free."

As a Christian and a philosopher, Hegel was horrified by such an attitude, and wrote in *The Philosophy of Religion* (Vol. I:62):

> The opinion that thought is injurious to religion and that the more thought is abandoned the more secure religion is, is the maddest error of our time.*

He was convinced that if religion were to survive it must be delivered from thoughtlessness, for "God is . . . the highest thought", and:

> Religion is divine knowledge, the knowledge man has of God. This is the divine wisdom, and the field of absolute Truth. . . . Religion is the knowledge of the highest truth, and this truth more precisely defined is free Spirit. In religion man is free before God, in that he brings his will into

* *Lectures on the Philosophy of Religion*, by Georg Wilhelm Friedrich Hegel. Spiers and Sanderson Translation. (Kegan Paul & Trench Trubner & Co. Ltd., 1895.)

conformity with the divine will, he is not in opposition to the supreme will, but possesses himself in it.

Therefore the knowledge of God and the nature of his will is essential to the practice of religion. Without thought of the very highest variety such practice is impossible. On the other hand, philosophy without God was an absurdity. "There was a time", Hegel reminded his readers, "when all knowledge was knowledge of God. Our own time, on the contrary, has the distinction of knowing about all and everything . . . but nothing at all of God."

He seems to be speaking of the present century when he writes:

> It no longer gives our age any concern that it knows nothing of God; on the contrary, it is regarded as a mark of the highest intelligence to hold that such knowledge is not even possible. . . . How, then, are we any longer to respect the commandment, and grasp its meaning, when it says to us: "Be ye therefore perfect as your Father in heaven is perfect" since we know nothing of the perfect one. . . ?

In other words, how can man hope to evolve to a higher species if he resolutely refuses to recognise and accept an evolutionary Goal, or Mark? Philosophy without religion, indeed, ceases to be Philosophy, for:

> Philosophy is not a wisdom of the world: it is not knowledge which concerns . . . empirical existence and life, but is knowledge of that which is eternal, of what God is, of what flows out of His nature. For this His nature must reveal and develop itself. Philosophy, therefore, only unfolds itself when it unfolds religion, and is unfolding itself in unfolding religion. Thus religion and philosophy come to be one. Philosophy is itself, in fact, worship; it is religion, for in the same way it renounces subjective notions and opinions in order to occupy itself with God.

Hegel recognised, with Inge, that the only pure religion was that of the mystic, the devotee who demanded immediate communion of mind with Mind. Therefore to maintain mental independence was essential to God-realisation. "To renounce independent thought", he said, is not within the power of the healthy mind." Of mystic knowledge he writes:

> Insomuch as this knowledge exists immediately in myself, all external authority, all foreign attestation is cast aside; what is to be of value to me must have its verification in my own spirit. It may indeed come to me from without, but any such external origin is a matter of indifference; if it is to be valid, this validity can only build itself up upon the foundation of all truth, in the witness of the spirit.

The spirit of Hegel certainly witnessed to deep understanding of the Wisdom-religion. His system was non-dualistic. For him, as for the wise men who preceded him, God was the one true Reality, and there was no other reality whatever. "God alone is."

> God is the absolute Substance, the only reality. All else which is real, is not real in itself, has no real existence of itself; the one absolute reality is God alone, and thus He is the absolute Substance.

God is the reality of all we perceive and of all that we are; which is not to say that what we see is real, or that we are what we seem to be. Beyond the ever-changing phantasmagoria presented by the external senses, God unchangeably *is*. As God is Spirit, "the manner of his manifestation must be itself a spiritual one, and consequently the negation of the natural". Man is idea.

Speaking of Vedanta in Vol. II:512, Hegel writes:

> Brahma is thought, man is a thinking being, thus Brahma has essentially an existence in human self-consciousness. . . Man is actually self-conscious thought . . . I am what thinks.

It is as a mental being that man can be conceived of as eternal:

> The eternal life of the Christian is the Spirit of God itself, and the Spirit of God just consists in self-consciousness of oneself as the divine Spirit. (Vol. II:57).

For Hegel, as for Plotinus, God, Spirit, being Substance, matter, its opposite, is absolute nothingness or non-being:

> God does not create out of anything material, for he is the Self, and not the immediate or material. . . . . The positing of nature . . . is the sinking of intelligence into sleep. (Vol. II:176.)

Hegel is the first European philosopher to accept the verdict of Plotinus and the Vedantists that material life is of the nature of a dream:

> What is distinguished from God has no right to be. . . . Inasmuch as it is something which has been posited, it also passes away, is only appearance. God only is Being, the truly real. Being outside of God has no right of existence.

Since the real man is a mental being:

> God exists only for the man who thinks, who keeps within the quiet of his own mind. The ancients called this enthusiasm; it is pure theoretic contemplation, the supreme repose of thought, but at the same time its highest activity manifested in grasping the pure idea of God and becoming conscious of this Idea.

It is only for the external senses that God is a Mystery, for they regard all things as material and so cannot conceive of God, who is Spirit, as being omnipresent.

> In the reason of sense knowledge two things cannot be in one and the same place; they are mutually exclusive. . . . In so far as God is characterised as Spirit, externality is done away with and absorbed, and therefore this is a mystery for sense.

But in truth "God is everywhere present, and the presence of God is just the element of truth which is in everything".

Hegel had an extensive knowledge of the Mystery Religions, as we find in Vol. II of his *Lectures*. He writes of the transition in human consciousness from the worship of the hosts of heaven to the worship of Wisdom, or the religion of Mind:

> The bright sun of Spirit makes the natural light pale before it. Thus we pass out of the circle of the Religion of Nature. . . . The peoples who have reached that stage in the development of self-consciousness in which subjectivity is recognised to be the ideality of the natural, have thereby crossed over into the sphere of ideality, into the kingdom of the Soul, and have come to the region belonging to the realm of Spirit. They have torn from their eyes the bandage of sensuous perception, escaped from the trackless maze which is devoid of thought, they have laid hold of thought, of the intellectual sphere, and have made and secured for themselves the solid ground in what is inward.

The ascent to God, such a closely guarded secret of the Mysteries, is clarified by Hegel in philosophic terms:

> To think of God means to rise above what is sensuous, external and individual. It means to rise up to what is pure, to that which is unity with itself: it is a going forth above and beyond the sensuous, beyond what belongs to the sphere of the senses, into the pure region of the universal. And this region is thought. (Vol. II:94.)

It is by means of thought that "I lift myself up to the Absolute beyond all that is finite, and am . . . infinite consciousness".

Hegel well understood the evolutionary urge, and realised that, in obeying it, man fulfils his destiny:

> It belongs to the very essence of Spirit to rise above nature (Vol. I:270). Humanity has within itself the requirement that it should rise higher, and hence it seems repugnant that this demand should be repressed, and man's aspiration tied down to continuance in ordinary finite existence. (Vol. I:52.)

That is what the materialistic Socialist States, with their demand for equality and for the devotion of thought to purely utilitarian projects, invariably demand. For Hegel exactly the reverse is the proper procedure, as he points out in a passage containing the essence of the Wisdom Religion, which might have been written by Plotinus. Referring to the idea held by the Ancients that "the spirit or soul has been forced into this world as into an element which is foreign to it", he goes on to say:

> This indwelling of the soul in the body, and this particularisation in the form of individuality, are held to be a degradation of Spirit. In this is involved the idea of the untruth of the purely material side, of immediate existence. On the other hand, however, the characteristic of immediate existence is . . . the final tapering point of Spirit in its subjectivity. Man has spiritual interests and is spiritually active; he can feel that he is hindered in connection with these interests and activities; in so far as he feels himself to be in a condition of physical dependence and has to provide for his own support, etc., his thoughts are taken away from his spiritual interests through his being bound to nature. (Vol. I:75.)

Hence the necessity for the simple, non-attached life, and the difficulty of combining spiritual evolution with an ordinary family life, the claims of dependants constantly demanding that thought should be kept upon earthly interests.

Salvation for Hegel is something that can only be achieved by individual effort. Man has to renounce what impedes his evolution and put on a higher mode of thought. He has, so to speak, to rethink himself:

> What, then, actually is it that man is to renounce? Man is to renounce his particular will, his passions and natural impulses. . . . Renunciation here means that I do not desire to regard certain deeds which I have committed as being my own, that I regard them as not having taken place, that is, I desire to repent of them.

By mental means man can nullify that which he does not desire to regard as part of himself, even as a butterfly repudiates the chrysalis that disguises its beauty.

In Hegel's non-dualistic system evil is not a secondary power; it is a negation, a nullity to be replaced with the realisation of the presence of the Good:

> In so far as evil appears when a man does what is evil, it is at the same time something which is implicitly a nullity over which Spirit has power, and this power is of such a character that Spirit is able to make evil to cease to exist, to undo it. . . . That what has happened can be made as though it had not happened, cannot take place in a sensuous or material way, but in a spiritual and inward way. (Vol. I:129.)

By a similar process Hegel believes that miracles can not only be explained but actually performed:

> Miracles are, speaking generally, effects produced by the power exercised by Spirit upon the natural connection of things . . . an interference with the cause and the eternal laws of nature. But the truth is that it is the Spirit which is this miracle, this absolute interference. Life is already an interference with those so-called laws of nature; it destroys, for instance, the eternal laws of mechanism and chemistry. The power of Spirit, and still more its weakness, have still more effect on life. Terror can produce death, anxiety, illness, and so in all ages infinite faith and trust have enabled the lame to walk and the deaf to hear, etc. Modern unbelief in occurrences of this sort is based on a superstitious belief in the so-called forces of Nature and its independence relatively to Spirit. (Vol. I:119.)

This superstitious belief should be replaced with the realisation of the omnipotence, as well as the omnipresence, of Spirit, for this is the truth that makes free, and is, in the Jesuine sense, to "have faith".

> Faith is essentially the consciousness of absolute Truth, of what God is in His true nature.

The foregoing citations constitute a very astonishing presentation of the spiritual healing that was to figure so prominently in America and Japan at the end of the nineteenth century. It is obvious that Hegel considered *materia medica* at least as inconsistent, for he remarks that "Brown treated with opium, naptha, spirit, etc., what was formerly cured by means of remedies of an entirely opposite nature". (Vol. I:302.)

Of death he writes: "Death takes away what is temporal, what is transitory in man, but has no power of control over that which he essentially is." (Vol. I:311.) And what he essentially is as a mental being, is the likeness of God:

> Man is exalted above all else in the whole creation. He is something which knows, perceives, thinks. He is thus the image of God in a sense quite other than that in which the same is true of the world. What is experienced in religion is God, He who is thought, and it is only in thought that God is worshipped.

He defines worship in the words: "Worship strictly speaking is the relation of self-consciousness to what is essential." (Vol. II:41.)

Right-knowing is, for Hegel, the supreme power, and to know rightly is to understand the unreality of the visible.

> Righteousness is the moment of negation, i.e., it makes manifest the nothingness of things. (Vol. II:183.)

He explains evil by explaining it away:

> God is only one Principle, one power, and the finite, and for that very reason, Evil, has no true independent existence. (Vol. II:74.)

Speaking of the Egyptian religion, he says that in it this Principle is represented by Osiris who is "Lord of the continuously existing soul . . . which has severed itself . . . from what is sensuous, perishable". He implies that in the Egyptian religion, it was understood that "Good has the power to assert itself, and to annihilate the non-existent, the evil". (Vol. II:101.) He quotes Herodotus as saying that the Egyptians were the first to declare that the soul of man is immortal, and speaks of the statue of Isis at Sais with its inscription: "I am what was, is, and shall be; my veil has been lifted by no mortal . . . but the fruit of my body is Helios." Here she declares herself to be the mother of the God first conceived of as the Sun, and then as the Wisdom, or Word of God.

Hegel makes an interesting point regarding the fabulous Golden age supposed to have existed under the rule of Saturn, but which really seems to have been the idealistic kingdom of God of the Pythagoreans. He argues that the mere fact that it is believed to have been lost proves that it was never, in the philosophic sense, "real", for "in divine history there is no past and no contingency", therefore:

> If the existing Paradise had been lost . . . it is something accidental . . . which must have come into the divine life from the outside. . . . The truly Divine, that which is in conformity with its essential nature, is not capable of being lost, is everlasting, and by its very nature abiding. (Vol. I:278.)

From this it follows that the Golden Age, as a true concept, is as eternal and omnipresent as the kingdom of God, an everlasting reality, always "at hand" for those willing to relinquish the shadow of the visible for the substance of the invisible. Heaven is, in other words, not a locality to which men go at some future time, but a state of pure consciousness to be realised inwardly at any time.

The essence of Hegel's exalted metaphysics is contained in the following lines:

> God is the Good, and man as Spirit is the reflection of God. (Vol. III:46.) . . . God is Spirit; in His abstract character He is characterised as universal Spirit which particularises itself. This represents the absolute Truth, and that religion is the true one which possesses this content.

While Hegel had a near-perfect cerebral concept of the Wisdom Religion, he still lacked the heart—the compassion that was the most outstanding feature of the teachings of Jesus Christ. This *lacuna* was abundantly filled by Schopenhauer (1788–1860) who in *The Basis of Morality* exalted it above all other qualities. For him it was at once the foundation and great mystery of Ethics—the *basis* of morality.

> Boundless compassion for all living beings is the surest and most certain guarantee of pure moral conduct.*

He points out that, in Europe, Christianity was the first and only religion to proclaim it as the queen of all the virtues, while, in Asia, with the exception of Islam, it has been so proclaimed for thousands of years. Yet even in Christianity compassion is denied to the lesser creatures. In Asia, in his time, secular laws did not have to be made for the protection of animals because universal compassion was a feature of the Hindu and Buddhist religions; but in Europe humane people have to demand the making of special laws for the purpose:

> The fact that Christian morality takes no thought for beasts is a defect in the system which is better admitted than perpetuated.

He points out that the ecclesiastical teachings that "there are no duties to be fulfilled towards animals" is a view of "revolting coarseness, a barbarism of the West, whose source is Judaism". He does not seem to realise that it also entered the Church via Mithraism, which included all the savagery of sun-worship, with its perpetual sacrifices of bulls and oxen; but he fully recognises that the Church is the chief culprit, and writes:

> European priestcraft knows no limits to its disavowal and blasphemy against, the Eternal Reality that lives in every animal. Thus was laid the foundation of that harshness and cruelty towards beasts which is customary in Europe, and on which a native of the Asiatic uplands could not look without righteous horror.

The materialistic viewpoint of philosophers such as Descartes whose emphasis on the radical difference between man and beast "was the necessary consequence of his mistakes", Schopenhauer also holds responsible. Descartes' arguments logically led to the conclusion that animals were not self-conscious, whereas it is quite obvious to anyone who has had anything to do with animals that their ego-consciousness is immense. On the Cartesian supposition that they cannot distinguish themselves from the external world, Schopenhauer comments:

> If anyone of the Cartesian persuasion, with views like these in his head, should find himself in the claws of a tiger, he would be taught in the most forcible manner what a sharp distinction such a beast draws between his ego and the non-ego.

* *The Basis of Morality*, by Arthur Schopenhauer. Translated, with Introduction and Notes by Arthur Broderick Bullock, M.A. (George, Allen & Unwin, 1915.)

Schopenhauer recognises that it is the Western departure from the concept of the unity of life which has led to this lack of compassion for other sentient creatures. He himself was well aware of the oneness of being; and although he evidently learnt of the Wisdom-Religion chiefly from Indian sources—a fact which, as we shall see, led to a certain lack of clarity in his philosophy—he had also traced it through the sources included in this book; and his witness, which I discovered after my own researches had been made, admirably confirmed my thesis.

His arguments were based upon what he considered Kant's triumph: his doctrine of the ideality of space and time, i.e., that they were both "the forms of our own faculty of intuition, to which they consequently belonged, and not to the objects thereby perceived". In reality, time and space are not, and if they are illusions, so also must multiplicity be:

> The web of plurality woven in the looms of Time and Space, is not the Thing in Itself, but only its appearance-form. Externally to the thinking subject, this appearance-form, as such, has no existence. . . . All plurality is only apparent. . . . In the endless series of individuals, passing simultaneously and successively into and out of life generation after generation, age after age, there is but one and the same entity really existing, which is present and identical in all alike.

This view, Schopenhauer points out, long preceded Kant, and was found in the Vedas, the Upanishads, Pythagorianism and the Neo-Platonists who teach that "all souls are one, because all things form a unity". He reminds us that this idea is also found among the Sufis of Islam, while Johannes Scotus Erigena presented it in the Christian idiom.

> In the West Giordano Bruno cannot resist the impulse to utter it aloud; but his reward is a death of shame and torture. And at the same time we find the Christian mystics losing themselves in it, against their will and intention, whenever and wherever we read of them.

He reminds us that Spinosa, also, stressed this fundamental unity of being, and finally that it was revived in Schelling's eclectic philosophy which included the systems of Plotinus, Spinosa, Kant and Jacob Boehme. As we have already seen, it was even more perfectly enunciated by Hegel. It is just this realisation of the oneness and unity of life, Schopenhauer points out, that produces compassion.

> If plurality and difference belong only to the appearance-form; if there is but one and the same Entity manifested in all living things, it follows that when we obliterate the distinction between the ego and the non-ego, we are not the sport of an illusion. Rather are we so, when we maintain the

reality of individuation—a thing the Hindus call Maya, that is, a deceptive vision, a phantasma.

It is this conscious or sub-conscious recognition of the oneness of life that is the actual explanation of compassion, for it is the recognition of ourselves in all, and who does not love himself? Hence the admonition to love our neighbour as ourselves. How otherwise, Schopenhauer asks, can we account for the giving of even the smallest offering to those in need, with no other object than to relieve their affliction?

> Such an act is only conceivable, only possible, in so far as the giver knows that it is his very self which stands before him clad in the garments of suffering; in other words, so far as he recognises the essential part of his own being, under a form *not his own*.

This argument, while it is true as far as it goes, betrays its Asiatic origin by not going further. We do indeed love our neighbour *as* ourselves, inasmuch as he is of the same essence as ourselves; but Schopenhauer fails to take into account man's higher allegiance to the Essence at its standpoint of perfection, which some, including the mystics of all Faiths, have loved *more* than themselves, so that they desire to lose all sense of separateness in entire identification with the object of their love. The deficiency in the philosophic concept here is that the Asiatics refuse to *define* God. Among the Greeks, and in the Mysteries, as we know, the Supreme Being was known positively as the Good, and unification with the Good leads to a higher and more inevitable almsgiving than that evoked by a sense of our unity with the fellow-man. For being at one with the Good involves at-one-ment with compassionate Love, and, embodying that Love, it is not possible to refuse to meet the brother's need.

It was the lack of this realisation that led to the pessimism which goes hand in hand with compassion in Schopenhauer's philosophy. While he believed in the existence of compassion in certain cases, he had a very poor opinion of human beings, as such. He points out that the conscience upon which men pride themselves is made up of about one-fifth, fear of men; one-fifth, superstition; one-fifth, prejudice; one-fifth, vanity; and one-fifth, habit. Here, once again, he shows a lack of understanding as to the outlook of the evolved man who recognises conscience as his connection with the Beloved, by means of which he is constantly measuring his thoughts and actions against the perfect model that he has accepted as his evolutionary goal.

This spiritual discipline is seldom taught in Eastern religions, and was evidently not understood by Schopenhauer, for he seems to believe that man has only his own jackboots by which to raise himself; therefore he is very dubious as to the possibility of arousing compassion in those who apparently do not possess it. He does not explain this lack of what, according to his own argument, should be innate in all who are part of the Unity, other than by showing that humanity has been misled by its teachers.

He shows a lack of understanding in his approach to this subject, for he speaks of the immense difficulty of "making" a man compassionate, whereas, even by his own showing, an innate compassion has not to be made but evoked. "It means", he says, "the turning round, so to say, of a man's heart in his body, the remoulding of his very being;" and then offers the not very confident solution that all one can hope to do is to "clear the intellect, correct the judgment, and so bring him to a better comprehension of the objective realities and actual relations of life".

Had Schopenhauer been a mystic, or had he not been so prejudiced against the Jews as to refuse to recognise the value of their greatest of all commandments, he would have known that obedience to this command alone can ensure the desired "turning round of a man's heart". For the surest and most enduring way of evoking compassion is the experience of the new birth which follows from loving the God of compassionate Love with all the heart, soul, mind and strength; for then to abandon compassion in any relationship would mean separation from the Beloved, which is unendurable to the lover of the Good.

Commenting on Kant's argument in the *Metaphysische Angfangs-grunder de Tugent Lehre*, that "to treat animals cruelly runs counter to the duty of man towards himself; because it deadens the feeling of sympathy for them in their sufferings, and thus weakens a natural tendency which is very serviceable to morality in relation to other men", he says:

> So one is only to have compassion on animals for the sake of Practice, and they are, as it were, the pathological phantom on which to train one's sympathy with men! In common with the whole of Asia that is not tainted by Islam (which is tantamount to Judaism) I regard such tenets as odious and revolting.

He points out that this philosophical morality is only a theological one in disguise, bringing one back to the argument that animals are only "things" to be used for man's convenience or pleasure, in vivisection, bull-fighting, horse-racing, hunting, etc., and remarks:

> Shame on such a morality . . . which fails to recognise the Eternal Reality imminent in everything that has life, and shining forth with inscrutable significance from all eyes that see the Sun!

He identifies woman with compassionate Love, saying that although she lacks justice, conscientiousness, etc., she surpasses man in loving-kindness, and is more susceptible to compassion than men. "Justice is more the masculine, loving-kindness more the feminine virtue." He himself so far tips the scales on the feminine side that there is in his philosophy a lack of balance which manifests itself at times in a lack of logic. Truth for him is not an absolute, though it is desirable. He feels with Plato and Clement of Alexandria that "a medicinal lie" is permissible, but that falsehood should be restricted to self-defence, otherwise it would result in dreadful abuses. But he argues that just as the law allows people to use weapons in self-defence, so one may defend oneself against violence or cunning by telling an untruth.

> The entirely unconditional and unreserved condemnation of lies as properly involved in their nature, is sufficiently refuted by well-known facts. . . . There are cases where a falsehood is a duty, especially for doctors.

This is what might be regarded, according to his analysis, as a "feminine" lack of conscientiousness; for to those whose God is Truth, as was the case with Mohandas Gandhi, a lie must always separate the liar from God; than which there is no worse fate. Also, the spiritual law of ends and means is violated by resorting to falsehood, so that men cannot, in the long run, produce by untruthfulness the good at which they aim.

But if Schopenhauer lacks full appreciation of the "male" virtues—and love of Truth seems originally to have been most pronounced in the masculine system of Zoroaster—he has the deepest appreciation of the "female" variety. He shows how impossible it is to be a good man without being compassionate by positing the statement: "This man is virtuous, but he is a stranger to compassion", and pointing out how at once the contradiction in terms is seen.

He shows the difference between the religious thought of the East, which understands and accepts the unity of being, and the West, which believes man to have been a special creation in space-time, by reminding us that no holy man of the East would ever appear, like John the Baptist, clothed in skins; and relates that the Royal Society of Calcutta insisted that their copy of the Vedas should be bound in silk instead of leather as was the Western custom. And he tells us that the old Indian dramas ended with the lovely prayer: "May all living things be delivered from pain."

In Schopenhauer's opinion, compassion covers all ethical necessities, for:

> In reality, what is generosity, clemency, humanity? Is it not *compassion* applied to the weak, to the guilty, or to the human race as a whole? Even

benevolence and friendship are seen to result from a constant compassion directed upon a particular object; for to desire that someone should not suffer is nothing else than to desire that he should be happy.... The more closely the living spectator identifies himself with the living sufferer, the more active does pity become.

But in so emphasising the compassion necessarily part of the Gospel of the Goddess, he overlooks the equally necessary virtue of Wisdom. Compassion without Wisdom can be as dangerous as knowledge without compassion. In seeking to aid others, we often harm them for lack of the wisdom that alone can reveal their true needs.

Again, his lack of logic mitigates against his very earnest and convincing plea for the Creed of Compassion when, after expressing the deepest concern for animals and their sufferings, and the utmost scorn for those who treat them as "things" made for man's use, he suddenly and surprisingly remarks:

We may observe that compassion for sentient beings is not to carry us to the length of abstaining from flesh, like the Brahmins.

The reason he gives for this extraordinary *volte face* is that such abstinence would create more hardship for men to refrain from animal food in a cold climate than it would cause pain to the animals who are quickly killed. But he was writing for his fellow countrymen who could have been vegetarian without any hardship whatever; and the rejection of this obvious "first step", as Tolstoy described it, on the path of a compassionate way of life somewhat invalidates his sincerity both as a philosopher and a humanitarian. But it does not invalidate the truth of all he has said as to the necessity for recognising the unity of life and the consequent duty of man towards the lesser creatures.

CHAPTER XVII

The Return of the Goddess

In spite of Schopenhauer's moments of illogicalness and his weakness in demonstration, it is obvious that he and Hegel, between them, recovered the two elements—the male Gnosis, or knowledge, and the female compassionate Love—which together form that Wisdom-Philosophy most perfectly expressed in the works of Plotinus and Porphyry, which at one time united the intelligentsia of both the Christian and pagan worlds.

As we have seen, ever since the establishment of the patriarchal system, first as Judaism and later as Judaic-Christianity, man has been equated with mind, the image and likeness of the Parent Mind, and women with the senses or emotions, as if these were antitheses and two totally divergent concepts, whereas in fact they are merely different expressions of the same essence. It is seldom realised that the only evidence we have of the existence of mind is thought and its effects which we believe to emanate from what we conceive of as an invisible but real power that we term "Mind". Without thought, nothing can be experienced. Emotions, feelings, sensitivity are as directly the result of thought, or mind, as philosophy. They are merely different modes of thought. It would therefore have done no harm to have regarded these two ways of thinking—the mental and scientific and the emotional and sensitive—as male and female, if the latter had not been considered evil as it was by the Jews. This fatal flaw in their logic stemmed from the erroneous beliefs that mind and emotions, or feeling, were antithetic, whereas, as the philosophies of Hegel and Schopenhauer bear eloquent witness, they are merely two ways by which mind is expressed.

As we see from Schopenhauer's *Basis of Morality*, the expression of emotion and feeling may not be evil, but may, on the contrary, constitute the highest morality. It is true that emotional feelings may be, and frequently are, expressed in sensuality and sexuality, but, on the other hand, they are also capable of producing the very highest God-quality known to man—compassionate Love. It is equally true that the Mind with which man is equated may reach the divine heights of the Wisdom-Philosophy, bringing its user into a relative kingdom of Heaven, or it may create a nuclear deterrent that will bring the world to an end in a veritable fiery furnace. Therefore, the philosophical confusion from which the Western world in general and its female members in particular, have suffered during the patriarchal period, has resulted from the loose logic and unreason of the primitive theologians who built up a completely erroneous hypothesis on entirely untenable foundations.

If we are going to equate man with Mind and woman with the emotions, let us at least make it clear that by this is meant speculative thought as distinct from emotional thought; and let it also be understood that emotion can be as sublime as philosophy, remembering that two of the greatest Teachers who ever lived, Gautama the Buddha and Jesus the Christ, were known not as Lords of Intellect but as Lords of Compassion. In other words, it was this womanly attribute that was most generally acknowledged and adored.

It was also false psychology to equate the emotional nature with the physical senses, for feeling is more often aroused by insight and instinct than by the evidence of these senses. It is true that the sight of suffering—the sensual evidence of another's misery—may, and usually does, precede the imaginative response to that suffering which arouses the impulse to give aid; but it is this response, this instinctive feeling and insight, which is responsible for the compassion that gives rise to the helpful act. The senses which Buddha truly called the Five Hindrances—as they certainly are when uncontrolled by the higher evidence of Wisdom—are not in themselves evil. They are misleading only to those who lack the Gnosis which corrects their evidence, and who consequently consent to the *maya*, or illusion, that they create. It is, therefore, the ignorant response to the senses which is evil, and that response is wholly mental, i.e. male!

Today, what we call science is a veneration and worship of sensual evidence. On this evidence the whole of the technological modern scientific age is founded—which explains its total moral failure. For the Divine Science which alone can ensure true morality is based on the rejection of sense-evidence and the certainty that spiritual Truth can never be found by an analysis of matter, or the "man" without the "woman", i.e. mind applied to matter, ignoring the need for instinct and insight which have informed Truth-seekers from the beginning of the search that salvation is gained by the application of Mind to Spirit.

We may say, therefore, that the modern world, dominated by the fear of extinction through its own violence, and the even deeper fear that by its moral depravity it has forfeited the right to exist, is the culmination of an age-old rejection of the woman, added to the appalling fact that when woman as a sex was partially liberated from male domination by her enfranchisement, and was free to choose, she herself aided in this rejection and threw the weight of her influence into the already overweighed masculine scale.

Shakespeare provides us with an example of the requisite Divine Equipoise in *The Merchant of Venice* where Justice, significantly symbolised by a Jew, is shown to be an evil without the balance of Mercy, symbolised by Portia: "For in the course of justice none of us should see salvation: we do pray for mercy. . . . " In the Court Room male and female are weighed in the scales of justice and two lives are saved by the establishment of *balance*.

If man is ever to evolve to a higher species, he must be given a philosophy that provides the Mark, or Model to which he must evolve. In the Christian religion, this Model was found in the man, Jesus Christ; and had he not been transformed into a sun-god by the over-zealous Paul, but had instead been presented as what he so obviously was, an androgynous, evolved man with male power and authority perfectly balanced by the compassionate love and wisdom of divine womanhood, his example, faithfully followed, could indeed have saved the world from its present state of almost undiluted violence and masculinity. But a patriarchal priesthood of Pauline Christianity never ceased to stress the male qualities of their man-god. The compassionate saving of the sacrificial animals by driving them away from the butcher-priests has been, for instance, represented as Christian authority for the use of violence. And, again, Jesus's words, "I come not to bring peace but a sword", all too well understood by those who have attempted to follow him as indicating the mental opposition that the evolving man always encounters from those who wish to remain in the sleep of the senses, have been taken literally, despite the obvious fact that they then not only contradict the explicit pacific instructions of the Sermon on the Mount, and the implicit teaching that violence is contrary to the will of God, in Luke 9:55, but also the whole spirit and meaning of one described as the Prince of Peace.

Without this Spirit, this feminine Paraclete, or divine Wisdom symbolised by the Dove, known to the ancients from the beginning of time, he could not have been the perfect man made in the image and likeness of the Father-Mother God, and so equally possessed of the male and female qualities of Deity. This divine Equipollence was, as we learn from Philo, symbolised by the male and female choruses performed by the Essenes, and most perfectly manifested in the character of the Prophet of Israel who taught from their sacred writings. But an all-male priesthood, in league with militaristic and power-loving States, deliberately upset this all-essential balance, replacing it with the Mithraic portrait found in Revelation 19:11–16, which runs:

> And I saw heaven opened and behold a white horse, and he that sat upon him was called Faithful and True, and in righteousness he doth judge and make war . . . and he was clothed with a vesture dipped in blood: and his

> name is called the Word of God. . . . And out of his mouth goeth a sharp sword, that with it he should smite the nations: . . . and he shall rule them with a rod of iron: and he treadeth the winepress of the fierceness and wrath of almighty God. And he hath on his vesture and on his thigh a name written King of Kings, and Lord of Lords.

This transmutation from a tender, loving, all-compassionate healer and teacher to a militaristic tyrant left man with an anti-Christ to worship, and woman with nothing to worship at all, unless she bent the knee to man's false demi-god.

For many centuries the Western female religionist managed to remain fairly true to her higher nature by manifesting the maternal love symbolised by the Mother of the Lord, but this tenderness and submissiveness was almost invariably exploited and despised by lovers of domination and power, with the result that woman's influence on man, her attempts to redress the balance by persuading him to subject his will and power to the dictates of compassionate love, miserably failed. It is not surprising that the slave eventually revolted and now bows down to the god of violence and materialistic Science who has given men such power. Yet, in a masculine world, torn by strife, nationalistic ambition, cruelty, greed and hate, what is needed beyond all else are the civilising and harmonising "feminine" qualities of pacific, tender, protective, compassionate Love. Instead of which, the human symbols of these divine qualities—women— have, since their liberation, been heaping fuel on the fire, not only, in many cases, encouraging men in their policies of violence but actually joining in the fray, going into uniform, marching with machine guns, entering into competition with men even in occupations that are most obviously suitable for men only; taking part in masculine sports, attending bull and prize fights, flaunting her sexual promiscuity and indulgence in narcotics and stimulants, and in every way apeing the toughness, callousness and downright bestial stupidity of the unredeemed, or unbalanced, male nature. By such misguided emulation she is rapidly eliminating in herself all the qualities of her higher nature which are precisely what she should be contributing to the world in order to adjust the balance of psychological power.

This is one of the unfortunate results of having had no philosophy or religion to provide her with a true sense of direction. Scientific materialism condemns her qualities as "soft" and reactionary, and quite unsuited to a competitive world. Lacking a higher divinity, she must, therefore, accept the God of men, or remain godless.

At the beginning of this century, before woman obtained her empty independence, the Irish mystic, George Russell, better known as A. E., perceived and commented upon the inappropriateness of the all-male religion that Christianity had become, for women, and wrote, in his beautiful essay, *Religion and Love*:

> I have often wondered whether there is not something wrong in our religious systems in that the same ritual, the same doctrines, the same aspirations are held to be sufficient both for men and women. The tendency everywhere is to obliterate distinctions, and if a woman be herself, she is looked upon unkindly. . . . The ancients were wiser than we in this, for they had Aphrodite and Hera and many another form of the Mighty Mother who bestowed on women their peculiar graces and powers.*

He argued that women should awaken worshipful love in men in order that they should perceive and adore the Goddess—the good qualities—in her, and strive to make them their own. He wrote:

> We remember that with Dante, the image of a woman became at last the purified vesture of his spirit through which the mysteries were revealed. . . . The man whose spirit has been obsessed by a beauty so long brooded upon that he has almost become that which he contemplated, owes much to the woman who may never be his.

For, as he pointed out:

> Spirituality is the power of apprehending formless, spiritual essences, of seeing the eternal in the transitory, and in the things which are seen the unseen things of which they are the shadow.

The need, as A. E. saw it, was for man to worship in woman what a purely patriarchal philosophy of life had taught him to despise—the harmlessness, beauty, gentleness, compassion and tenderness which were once believed to be essentially "feminine"; the civilising qualities that undoubtedly originated with the mothers of the race who worshipped the Mother-Goddesses and modelled themselves on these peace-loving deities.

But since A. E. saw this necessity for men, it has become equally necessary for women. They, too, must return to the worship of their own Divinity, the Goddess within, whom they have abandoned in order to join men in their power-worship, thus utterly destroying the balance of Being. A. E. visualises this return in the words:

> Woman may again have her temples and her mysteries, and renew again her radiant life at its fountain, and feel that in seeking for beauty she is growing more into her own ancient being, and that in its shining forth she is giving to man, as he may give to her, something of that completeness of Spirit of which it is written: "Neither is the man without the woman, nor the woman without the man in the Highest."

* *Imaginations and Reveries*, by A. E. (Macmillan & Co. Ltd., 1925.)

Man in the image and likeness of the Divine Parent, the Father-Mother God, can never be whole and complete, as he eternally is in the eyes of The Good, unless he manifests the perfect balance of male-female qualities. For this it is not necessary nor desirable for women to compete with, and to ape, the man, which they have been doing increasingly and fatally since their enfranchisement, nor for men to become "effeminate" by apeing woman's lower nature with its seductiveness, illogicalness and treachery; but both should recognise and seek to embrace and emulate the divine qualities in one another, and so learn how to establish the Divine Equipollence in themselves. Feminine compassionate Love needs the support of the masculine will and strength; masculine knowledge and power needs feminine wisdom to ensure their harmlessness. The two must be one in operation in order to, as Vivekananda put it, "restore the essential balance in the world between the masculine and feminine energies and qualities. The bird of the spirit of Humanity cannot fly with only one wing."

Woman has failed to play her part in the evolution of mankind because she has not been true to the highest, the Divinity, within her. Her long awaited contribution to the human race has still to appear.

In his *Answer to Job*, the late C. G. Jung, who seems clearly to have understood the need for the return of the Goddess, gave this timely warning:

> Everything now depends on men: immense power of destruction is given into his hand, and the question is whether he can resist the will to use it, and can temper his will with the spirit of Love and Wisdom.

But "male" will and power can only be subordinate to "female" Love and Wisdom when man has learned to worship these womanly qualities. And how can he worship them if he never finds them embodied in the sex which was originally—in the days of the Mother-Goddess—believed to be equated with them? How can he evolve without an evolutionary model? Woman, originally intended to be man's help-mate (and we can only be helped from "above") should be providing that model. The happiness, even the continuance of the human race depends on her providing it and so restraining the will-to-power of men, as Cybele restrained the over-procreative Attis. Thus a tremendous responsibility rests upon women who do not seem to have begun to realise the immense importance of the part they should be playing in the present scheme of things. Jung wrote of the effects of the present lack of equipoise:

> The more the feminine ideal is bent in the direction of the masculine, the more the woman loses her power to compensate the masculine striving for

perfection, and a typically masculine ideal state arises which, as we shall see, is threatened with an enantiodromia. . . .

Jung believed that the late Pope, Pius XII, was acutely aware of the necessity for the reinstatement of the Wisdom-Goddess both externally and internally. He writes of the Assumption of the Virgin Mary being made dogma in 1950:

> It was recognised even in prehistoric times that the primordial divine being is both male and female. But such a truth eventuates in time only when it is solemnly proclaimed or rediscovered. It is psychologically significant for our day that in the year 1950 the heavenly bride was united with the bridegroom.*

In other words, the Church, rather late in its history, has remembered a truth that it should never have allowed its congregations to forget—the supreme importance of the Divine Equipollence being manifested in the human psyche.

It is vital that woman should awaken to the fact that her legal emancipation has brought her not liberation but an increase of slavery. The latest evidence of this is the world-wide campaigns to persuade her into working both inside and outside the home. The chance to be a professional woman, plus home-maker, is represented as being a "privilege", a sign of her "equality" with man who, however, seems quite satisfied as a rule to have only one occupation for which he demands ever shorter hours and ever increasing remuneration. With their life-partners working with the diligence of ants, it is difficult to imagine what men will do with their increased leisure. It is quite certain that if woman continues to regard unceasing materialistic labour as a proof of progress, she will not only be unable to share this leisure but will have no time to civilise—even when she is capable of it—either her husband or children. Moreover, by such blind acquiescence to the plans of our modern Pharaohs to turn the world into a large State-termitary, she is rapidly losing her soul, or divinity, as A. E., would put it: her sense of spirituality, her natural response to beauty, her innate womanliness most perfectly expressed in selfless maternal love.

The modern woman has exchanged worship of the Highest for a veneration of commodities and gadgets; her ideals take the form of refrigerators and washing machines; her sense of beauty is expressed in blood-red talons and artificial eye-lashes; in the cultivation of body

---

* *Answer to Job*, by C. G. Jung, translated from the German by R. F. C. Hull. (Routledge & Kegal Paul.)

instead of the cultivation of mind. She no longer sings as she goes about her work—the "pop-singers" do that for her. She has ceased to rejoice in her femininity, her aim being to ape the male. For lack of a Divinity, a feminine Ideal, or Goddess, woman is becoming a dying species. Unless she awakens and returns to herself, her true being, she will find herself in that typically masculine State visualised by Jung, lacking all grace, beauty, compassion, mercy and joy.

We can therefore only unite with A. E. in the hope that there may be:

> Some renewal of ancient conceptions of the fundamental purpose of womanhood and its relations to Divine Nature, and that from the temples where women may be instructed she will come forth, with strength in her to resist all pleading until the lover worship in her a divine womanhood, and that through their love the divided portions of the immortal nature may come together and be one as before the beginning of the world.

BIBLIOGRAPHY

THE ORIGIN OF SPECIES, by *Charles Darwin, M.A.* John Murray.

RELIGIOUS SYSTEMS OF THE WORLD. Swan Sonnenschein & Co.

THE HISTORY OF HERODOTUS, translated by *George Rawlinson.* J. M. Dent & Sons Ltd.

THE WORKS OF PHILO JUDAEUS, translated by *C. D. Yonge, B.A.* George Bell & Sons.

LASCAUX. Paintings and engravings by *Annette Laming.*

THE TWO BABYLONS, by *Alexander Hislop.* S. W. Partridge & Co.

THE ANTIQUITIES OF THE JEWS, by *Flavius Josephus.*

THE CONFESSIONS OF ST. AUGUSTINE, translated by *Sir Tobie Matthews, Kt.* Collins, Fontana Books.

THE CITY OF GOD, by *Augustine*, translated by *John Helsey.* J. M. Dent & Sons.

THE GOLDEN ASSE OF APULEIUS, translated by *Wil Aldington,* 1566. Guy Chapman.

PLUTARCH'S LIVES, translated by *Bernadotte Perrin,* Heinemann.

PLOTINUS: THE ENNEADS, translated by *Stephen MacKenna.* Faber & Faber.

CHRISTIAN PLATONISTS OF ALEXANDRIA, Bampton Lectures, 1886. *Charles Biggs, D.D.* Oxford, 1913.

ALEXANDRIAN CHRISTIANITY, *J. E. L. Oulton, D.D.* and *Henry Chadwick, B.D.* S.C.M. Press Ltd.

FIRST PRINCIPLES BY ORIGEN (Koetchau's Text of De Principiis), translated by *G. W. Butterworth,* S.P.C.K.

ORIGEN AND GREEK PATRISTIC THEOLOGY, by *the Rev. W. Fairweather, M.A.* T. and T. Clark.

PRAYER: EXHORTATION TO MARTYRDOM, by *Origen*, translated and Annotated by *John F. O'Meara.* Longmans, Green.

JUSTIN MARTYR: THE DIALOGUE WITH TRYPHO, translation, introduction and notes by *A. Lukyn Williams, D.D.* S.P.C.K.

CHRISTIAN ETHICS AND MODERN PROBLEMS, by *W. R. Inge.* Hodder & Stoughton.

THE USES OF THE PAST, by *Herbert J. Miller.* A Mentor Book, 1954.

DAS WESEN DES CHRISTENTHUMS. Harnack.

THE TEACHING OF THE TWELVE APOSTLES. A translation with notes by *Canon Spence. M.A.* James Nisbet & Co.

THE SIBYLLINE ORACLES, by *the Rev. H. N. Bate, M.A.* S.P.C.K.

ORIGEN: CONTRA CELSUM, translated by *Henry Chadwick.* Cambridge University Press.

SELECTIONS FROM THE COMMENTARIES AND HOMILIES OF ORIGEN, by *R. B. Tollinton, D.D.* Macmillan, S.P.C.K.

PLATO, translated by *W. R. M. Lamb,* William Heinemann. Loeb Classical Library.

THE REPUBLIC OF PLATO, translated by *A. D. Lindsay, M.A.* Dent's, Everyman's Library.

BIBLIOGRAPHY

FIVE DIALOGUES OF PLATO, translated by *Floyer Sydenham*, Dent's Everyman's Library.

THE VARIETIES OF RELIGIOUS EXPERIENCE, by *William James*. Longmans, Green & Co.

THE WORKS OF THE EMPEROR JULIAN, translated by *Wilmer K. Wright, Ph.D.* Heinemann, The Loeb Classical Library.

THE DIVINE LEGATION OF MOSES, by *W. Warburton, D.D.* J. & P. Knapton, London, MDCCLV.

THE GNOSTICS AND THEIR REMAINS, by *C. W. King*. David Nutt.

THE RISE OF CHRISTIANITY, by *Ernest William Barnes*. Longmans, Green & Co.

THE MYSTERIES OF MITHRA, by *Franz Cumont*, Kegan Paul, Trench, Trubner & Co. Ltd.

OLD AND NEW TESTAMENTS.

THE BOOK OF ENOCH, translated by *R. H. Charles, D.D.* S.P.C.K.

THE WORKS OF NATHANIEL LARDNER, D.D., Life by *Dr Kippis*. James Ogle Robinson.

CRUDEN'S COMPLETE CONCORDANCE.

THE METAMORPHOSES OF OVID, translated by *Mary M. Innes*. The Penguin Classics.

VITA CONSTANTINI, by *Eusebius*, Bishop of Caesarea.

DISCOURSE ON METHOD, ETC., by *René Descartes*. Translated by *John Veitch, LL.D.* Dent's Everyman's Library.

ETHICS: SPINOSA, introduction by *T. S. Gregory, M.A. Oxon.* Dent's Everyman's Library.

CRITIQUE OF PURE REASON, by *Immanuel Kant*. Translated by *J. M. D. Meiklejohn*. Bohn's Philosophical Library.

THE BASIS OF MORALITY, by *Arthur Schopenhauer*. Translated by *Arthur Bullock, M.A.* George Allen & Unwin Ltd.

LECTURES ON THE PHILOSOPHY OF RELIGION, by *G. W. F. Hegel, Speirs and Sanderson* translation. Kegan Paul, Trench, Trubner & Co. Ltd.

PLUTARCH'S LIVES (Dryden edition revised by *Arthur Clough*). Dent's Everyman's Library.

PLATO, translated by *The Rev. R. G. Bury, Litt.D.* Heinemann.

THE SCROLLS FROM THE DEAD SEA, by *Edmund Wilson*. W. H. Allen.

THE HISTORY OF THE DECLINE AND FALL OF THE ROMAN EMPIRE, by *Edward Gibbon*, with notes by *The Rev. H. H. Milman*. John Murray, 1846.

THE ECLOGUES AND GEORGICS OF VIRGIL, translated into English verse by *T. F. Royds, M.A.* J. M. Dent & Sons Ltd., E. P. Dutton & Co., New York.

IMAGINATIONS AND REVERIES, by *A. E.* Macmillan & Co. Ltd., 1925.

ANSWER TO JOB, by *C. G. Juno*. Translated from the German by R. F. C. Hull. Routledge and Kegan Paul.

INDEX

INDEX

INDEX

INDEX

Proclus, 27
Prometheus, 180
Proserpine, 28, 30, 31, 40, 45
Protestants, 229, 231, 234
Proteus, 197
Protoevangelium of St. James, 167
Psychosomatic healing, 79
Ptolemy, 126
Pythagoras of Samos, 11, 39, 59, 66, 71, 73, 74, 99, 149, 186, 192, 194, 196, 198
Pythagoreans, 61, 185, 196, 199
Pythia, 52
Pythius, the Lydian, 94
Pythoness, the, 52, 53, 56, 57

Q., 166, 233
Queen of Heaven, 25, 30, 31, 32, 41, 43, 46, 53, 91, 99, 105, 111, 116, 159, 200, 227
Quexalcoatl, 23
Qumran, caves of, 123

Rachael, 107
Realm of Process, 208, 211, 212
Reincarnation, 185,
  theory of, 175
Republic of Plato, The, 31, 64, 73, 74, 76–78, 81, 83
Reserve, the, 95, 134, 191
Resurrection, 192, 224
  body, 163, 177
Revelation of John, the, 267
Rhea, 23, 25, 29, 103
Roman Empire, 71, 96
Romans, 67, 69
Romulus, 32, 65–67, 70, 71
  and Remus, 68

Sabines, 69, 70
Sabbath Day, 131
Sabbath, the, 132
  of rest, 226
  perpetual, 132, 171, 174
Salome, 178
Salverté Eusèbe, 51
Saoshyant, Messiah, 163
Saturn, 28, 258
Saul, meaning of, 156
Saul of Tarsus, 129, 131, 156
Schopenhauer, 237, 248, 251, 258–263, 265
  Basis of Morality, 246, 258, 265
Science, 127, 181, 247
  Divine, 176, 181, 266
  materialistic, 190, 203, 210, 211, 268
  mysterious, 186
  pure, 203
Scientific materialism, 241
Scrolls from the Dead Sea, The, 123
Second Council of Constantinople, 183, 192
Secrets of Enoch, The, 160
Semele, 30, 168
Semiramis, 22–24, 32–34, 50, 89, 90, 216
Serapis, 30, 45

Sermon on the Mount, 267
Serpent, 51, 52, 57, 112
Sesostris, 55
Seven, heavens, 160
  number, 37, 45
  planets, 38
  spirits of God, 38, 68, 114
Seventh heaven, 160, 164
Severus Lucius Septimus, 194, 198
Sexual intercourse, 178, 179, 232
Shakespeare, 260
Shamash, 24
Shaw, George Bernard, 127
Shepherds and Kings, 154
Shinar, Land of, 19
Sibylline books, 49
  Oracles, 50
Sibyl of Cumae, 49, 92
Sisyphus, 225
Socrates, 73–87, 97, 149, 198, 250
Sodom and Gomorrah, 145
Sol, 28
Solomon, 67, 88, 115–119, 182
  Wisdom of, The, 119
Sophia, 98, 104, 169
Soul, 75, 79–81, 83–86, 176, 177, 188, 203–213, 258
  descent of the, 184, 189
Spanish Inquisition, 234
Spartans, 53, 56
Spinosa, 242–246, 251, 260
Spirit, 40, 100, 146, 148, 165, 166, 183, 208, 252, 254–258
  God is, 145, 254, 258
Spiritual healing, 79, 80, 119, 154, 172, 176, 187, 188, 198, 257
Stephen, 159, 163
Substance, 238, 240, 243, 254
Summit, of our being, 203, 204
Sun, 22, 29, 30, 44, 45, 61, 62, 91, 94, 110, 114, 255, 258, 262
  city of the, 110
  chariots of the, 120
  symbol of the, 52
  Syrian worship of the, 196
Sun-god, 91, 96, 103, 106, 108, 114, 157, 267
Sun temple, 114, 116
Sun-worship, 91, 106
Swedenborg, 247
Symposium, The, 77, 81
Syncellus, George, 7

Tammuz, 22–24, 31, 91, 152, 158, 174, 221
Tantalus, 225
Tara, 23
Tatia, 66
Tatian, 177
Taurobolium, 41
Taw, 171
Teaching of the Twelve Apostles, The, 131
Telepathy, 247
Teletae, 26